Roger Hutchinson is an author and journalist. After working as a magazine editor in London, in 1977 he joined the *West Highland Free Press* in Skye. Since then, he has published fifteen books, including *Polly: The True Story Behind Whisky Galore*. He is still a columnist for the *WHFP*, and has written for BBC Radio, *The Scotsman*, *The Guardian*, *The Herald* and *The Literary Review*. His book *The Soap Man: Lewis, Harris and Lord Leverhulme* was shortlisted for the Saltire Scottish Book of the Year, and the bestselling *Calum's Road* was shortlisted for the Royal Society of Literature's Ondaatje Prize.

He has lived in Raasay since the end of the last millennium.

Praise for Roger Hutchinson

Calum's Road

'A great read – a terrific story of courage and endurance'
Andrew O'Hagan

'Uplifting and life-enhancing'
The Guardian

'Wonderful, elegant and serious'
Daily Telegraph

The Soap Man: Lewis, Harris and Lord Leverhulme

'Readable as a novel … rich in insights'
The Herald

'A wonderful little book about what happens when righteous ambition meets stubborn culture'
Scotland on Sunday

Polly: The True Story behind 'Whisky Galore'

'A delightful dram of a book'
Daily Mail

'Riveting . . . a legendary tale, full of humour'
West Highland Free Press

Island of Roe Deer

THE STORY OF RAASAY

Roger Hutchinson

ORIGIN

First published in 2026 by
Origin, an imprint of
Birlinn Limited
West Newington House
10 Newington Road
Edinburgh
EH9 1QS

www.birlinn.co.uk

ISBN: 978-1-83983-092-1

British Library Cataloguing-in-Publication Data
A catalogue record for this book is available from the British Library

Typeset by Lexis Books

MIX
Paper | Supporting responsible forestry
FSC® C018072

Printed and bound by Clays Ltd, Elcograf S.p.A.

Contents

To all the smaller islands, where the bigger things live

"Raasay … offers, in one small unit, an opportunity to see almost all the major influences and trends in the history of the Western Highlands and Islands"

— Richard Sharpe, 1976

Preface and Acknowledgements

Foghar Dhonnchaidh

"He risked there not being a week of good autumn weather, but there always is."

ON ONE of those still and clear October mornings in the Hebrides, when the sea sparkles and the hills turn black in the sun, I walked up to Raasay Stores and bumped into the fisherman, ferryman and Fladdach, Calum Gillies.

I commented on the fine weather. Calum grinned and said, "Yes. Foghar Dhonnchaidh."

"Duncan's what?"

"Foghar. Harvest. Duncan's harvest. It's what we call this week of good weather in autumn. Duncan never harvested his croft in late summer, when everyone else did. He waited for foghar Dhonnchaidh. That way he had a few extra weeks' growing time … and the help of his neighbours, who had already finished their harvests. He risked there not being a week of good autumn weather, but there always is."

The former Kenyan civil servant, district councillor, Justice of the Peace, ferry skipper, hotelier and native of Eilean Taighe,

Alastair Nicolson had strolled down the road and joined us. The two offshore island men were of an age, and it was a good age. Calum nodded to Alastair, "foghar Dhonnchaidh?" Alastair looked up at the sun and the blue sky, and nodded back.

"Aye. Foghar Dhonnchaidh," he said.

"Was Donnchadh a real person?" I asked.

"Oh yes. Duncan MacLeod. Up in Fearns, I think."

Every single Ratharsach, as well as probably every other Gael north and west of Stirling, was clearly familiar with foghar Dhonnchadh. I wondered if the great Victorian folklorists, Alexander Carmichael or John Francis Campbell, could have picked up the legend 150 years ago.

"When?" Fifteenth century? Early medieval?

"Oh, it was a while ago … 1950s? 1930s …?"

Having devoted fifty years to it, I can attest to one advantage that a full time incomer to Hebridean islands has over the natives. It is that life becomes an endless voyage of discovery about your new home, a voyage which is piloted and crewed by your neighbours, those same indigenes.

I never intended to write a book about Raasay. Arriving wide-eyed in Drumfearn in Skye half a century ago, I did not intend to write books about any part of the Highlands and Islands. My proscription of Raasay surrendered seven years after I moved to live on the island in 1999. Twenty years after that, it is holding up its hands again. There is, as I hope you will agree, just too much good material to ignore for very long.

As I was settling into Drumfearn in the last quarter of the old century, my contemporary, Richard Sharpe, was publishing in two volumes his dissertation on the history of Raasay. Sharpe, who would proceed to a distinguished academic career at Oxford University before his sudden death in 2020, was one of the first to suggest that Raasay uniquely offered the chance to study the Highlands and the Hebrides in miniature.

It is a tempting proposition. All islands, and most Highland parishes, are the same, and all are different. The mighty waves which crash over one, usually also invade the beaches of the others.

The problem with the microcosmic theory is that both oral and written histories are selective and sensational. They reflexively feature big bad things – the tsunamis that leave dead, injured and mourning people in their wake – such as the eighteenth-century Jacobite Risings, the last pitched battle between two armies fought on British soil, the Highland Clearances, the efforts to introduce the delights of the individual revolution to this most stubbornly rural of European regions, and the twentieth-century scourge of absentee private landlords – Raasay having featured in that role a villain straight from central casting.

Raasay experienced all of those phenomena in vivid technicolour. But the island also stood almost alone in the shape and character of its resistance. Its crofting community maintained its Gaelic language and culture – as well as its crofting community! – against all the odds into the twenty-first century. It was a proudly Christian island from the sixth to the twenty-first centuries, which gave to the world a denomination whose word is still heard in Africa, Ukraine, Texas and London, as well as elsewhere in Scotland and the Hebrides. It delivered an extraordinary musical repertoire, a library shelf of memoirs, one of Scotland's greatest poets and probably the country's greatest poem. The island's response to governmental neglect became internationally celebrated in the piece of practical twentieth-century landscape art which is known as Calum's Road.

All of that while losing disproportionate numbers of its young in the shell craters of Flanders, while spearheading the victorious nineteenth- and twentieth-century land wars, and while shaping, refining and retaining an identifiable character of its own.

In some of those ways Raasay is more typical than such of its demographic equivalents as Eriskay, Vatersay and Eigg. In others it is markedly unique. No other island fought with the Jacobite army at Culloden, helped Charles Edward Stuart to escape and just 150 years later founded the Free Presbyterian Church of Scotland,

and no other island could have done so without acknowledging the slightest contradiction or incongruity. There are no effects without causes, and untangling those causes makes writing a book like this one such a joy.

For obvious reasons, I owe acknowledgements to everybody who has ever lived in Raasay, before, after and even during the last Ice Age, with particular salutes to those who are mentioned in the following pages.

In my time, I have profited personally from the wisdom, company and generosity of Calum Gillies, young and old, beag 's mor, John Allan Gillies, Alasdair Iain Gillies, Rhona Gillies, Wilma Duncan, Nairn Duncan, Donalda MacKenzie, Calum "Ban" MacLeod, Calum "Arnish" MacLeod, Donald MacLeod, Christine MacLeod, Lyn Rowe, David Croy, Freya Croy, Lexy MacLeod, Jen Burnett, Ian Hill, Artemis Pana, Julie Allan, John William "Bradan" Gillies, Andrew "Cuddy" Gillies, Ann Gillies, James "Emby" Gillies, Stuart Brown, Gina Ferguson, Morag Ferguson, Ally MacLeod, Donnie MacLeod, Alex MacLeod, Calum Don MacKay, John "the Caley" Nicolson, Sadie MacLeod, Angus Gillies, Donnie Oliphant, Ann Oliphant, Jessie Nicolson, Sandy MacLeod, Alastair Nicolson, Chrissie Nicolson, Chrissie Gillies, John Ferguson, Margaret Ferguson, Norman Gillies, Seonaidh Cumming, John "Korea" MacLeod, Reverend James Tallach, Calum Tom MacLeod, Margaret Moodie, Alec Moodie, Stephen Bungard, Rosemary Bungard, Finlay MacLennan, Bella MacLennan, Davie Carslaw, Donald Malcolm MacLeod, Catherine MacPhee at Skye and Lochalsh Archive Centre, all at the West Highland Free Press from its birth to the present day.

For their company on so much of the journey, Derek Cooper, Angus Peter Campbell, Brian Wilson, Torcuil Crichton, Jim Hunter, Cailean Maclean. For her partnership on all of the miraculous passage, Caroline MacKechnie.

I hope that the eponymous eighteenth-century neighbour of the Royal Literary Fund in Johnson's Court, EC4, would approve of this book in particular.

Hugh Andrew, Jan Rutherford, Andrew Simmons, James Rose and all at Birlinn … thanks for everything. Without you guys, it's just characters on a screen.

Roger Hutchinson
Raasay, 2026

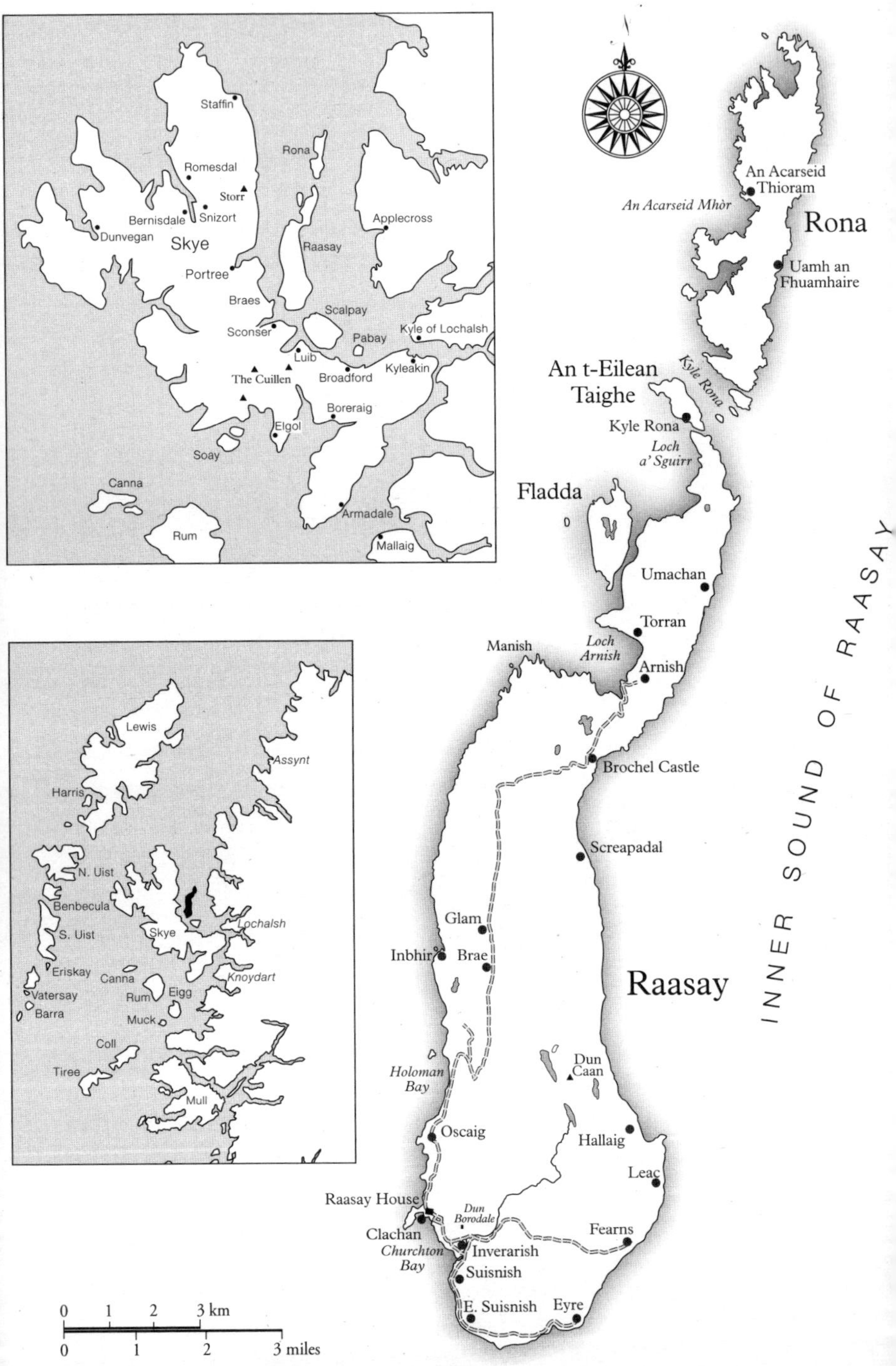
Staffin
Rona
Romesdal
Storr
Bernisdale
Snizort
Applecross
Dunvegan
Skye
Raasay
Portree
Braes
Scalpay
Sconser
Pabay
Kyle of Lochalsh
Luib
Kyleakin
The Cuillen
Broadford
Boreraig
Elgol
Soay
Canna
Armadale
Rum
Mallaig
Lewis
Assynt
Harris
N. Uist
Benbecula
Lochalsh
S. Uist
Skye
Eriskay
Canna
Knoydart
Vatersay
Rum
Eigg
Barra
Muck
Coll
Tiree
Mull
An Acarseid
Thioram
An Acarseid Mhòr
Rona
Uamh an
Fhuamhaire
An t-Eilean
Taighe
Kyle Rona
Kyle Rona
Loch
a' Sguirr
Fladda
Umachan
Torran
Manish
Loch
Arnish
Arnish
INNER SOUND OF RAASAY
Brochel Castle
Screapadal
Glam
Inbhir
Brae
Raasay
Dun
Caan
Holoman
Bay
Oscaig
Hallaig
Leac
Raasay House
Dun
Borodale
Clachan
Fearns
Churchton
Bay
Inverarish
Suisnish
E. Suisnish
Eyre
0 1 2 3 km
0 1 2 3 miles

1

The Hebridean Walter Mitty

"Scotland has had issues with the identity of its Norse and Gaelic northern and western peripheries since the departure of the Romans."

In 1996, the journalist Andrew Neil became editor-in-chief of Press Holdings, a company whose media assets then included *The Scotsman*, a storied daily broadsheet newspaper in the capital of the Scotsman's country.

Neil, who was born and raised in Paisley, sixty miles west of that newspaper's Edinburgh offices, enjoyed his excursions back home, cultivating new friends and reviving past connections. In 2001 he addressed the annual prize giving ceremony of Dollar Academy, a 200-year-old private school whose rector was a fellow alumnus of Glasgow University and an old acquaintance.

On 28 June 2001, the very morning of Andrew Neil's speech to its thousand pupils, there appeared in *The Scotsman* an awestruck profile of the most remarkable member of staff at Dollar Academy, or at any other Scottish school.

Scott Peake was Dollar's 33-year-old principal teacher of classics. He was also, he told *The Scotsman*'s feature writer, a native Gaelic speaker from the Hebrides who had known no other language before entering primary school. His connections with his native tongue were undiminished. Scott Peake was still, he pointed out, a Gaelic broadcaster and an occasional actor. He was a natural athlete, a cricket cap for Scotland and an accomplished shinty player, a Scottish internationalist at the sport, who earlier in that summer of 2001 had represented his country in a match against Canada. Shinty is a famously physical game and such exertions had taken their toll. "I'm just about to have a bolt put into my toe," he told *The Scotsman* ruefully, "the old cheek is playing up and my hands are getting weary. I've got four pieces of metal in me."

Scott Peake had also, he said, been honoured by the Turkish government for his heroic rescue efforts following a murderous Anatolian earthquake in August 1999, when Peake had fortuitously been in the vicinity. More prosaically, he had recently emerged from several months spent on important archaeological digs with Corpus Christi College in Oxford.

As a result of those and other accomplishments, Scott Peake had not only been welcomed behind the Doric pillars of Dollar Academy but had also been made a member of two government quangos: the Ancient Monuments Board for Scotland and the Battlefields Trust for Scotland, of which he was convener.

In June 2001, shortly before Andrew Neil's prize-giving speech at Dollar, this Caledonian Indiana Jones was appointed as the salaried director of the Saltire Society, a comfortable Edinburgh body which existed "to promote and celebrate the uniqueness of Scottish culture and Scotland's heritage, and to reclaim Scotland's place as a distinct contributor to European and international culture".

It was all owed to his Hebridean identity, Peake said.

He had been born in the island of Raasay in 1968. He was raised a monoglot Gaelic speaker in a Free Presbyterian household. Before leaving Raasay "to find my own way", he had first attended Raasay Primary School, and then the High School at Portree in the larger neighbouring island of Skye.

He had won the prestigious Saltire Society position, Scott Peake modestly assumed, because of his shinty experience.

The society, he said, "wanted someone to look at areas which the society hadn't really thought of in the past. And sport is one. After all, if you're a Highlander, what's the most important cultural gathering you have? Your shinty group."

In 2001 the island of Raasay was still populated by his contemporaries, Gaelic-speaking Gillieses and Nicolsons, MacLeods and MacKays, all of whom could read newspapers and none of whom had ever heard of Scott Peake. To compound matters, there was an actually existing Scottish national shinty team, to whose players, coaches and directors the name of Peake was quite unknown.

A local newspaper, the *West Highland Free Press*, which covered both Raasay and shinty, was alerted to the mystifying case of the eminent Hebridean who never was. Under investigation, Scott Peake's autobiography fell apart.

Nobody of his name had ever played cricket for Scotland.

Not only had no Scott Peake ever played shinty for Scotland either; the Scottish national shinty team had never played against Canada. Authorities considered it doubtful that the nation of Canada possessed the twelve shinty players necessary to form a team. Within the small worlds of Gaelic drama and broadcasting, Scott Peake was equally unknown.

The Turkish government refused to comment on the distribution of its national honours, but Corpus Christi College was less discreet. "I don't have anyone of that name on my lists," said an Oxford University official, "and I would have had if he was doing work for us in the past year."

"I am forty years old," said a Raasay man. "I have lived in Raasay all my life. I spoke only Gaelic before going to Raasay Primary and Portree High School. The population of Raasay now is just under two hundred people, and I'd say I know every one of them. Not only have I never met anybody called Scott Peake, until that *Scotsman* article appeared I had never so much as heard the name."

There were indeed no records at the General Registrar's Office in Edinburgh of a Scott Peake being born in Raasay, or anywhere else in Scotland, in 1968, or any other year in the twentieth century.

There was, however, a Scott Peake born of thoroughbred English stock in Woolwich in south London on 7 February 1964. That Scott Peake graduated in 1986 from the Royal Holloway and Bedford New College in Surrey with a BA in Latin and Ancient History. He later enrolled at St Andrews University in Scotland, which institution confirmed that Scott Peake completed a PhD in 1991. Poignantly, Peake did occasionally play shinty for the scratch St Andrews University team, and there on the coast of Fife he was remembered as claiming Hebridean origins in a soft, low voice which obscured his London accent.

He fell even more quickly than he had risen. Within hours of his exposure in the *West Highland Free Press* on 22 November 2001, and subsequently in almost every other media outlet in the United Kingdom, Dr Scott Peake was relieved of his memberships of both the Scottish Battlefields Trust and the Ancient Monuments Board. He was peremptorily sacked from the Saltire Society. He was put on notice by Dollar Academy and he shortly afterwards departed to take up positions on the circuit of unsuspecting and undemanding English private schools. In 2014, he entered the debate which preceded a Scottish independence referendum by writing to a national newspaper expressing his support for independence because "Scotland remains the only country not to teach its own children its history."

His had been a brief, bright fantasy which revealed more about Scotland's relationship with its residual north-western Gaidhealtachd than Scotland was ready to admit. Scott Peake was no everyday Walter Mitty. He was an astoundingly successful Walter Mitty within a small and self-regarding metropolitan society. He parlayed his mythology into positions of prestige and influence and even power, not because he was an outstanding character actor, but because it was a mythology which many Scots were prepared uncritically to embrace. The rest of Scotland has had issues with the identity of its Norse and Gaelic northern and western peripheries since the departure of the Romans. Over the centuries it attempted to resolve them by conquest, by political and cultural subjugation, by mockery, by forced clearance, by condescension and by mimicry. Resolution was impossible for as long as Scotland denied the objective historical fact that of all the many bad things that had been done to Hebrideans, most of them were devised in Edinburgh.

Those issues were still, at the time of the Scott Peake affair, alive and nagging at the country's identity. In 2001, the pre-eminent arbiter of Scottish cultural identity, Edinburgh's main national daily newspaper and its editor-in-chief, perhaps the most visible of modern Scottish journalists, were all unable to distinguish a native of south London from a son of the Inner Hebrides.

Why, though, out of three dozen inhabited western islands, had Scott Peake chosen Raasay?

In 1976 the Cambridge University student Richard Sharpe, a future history professor at Oxford University, devoted his Bachelor of Arts thesis in Anglo-Saxon, Norse and Celtic to the island of Raasay. In the following year, as Sharpe graduated with a First, his thesis was published in two volumes by the small, scholarly, London bookseller-turned-publisher Grant & Cutler. For several years, Sharpe's *Raasay: A Study in Island History* stood alone as a rare objective, academic study of the island's past

Richard Sharpe had chosen Raasay largely because he nursed in the north of England a boyhood fascination with the island, which had drawn him into dusty archives and a lifelong fascination with historical manuscripts and documents.

Sharpe also identified Raasay as an archetypal Hebridean settlement, which had experienced "almost all the major influences and trends in the history of the Western Highlands and Islands".

It was an extravagant claim. West Highland parishes share a tumultuous past while retaining individual identities. But Sharpe's characterisation of Raasay held enough water to become established into the following century. From megalithic monuments to

– at the time of Richard Sharpe's study – an absentee landowner who was actually nicknamed after a James Bond villain, it seemed that the good, the bad, the beautiful and the ugly of Hebridean history had all, over the millennia, washed up on Raasay's stony shores.

A few years later, searching for an adoptive Scottish home, Scott Peake either sensed or learned as much about the island of Raasay. If he was going to become an *echt* Hebridean, as he surely was, he must settle for no less than quintessential Hebridean roots.

He did his homework, and he found those perfect origins on twenty-four square miles of seabound granite, sandstone and shale between the island of Skye and the mainland peninsula of Applecross.

2

Fire and Ice

"The tensions between itinerant hill people and the settled cultivators of the grassy plains have been a human flashpoint and a narrative trope since Cain and Abel."

FOUR hundred million years before Scott Peake arrived at the Saltire Society, the land masses of primeval Scotland and northern Ireland, which had been engaged in a stately waltz across the surface of the planet, collided with those of England and southern Ireland.

Scotland and northern Ireland were one island afloat on a prehistoric ocean. England and Wales and southern Ireland were another. It was a very long time before the Acts of Union, and none of them had designs on the other.

From the geological and fossil record, Scotland seems to have spent several million years touring the southern hemisphere, the tropics and the eastern seaboard of North America, while England was exploring the coast of Antarctica. According to the geologist Alan McKirdy, the petrified residue of desert sands from that distant episode in the tropics can be found where they were first laid down, "east of Stornoway" in the island of Lewis. It may help to think of our earthly adventure as a perpetual world cruise. Tomorrow, Great Britain could be anchored off Shanghai, or forming a new peninsula of Patagonia, accumulating worthless but sentimental souvenirs as it drifts through time.

The basic foundation stones of Scotland were already laid when, over several hundreds of millions of years, the country bumped into the north of England. The locus of the collision was suspiciously close to the later site of Hadrian's Wall. It buckled the earth's crust and threw up the mountains of central and north-western Scotland, which were also under pressure from the west and which in their infancy were at least as tall as the modern Alps.

Those high lands were thrown up with whatever materials happened to be in the vicinity. The jagged hills of the island of Skye were built mainly from volcanic lava. The Outer Hebrides were chiefly constructed from an ancient form of granite called, after the largest Hebridean island, Lewisian gneiss. So too was a peculiar outrider, a finger of granite and sandstone in the water between Scotland and Skye which came to be known as Raasay.

The rough geological union created scarps, bluffs and cliff faces running east to west across Northumbria, which, millions of years later, the Romans cheerfully utilised when they built their frontier wall.

They did not necessarily believe that Zeus had welded together different countries at that part of the landscape, although they may have had their suspicions. They will have been equally attracted to the location because it offered an isthmus, the shortest coast-to-coast distance in that part of Britannia.

But the politics of geology are inescapable. At their most basic, the tensions between itinerant hill people and the settled cultivators of the grassy plains have been a human flashpoint and a narrative trope since Cain and Abel, and the Lapiths and the Centaurs. Different terrains demand different ways of life. They are not always complementary and are sometimes incompatible.

The geological coupling of Scotland and England was far from the only major influence on the Highland landscape. While the two masses were snuggling together around the Solway Firth, a crack opened in the earth's tectonic plates in the region of Skye and St Kilda. We know the results because we live with them. Fire and molten lava from the planet's core erupted into the night sky. Whole islands were created and rebuilt.

The twentieth-century travel writer H.V. Morton described the Cuillin ridge as "Wagner's 'Ride of the Valkyries' frozen in stone and hung up like a colossal screen against the sky". That is very good, but what the Cuillins truly depict is what they are: a young volcanic panorama before time and the weather sandpaper their sharp edges.

A further 200 million years after the collision, wind and water had eroded the highest peaks, and much of what is now the north-western archipelago and seaboard of Scotland lazed peacefully beneath a warm and shallow sea. That water ebbed and flowed as the millennia passed. Throughout the long Jurassic period, Skye was mostly inundated while the Outer Hebrides of Lewis, Harris and Uist were mainly left high and dry. Orkney was submerged but Shetland was above high tide. Most of the present western mainland was also overground, and the island of Raasay lay on an aquatic borderline, half underwater, half drying in the sun. The sea teemed with shellfish, corals, ammonites, belemnites and such marine reptiles as ichthyosaurs and plesiosaurs. The land was stalked by dinosaurs.

Some of those creatures, such as molluscs and crabs, would survive to play a substantial part in the economy of the human era. Others, such as the three-toed hadrosaur, left only their immense footprints in ossified mudflats on the coastline of Skye. Many more were captured whole and alive in the layer cakes of rock formations in places such as Raasay, becoming fossils for the amusement of generations of children and geologists, and a lesson to all sentient beings that their own inescapable fate was to be fossilised and pressed into a thin layer of rock, to the delight of future intelligent life forms.

A survey of the island in 2015 concluded that "An unusually wide range of lithologies is seen in close proximity, juxtaposed by large-scale faults, which allow nearly 3 billion years of Earth history to be condensed onto one small island." By 2015 that wide range of stones had attracted geologists to Raasay for 200 years. It had become known that if you cut the island, it bled such semi-precious deposits as feldspar, mica and quartz. Tectonic activity had also given the island an unusual number of fissures, sinks, rifts and potholes, which would prove fascinating to speleologists but hazardous to dogs, sheep and unwary humans.

One of Raasay's unusually rich and varied mineral deposits would later have a dramatic effect on human fortunes on the island. It was recognised in the nineteenth century that the south of Raasay contained substantial quantities of oolitic iron ore, a sediment which had been slow cooked in the witches brew of the warm, shallow Jurassic Hebridean sea. Early in the twentieth century that iron ore would, in a roundabout way, help to keep people living in an embattled island.

In so much as geology creates environments, it also helps to form human characteristics. It is unlikely to be an accident that the medieval border between England and Scotland lies only a few miles from where two distinct geological formations met and merged hundreds of millions of years ago. The same species of *Homo sapiens* reclaimed both territories after the last Ice Age, but once humans were established north and south of the Southern Uplands Fault, and more particularly of the Highland Boundary Fault, they were obliged to pursue different ways of life.

It may be coincidental that in the twenty-first century an outcrop of Lewisian gneiss eighty sea miles from Lewis and just two miles from Skye should contain more natives of Lewis and the other Outer Hebrides than immigrants from its neighbouring Inner Hebridean island of Skye. Those Lewis people in modern Raasay will not consciously have emigrated to that particular place to feel a familiar granite floor beneath their feet. They will no longer have crossed the sea simply because in the Middle Ages the island of Raasay was a fiefdom of the MacLeods of Lewis, rather than of some other clan in Skye. It should be asserted that there have usually been few economic reasons for a person from Skye to relocate in Raasay, but several economic reasons for somebody to go the other way. It should also be pointed out that not all of Raasay is made of Lewisian gneiss, and that the exceptional part is more fertile and attractive to new settlers. It should be understood that the men of Raasay were traditional seafarers who were long accustomed to making friendships and more intimate affiliations with Gaels in other, distant Hebridean islands, regardless of their geology.

But a human relationship which dates far back in recorded time, and which has been constant for a millennium, between the inhabitants of geologically twinned islands separated at birth, deserves cautious attention.

The first humans to arrive at the virginal refuge of Raasay in the centuries after the retreat of the last Ice Age travelled there from southern and eastern Britain, and from continental Europe. Some families and groups will have walked over Doggerland, the low-lying mass of fen and bog which at its greatest extent connected Britain to the rest of Europe, between Flamborough Head and Kent in the west and Denmark and northern France in the east.

Until recently it was assumed, on the evidence of prehistoric human settlements elsewhere in Scotland and the supposition that the Hebrides would be among the last regions to be populated, that our ancestors arrived here as recently as 6000/7000 BC, 8,000/9,000 years ago.

In the district of Assynt, on the western Scottish mainland north-east of Raasay, substantial evidence of pre- and post-Ice Age habitation has been found in a subterranean complex known as the "bone caves". Those natural catacombs have so far delivered the remains of lemmings, arctic fox, bears and lynx, as well as human beings, revealing details of Highland fauna before, after and possibly during the last Ice Age.

If the first post-Ice Age humans were in residence at the time of those animals, it throws back our estimate of the dawn of our species' modern reoccupation of north-western Scotland by a millennium or two.

If the bones in the bone caves are the remains of human middens rather than lynx and lemming graveyards, the Assynt remains suggest that having traipsed across Doggerland from Belgium 11,000 years ago our ancestors were effectively bivouacking at the edge of the retreating ice.

In April 2025, Karen Hardy, the Professor of Prehistoric Archaeology at the University of Glasgow, announced that her team of archaeologists and scientists had discovered at an undisclosed location in north Skye stone tool heads from the Late Upper Palaeolithic period between 11,000 and 11,500 years ago.

"This is a hugely significant discovery which offers a new perspective on the earliest human occupation yet known of north-west Scotland," said Professor Hardy.

"During the LUP period when the tools are believed to have been made," commented the BBC, "much of western Scotland was buried under ice. Groups of nomadic hunter-gatherers, most likely of the Ahrensburgian culture from northern Europe, would have crossed the Doggerland area now covered by the North Sea and established themselves on Skye."

"The journey made by these pioneering people who left their lowland territories in mainland Europe to travel northwards into the unknown is the ultimate adventure story," added Professor Hardy.

"As they journeyed northwards, most likely following animal herds, they eventually reached Scotland, where the western landscape was dramatically changing as glaciers melted and the land rebounded as it recovered from the weight of the ice."

When the world was young those few pioneers, and their parents and grandparents, their children and grandchildren, negotiated wonderlands. They navigated pristine forests and unspoilt seas. They roamed in the company of aurochs, lemmings, Irish elk, wild horses, bears and wolves. They pulled plentiful fish from both fresh and salt water.

More than 60 per cent of Scotland was covered by Scots pine, oak, rowan, birch, hazel, alder, aspen and willow. That low forest offered sustenance and shelter to all living creatures, including humans. As the millennia of warm, wet weather passed, in large parts of the north and west of the land it also laid down a fuel dump and carbon sink for the future. Vegetable matter had been dying and decomposing since the retreat of the ice. After a few thousand years it formed ever-deepening peat bogs which, at the rate of approximately one millimetre a year, came to cover a quarter of Scotland and more than half of parts of the Scottish Highlands and Islands. It must soon have become obvious to the new human settlers that dried peat was a plentiful source of slow-burning domestic fuel.

Just as the marshy expanse of Doggerland connected the hammerhead of mainland Britain to the coasts of Denmark, Holland, Belgium and Normandy, it is also possible that Raasay was still linked by land to Skye, and that the two of them were joined to the mainland hills of Lochalsh and Applecross, forming a blunt little peninsula on the north-western littoral of continental Europe.

Around 7000 BC, as vast quantities of melted ice was dispersed around the northern oceans, sea levels quickly rose again, creating an astonishing archipelago from the English Channel to the Scottish islands. Most of the Hebridean surface topography was already in place. To its first settlers, the profile of Raasay already resembled what much later generations would identify as a submarine, with its 1,500-foot volcanic plug of Dun Caan as a giant's conning tower.

We know that they were seagoing people, for they colonised the Outer Hebrides and paddled from there over the horizon to St Kilda. We know that they built rafts, and that they used light, hide-and-wood canoes which the people of the west coast of Ireland would familiarise as curraghs. They probably voyaged north by sea, hugging the serrated shore, and walked through hills and glens, building from skins and branches their vessels for local use upon arrival. They often did both. There are at least seventeen places which are still called Tarbert in the north-west Highlands and Islands of Scotland. One of them is in the north of Raasay. A tarbert, or tarbet, or tairbeart, is the Scottish and Irish Gaelic term for an isthmus, a neck of earth and rock between two stretches of water. They were traditionally valuable as land bridges where boats could be hauled from one seaway to another, to avoid sailing or rowing a long way around.

Those earliest humans will have led lives replete with marvels and miracles, unseen dangers, terrible afflictions, thrills, panics and novelties which were related as living history by parents to children. All subsequent human generations would inherit nostalgia for the savage innocence of that garden, would memorialise it in their spiritual rituals, would sketch it and paint it in words and pigment even as they vandalised its remains.

They were Palaeolithic hunter-gatherers. Their earliest numbers have been estimated as low as seventy men, women and children in the whole of Scotland. Although that figure has been dismissed as an underestimate – during most of the 8,000 years of Palaeolithic and Mesolithic Scotland there was probably a drifting population of several hundred people – it must have been accurate at some early point in the resettlement, as a stopped clock is right twice a day. The north-western seaboard is a small part of Scotland, and the peninsula/island of Raasay is even smaller. Among a few hundred first Scots it is unlikely that many made their permanent homes within sight of Dun Caan. Among a few hundred peripatetic and boundlessly inquisitive hunter-gatherers, however, it is certain that over thousands of years many made at least a temporary landfall.

We know from their fossilised footprints across Europe, Africa, Asia and Australasia that they travelled in family groups of differing sizes, which units were the origin of the Highland clan (the Irish and Scottish Gaelic word *clann* itself means children). We know from the same sources that they could accelerate quickly and maintain a high running speed over middle to long distances. Over a short distance they were perhaps as fast as a 21st-century sprinter such as Usain Bolt.

By later standards they did not live for very long. Infant mortality was as high as 40 per cent, and any survivors who passed their fortieth birthday were unlikely to live much longer. Young women in particular were liable to die, from the complications of childbirth, from other infections and from vulnerability to violence.

They ate from the land and the sea. Much of their diet is still identifiable from Hebridean Stone Age middens. It consisted of fish, with which the sea was liberally stocked, shellfish and the venison of the roe deer herds. They roasted and ate hazelnuts, they will have foraged for berries, roots, leaves, herbs and mushrooms. Several aspects of their diet and lifestyle would never disappear. Just as nobody who uses a pestle and mortar has entirely left the Stone Age, so the inhabitants of Raasay would never cease from eating freshly caught fish, slaughtered venison and berries from the wild shrubs.

They talked, sang and shouted to one another using a sophistication of phrasing and a breadth of vocabulary, which helped to ensure the survival of this physically weak and awkward species, and later to establish its primacy. They must have had what would be termed a "language", and it was probably a prototype of the British Celtic tongue which, when such things were first noticed and recorded, was spoken in different highly evolved dialects across almost all of the archipelago and on the neighbouring continent. Somebody, at some time in the prehistoric aeons before the birth of Christ, first called a British river an "arvon" and a dwelling place a "ty".

Their lives may have been short, but they were not always nasty and brutish. Hunter-gatherers have been credited with a better and more healthy lifestyle than early settled farmers. An agriculturalist's grinding daily husbandry of crops and animals was never done. Hunter-gatherers, on the other hand, may have needed to hunt and gather for as little as three hours a day, leaving themselves a lot of time to whittle hazel rods for curragh struts, roast nuts and watch the sun set over Skye. That theory of an "original affluent society" has been criticised for many things, not least its failure to consider the time spent foraging for fuel, which was even more important in the wet and chilly Scottish Hebrides than in the Kalahari savannah. It also overlooked the fact that as a large expanse of territory was essential to maintain Palaeolithic leisure societies, early humans spent much of their down time fighting each other over boundaries. The shattered skulls of Stone Age skeletons were not all caused by cliff falls.

As coastal itinerants they were also vulnerable to such unpredictable natural disasters as the Storegga tsunami, which in about 6220 BC surged through the North Atlantic Ocean, may finally have inundated what remained of Doggerland and simultaneously created the North Sea, the English Channel, and consequently the British islands. It also flooded the most northerly of those islands for several miles inland.

Anybody sheltering on the shoreline of Raasay when the Storegga tsunami struck would have stood little chance of survival. Some people, in however small a family band, were almost certainly there and were almost certainly extinguished. We know that because they left behind their household waste.

As part of a peninsula and as an island, Raasay was sandwiched by two other known Palaeolithic and Mesolithic sites. At Sand, a small, hospitable beach north of Applecross on the Scottish mainland, which looks at Raasay over a couple of miles of sea, between 7500 BC and the Middle Ages people occasionally camped in a rock cave. The earliest, Stone Age, settlers deposited immense quantities of stone and antler bone weapons and tools at Sand, including a harpoon and a knife.

The butchered bones of food included inshore wrasse and cod, and such shellfish as crab, limpets, winkles and mussels. Some scallop and cowrie shells were pierced as if to suggest jewellery, and dogwhelks may have been harvested for dye.

Bloodstone artifacts from twenty miles away on the island of Rum were found at Sand, and sharp mudstone tools were sourced to a site ten miles away at An Corran, in the Staffin district of

Skye. A rock shelter at An Corran, a headland between dark, sheer cliffs and the low green shelter of Staffin Island, relinquished stone and antler bone tools, including scores of the mudstone blades which found their way to Sand. An Corran safeguarded, until they were excavated at the very end of the twentieth century AD, certain surviving fragments of menus featuring cormorants, guillemots, puffins and great auks – the latter being a large, clumsy and flightless Atlantic seabird which somehow avoided being hunted to extinction in the Scottish Hebrides until the middle of the nineteenth century AD.

In the vicinity of An Corran there was also found some of the remains of five prehistoric human beings. Two were children: one was younger than twelve months old, the other was never to see their sixth birthday. One was a teenager, one was in their mid-thirties and one was over forty years of age. The oldest, the forty-something, suffered from osteoarthritis of the cervical spine. On the shore directly below An Corran cave, where those children may have played while their parents knapped mudstone tools, lay the fossilised footprints of a three-toed Hadrosaur. The stony evidence of a previous species to dominate Earth stood witness to the emergence of its successor.

The sites at Sand and Staffin bookmarked Raasay. They sat almost equidistant from the island, overlooking it from the east and the west, occupying the same close neighbourhood. They were within sight of each other in all but the worst of weather. At their backs were the broad, unfenced estates of Wester Ross and Skye. Between them was the generous sea, and in the middle of that sea lay the private insular deer park of Raasay.

They were almost certainly not alone. There will have been other rock shelters, other way stations, other hunting and fishing grounds at Rum and even further afield, which were known intimately to the few Palaeolithic and Mesolithic people who occupied the north-west of Scotland. They present evidence of a sparse but busy and comfortably sustained Stone Age community. The sea sounds between Applecross and Raasay and between Raasay and Staffin could be hostile, but they were not the open ocean. Curraghs and rafts could evidently navigate the short distances with confidence. Over the earliest unrecorded millennia of human time they may have done so regularly, as small parties of hunter-gatherers made their seasonal peregrinations from one familiar source of food and shelter to the next. For the following several thousand years, until the twentieth century AD, seaways were at least as quick and busy as highways in the north-west of Scotland, and Raasay was not an especially remote or isolated part of its region.

The oldest evidence so far unearthed of human settlement on Raasay dates, unsurprisingly, to roughly the same period as the camps and middens at Sand and Staffin, a thousand years before the Storegga tsunami. Between 7629 BC and 7245 BC people lived for at least part of the year in a rock shelter by the side of Loch a' Sguirr in the north of the island. Loch a' Sguirr is a sheltered inlet surrounded by low hills of Lewisian gneiss, which leads onto a wide basin of water surrounded on three sides by the small islands of Fladda, Eilean Taighe and the home island of Raasay itself.

The rock shelter is on the Raasay coast, rather than the shores of Fladda or Eilean Taighe. That holds no great significance, it is likely to have been selected as much for its commodious shelter as for its situation. Fourteen such Mesolithic campsites have been identified in Raasay. They are all on or overlooking the coast. That is partly because cliffside overhang shelters are most likely to be coastal. It also reflects the occupants' desire to be close to the fishing grounds and highways of the sea, and to keep watch over the traffic on their own inshore roads. The same antler bone tools were identified at Loch a' Sguirr as at Sand and Staffin, which is evidence of deer hunting in the hinterlands. But the primacy of the open ocean is obvious. Like their successors across countless generations, the Stone Age occupants of Raasay were seafarers and fishing people.

So passed several thousand years of permanent or occasional human residence in the bays and among the hazel woods of Raasay. In around 4000 BC, some 3,000 to 4,000 years after the first settlements, the small population turned its attentions to crop and animal husbandry.

That momentous change from hunting and gathering to farming, from Palaeolithic and Mesolithic to Neolithic, did not occur overnight. Hunter-gatherers will always have owned a fascination with growing plants, and agriculturalists never stopped augmenting their cultivated and domesticated diet by killing wild game, fishing, and collecting nuts and berries.

Gradually, across millennia, the responsibilities and relative securities of husbandry overtook the thrills, dangers and uncertainties of the chase.

Families, in short, settled down. In Applecross, in Skye and in Raasay they moved out of the rock shelters into huts of wood and stone and thatch. They delineated territory in which to plant their own crops and graze their own domesticated beasts.

Newcomers introduced them to the wheel. As their encounter with the unspoiled planet seeped into their faith traditions, so also the lengthy childhood of their species spent as vagabond free spirits of the earth and sea would never be forgotten by *Homo sapiens*. It would haunt their folk memories and inform their mythologies, but they did not go back.

It took settled societies to create the megalithic structures which flowered across Europe in the later millennia of the Stone Age. Only people who were established in one place had the means or the inclination to design and erect standing stones, Herculean public buildings and personal tombs. They went up all over the continent after 5000 BC. Some 35,000 menhirs, dolmens and stone rows, cyclopean walls and circles survive in Europe. There is a concentration of their remains on the Atlantic seaboard, in Iberia, France and the British Isles. Their most famous manifestations, such as the assemblies of megaliths at Filitosa in Corsica, Stonehenge in England and Carnac in Brittany, open windows on the origins of monumental architecture and statuary.

Megalithic culture was enthusiastically embraced by the recently settled hunter-gatherers of the northern and western islands of

Scotland. In Shetland and Orkney, stone circles were thrown up. On the west side of Lewis, in around 3000 BC, the spectacular Callanish cruciform was raised.

At the same time, a dolmen was built at the southern tip of Raasay.

Dolmens are elementary structures of three or more large flat rocks, consisting of a capstone balanced on supporting walls. They appear in silhouette like a massive, three-dimensional Stone Age representations of the Cyrillic pi symbol. They were as fundamental to the megalithic world as the stone circle and the standing stone. They are still to be found on sun scorched plains in Portugal, in old French forests and on Irish moors, as well as being littered plentifully around the unspoiled coast of the Black Sea. In southern Europe dolmens have had Christian chapels grafted onto their sides, partly because a readymade gable wall was not to be spurned, probably also in acknowledgment of their role as the first sarcophaguses or mausoleums, as burial chambers to safeguard the mortal remains of human individuals or family groups.

Three Neolithic dolmens have so far been uncovered in Raasay. Two of them are still mostly submerged in the earth. The third stands proud, as it has for five millennia, on an unusually broad expanse of turf at Eyre on the southern tip of the island. Some person or persons unknown is buried in its unexcavated chamber. Its capstone, which is only slightly askew after fifty centuries of Hebridean wear, had been hacked out of a nearby rock face and hauled down to the machair. It looks out across the sea at a landscape in which the occupants would be instantly and completely at home, which is at least part of the structure's purpose. To the east, at the far side of the Inner Sound of Raasay, the slopes of Applecross loom up towards the sky and what would become known as the Scarp islands scatter across Broadford Bay. To the west the bare hills of southern Skye dominate the near horizon.

Many European dolmens have collapsed or been dismantled, their component stones reused in later building projects. The dolmen at Eyre lies between two twentieth-century crofthouses, in the middle of a settlement which dates back to the Neolithic period, on top of some of the best agricultural land in the island, but its presence has been respected and its dignity undisturbed by 200 generations of human inhabitants.

The Raasay chambered tombs were built 3,000 years before the birth of Christ. They therefore give us the first records of permanent human residency on the island 5,000 years ago. It is not a perfect record. Even if there are no older dolmens still to be discovered, it is likely that a small human settlement had been present for some time, perhaps a millennium or two, before it got round to building megalithic tombs. It is also possible, although less likely, that people who had not actually lived there were buried in Raasay by their equally alien families, inside weighty slabs of rock beneath several tons of granite.

But Occam's Razor, the balance of probabilities, suggests that the tombs were for respected occupants of the island who were anxious to spend their afterlives in the same heavenly surroundings which had cradled them from birth to death, still keeping a weather eye on the distant hills and the restless sea.

It would always have required several pairs of strong hands to dislodge and carry and then lift and re-lay the capstones on the dolmens at Eyre and elsewhere. "Raasay is supposed to have been very long inhabited," wrote the eighteenth-century man of letters Samuel Johnson. "On one side of it they show caves, into which the rude nations of the first ages retreated from the weather ..."

Johnson visited Raasay as a guest of John, 11th MacLeod clan chief of the island, for four days and nights in the September of 1773. "A proof much stronger of the distance at which the first possessors of this island lived from the present time," he continued, "is afforded by the stone heads of arrows which are very frequently picked up. The people call them Elf-bolts, and believe that the fairies shoot them at the cattle. They nearly resemble those which Mr. Banks has lately brought from the savage countries in the Pacifick Ocean, and must have been made by a nation to which the use of metals was unknown."

Stone Age arrowheads, axes and knives, similar to those which the botanist Joseph Banks had carried on Captain James Cook's *Endeavour* from Australia to London in 1771, were regularly found in Raasay throughout the centuries. They indicated a busy prehistoric population. The residue of their dwelling places and monuments suggest that Stone Age people settled all over the twenty-four square miles of Raasay. The vestiges of more than a dozen prehistoric communities, some of one household, others of three or four, are scattered from the shore of Loch Arnish in the north to Fearns in the south. At Doire Domhain, between Manish and Glam on the west coast, early rig and furrow systems of communal agricultural troughs have been identified between the circular walls of huts and cairns. In those prototypes of the lazy-beds which would later corrugate the hillsides of the Highlands and Islands of Scotland, the region's first bere, or barley, was cultivated, and certain edible wild grasses were trained to be domesticated oats.

No censuses were conducted in the Stone, Bronze and Iron Ages, as newly agricultural Britons moved out of the millennia before Christ, and into the centuries before Christ. The population was by later standards young and vulnerable, and prone to the drastic shrinkages caused by extreme weather events, harvest failures or epidemics. It has been suggested that during the Scottish Iron Age, which is to say the years from approximately 800 BC to AD 400, some 2,000 or 3,000 people lived between the Solway Firth and the Northern Isles. If they were evenly spread, five or six large family groups in Raasay would be a generous but not unreasonable guess for an easily defensible place with abundant natural resources. The local and national numbers could of course have been smaller or larger, and at times in the distant centuries they will have been both.

In the middle of the First World War, in about 1916, a crofter found "in a natural rock shelter beneath the cliffs" at Eyre, close to the district's surviving dolmen, a large metal spearhead. The leaf-shaped blade was a foot long and 2.5 inches at its broadest. It had a "fine, dark green patina" and was in good condition other than a severed tip and a broken rivet-hole in the socket. Raasay crofters were not unfamiliar with weapons of war. Spears had been carried and used in the island by locals and by hostile visitors from the Dark Ages to the nineteenth century. In 1922 this discovery was given as a children's toy to a friendly neighbour. At some point in the following sixty years playful youngsters accidentally snapped off its tip, and in 1975 John MacLeod, the son of the boy who received it as a gift in 1922, sold it to the National Museum of Scotland in Edinburgh.

Its true antiquity was only then confirmed. The Eyre spearhead was a beautifully preserved relic of the Scottish Bronze Age; it was dated to between 950 and 750 BC. It had been carried and used by, in the words of the National Museum, "an elite Late Bronze Age warrior" to shed human or animal blood in the island of Raasay not only long before Culloden or Waterloo, but also several centuries before the Battle of Thermopylae.

The Eyre spearhead was contemporaneous with the first bright flames of Celtic activity in the British Isles, and may therefore be among the earliest manifestations of a culture, a language and a people which would inhabit the island of Raasay for a further three millennia until the twenty-first century after Christ.

Whoever abandoned or lost their spearhead in Raasay in the centuries before Christ is likely to have been familiar with an industrious Bronze Age and Iron Age community. They will have known, if not built and occupied, the broch on a hillock at Dun Borodale, a mile away from Eyre. They will have crawled inside the souterrain at Suisnish for supplies or shelter.

Brochs and souterrains were signature features of the architecture of the Scottish Iron Age. They are to be found in various stages of disrepair across the Highlands and Islands. Brochs were formidable defensive structures: round stone towers which served as prototypical castle keeps, with layered cavity walls and small protected doorways at ground level.

Souterrains are less transparent to later eyes. They are found across western Europe (their etymological origin, *sous terre*, is of course French for "underground"). Shallow, lined galleries beneath the surface of the earth, souterrains contain no evidence of human burial or human habitation. They may have occasionally been deployed as hideaways from rude invaders, but were neither defensible nor well concealed and were probably conceived as communal storage facilities. They were early rural lock-ups, and over 700 of them have been located in Scotland in different shapes and sizes and in varying stages of collapse and good repair.

There are two uncovered souterrains in Raasay. They date from the thousand-year-long Hebridean Iron Age between 500 BC and 500 AD.

One of them is a short walk from Raasay House. It is no more than a broad cleft in the rock, which was tidily roofed with stone lintels and topped off with earth and turf. Its name, Uamh nan Ràmh, "Cave of the Oars" suggests that although it was originally constructed in the Iron Age, in later centuries it was utilised as a boat shed. In 1773 Samuel Johnson was offered a dubious backstory of Uamh nan Ràmh by the MacLeods of Raasay House.

"There is still a cavity near the house called the oar-cave," wrote Johnson, "in which the seamen, after one of those piratical expeditions … used, as tradition tells us, to hide their oars. This hollow was near the sea, that nothing so necessary might be far to be fetched; and it was secret, that enemies, if they landed, could find nothing. Yet it is not very evident of what use it was to hide their oars from those, who, if they were masters of the coast, could take away their boats."

"A little from the shore," added Johnson's amanuensis James Boswell, who was with him in Raasay, "… is a kind of subterraneous house. There has been a natural fissure, or separation of rock, running towards the sea, which has been roofed over with long stones, and above them turf has been laid. In that place the inhabitants used to keep their oars."

Less than a mile south of Uamh nan Ràmh, on a bluff above the Sound of Raasay, is a well-constructed underground chamber. It is anonymous and partly collapsed, but undoubtedly a souterrain. It stands hard by the old township of Suisnish, which in the middle of the nineteenth century was cleared to make way for a sheep farm, suggesting that it could have been a community asset for almost two millennia.

The construction of a broch and souterrains in a couple of square miles of southern Raasay 2,000 years ago teaches a similar lesson to that of the dolmens 5,000 years ago. Not only would a broch and a souterrain have required many strong hands to build and maintain; they could only have been imagined to serve a substantial settlement. However many there were, and whatever they called themselves, the Iron Age people of Raasay were on the island to stay.

We cannot yet know how those ancestors understood themselves, their home or their culture. The human phenomenon known to the Greeks as Keltoi and to the Romans as Celtae, was by the last millennium before Christ reaching tentacles out of France and the Low Countries and into the British Isles.

Even in the distant Scottish islands, prehistoric people rarely existed in isolation from the European continent. The presence in the Hebrides, in Shetland and in Orkney, of megalithic structures proves that from the earliest times cultural influences crossed seas and mountains. If such features as dolmens, aligned stone circles and souterrains could make their way from France and Iberia to Lewis and Raasay, so also could language and spiritual affirmation. It may be significant that the terms dolmen and menhir derive from Brittanic Celtic, Welsh, Cornish and Breton words for a table stone and a tall stone.

It has been suggested, firstly by the Greek historian Ephorus in the 4th century BC, that the traffic went the other way, that Celtic culture originated in the islands off the mouth of the Rhine and spread eastwards from there into continental Europe. Such a counterflow did in places occur. It is often proposed that, as their name implies, the Bretons of Brittany in north-western France migrated there from south-western Britain, from Cornwall, Devon, Dorset and Wales rather than the other way round.

But there was not necessarily an invasion and subsequent cultural colonisation from east to west or vice versa. The process over millennia could have been, and probably was, symbiotic and synchronous, as the people of the Continent and the archipelago sailed to and fro and fed off each other. As we do not know, it is lazily conceded that the British Isles became "Celtic" early in the first millennium BC, perhaps 700 or 800 years before the birth of Christ. That loosely coincides with the flowering of the Bronze Age, the use of metal weapons and tools – the Celts were notable metalworkers – and the creation of souterrains.

The matter is complicated by the fact that while Greek and Roman historians and chroniclers recognised by name the Keltoi and Celtae of continental Europe by 500 BC, it was not until 2,300 years later that anybody attached the term to the people of the islands in the North Atlantic mist.

Before AD 1707, when the scholar Edward Lhuyd first described them in print as Celts, the early inhabitants of the British Isles – of all of the British Isles from Kent to Anglesey, Caithness to Raasay – were known by ancients and moderns alike as Pritanoi, or Brittanic/Brythonic, or British.

That does not mean that the Pritanoi were not a branch, or several branches, of the European Celtic tree. The god called Lugh, or Lugus, or Lug, or Llew, or a score of other dialectical derivatives, was a powerful pan-Celtic deity. His name was given at their foundation to the towns of Loudun and Lyon (which under Roman administration became Lughdunum) in France, to London and Luton in England, to Dinlleu in Wales, to Leiden in Holland, to Lugones in Spain, to Louth in Ireland, and to Lothian and Loudoun in Scotland. In some mythologies Lugh became the father of Cú Chulainn, who left his name on the Cuillin mountain range of the Scottish island of Skye.

He is also recalled seasonally. The Irish harvest festival is celebrated as Lughnasadh. In such parts of Gaelic Scotland as the island of Raasay, the eighth month of the year is known as Lunasdal. When 21st-century Raasay Gaels refer in their native language to August, they invoke a pre-Christian, and pre-Roman, past which their ancestors shared with the people of Lugo in Galicia and Lyon in the foothills of the Alps.

The name of the Raasay broch known as Dun Borodale tells a similar story. "Dun" is another common Celtic word. In Scottish and Irish Gaelic it denotes a fort. "Dun" had the same meaning when the defensive bastions of London and Loudun were christened with a god's name in England and France. Its Welsh equivalent is "din", which in that country gives us Dinlleu. Tintagel, the name of the postulate Arthurian castle in Celtic Cornwall, is a corruption of Dintagel.

There are endless clues to a shared history. The Iron Age spearhead found in southern Raasay is not unique in the Hebrides to that island. Almost identical survivals have been discovered elsewhere. At Glendale in Skye a spearhead of similar antiquity was found in a freshwater spring. Abandoned spearheads have emerged in peat bogs at Struan in Skye and at Carinish in North Uist, where in the 1970s four were found together. The Raasay artefact was unearthed in a dry site. Its equivalents in Skye and Uist were deposited in bogs, or what became bogs, and in a water source. That places them securely in a European Celtic tradition of immersing swords and spears, at the end of their or their owners' useful life, in a watery grave. In that light the Glendale, Struan and Carinish spearheads were Hebridean equivalents of the thirteenth-century French romance that the dying paladin King Arthur's sword Excalibur was thrown at the last by his companion into a lake, as well as of the caches of assorted weaponry which have in modern times been retrieved from lochs and lagoons in Scotland, England, Wales, Ireland, France, Poland, Germany and elsewhere.

Bryan Sykes, Professor of Human Genetics at Oxford University, argued that analysis of mitochondrial DNA, and the Y chromosome indicated that most of the Celts who colonised the British Isles in the Bronze and Iron Ages sailed from Galicia in north-western Spain. His genetic evidence was supported by historical revelations of the development of ocean-going boats in Galicia in the centuries before Christ, and by the cultural and linguistic connections between the Gallaeci tribes who populated the region and the people of Ireland, Wales, England and Scotland. They built in northern Spain circular drystone brochs which they knew as "brixs" or "duno". At its most basic, the "gal" in Gallaeci and Galicia shares a root with Galway in Ireland and Galloway in Scotland.

Bryan Sykes contended that Celtic DNA from the Atlantic coasts of Spain and France was still in the twenty-first century the most popular gene throughout the British Isles, overwhelming even in England such latecomers as Roman, Anglo-Saxon, Norman and Norse. Many of his conclusions were challenged by later genetic surveys and scientists, but the primacy of a Celtic cultural past from Carloway to Cornwall is now clear.

Although Celtic hegemony in Gaul, or modern France, was famously replaced by Roman Latin ascendancy in the decades following Julius Caesar's defeat of Vercingetorix and his Gallic allies at Alesia in 52 BC, the French Celts themselves did not then disappear from the face of the land. They remained in groups and tribes of greater or lesser size and seclusion, gradually adopting new rulers, customs, languages and cultures until a series of fresh ideas of France were presented to the world.

Those ideas included such telltale hangovers as the "Asterix the Gaul" comic strip and the presence in the later French idiom of such Celtic trace words as *gobelet*, meaning a drinking beaker, which shares the root of the word for mouth, "gob", with Irish and Scottish Gaelic, and Welsh, as *gober*, which means to guzzle from a beaker, as *cabane*, *chemin*, *truand* and *mouton*, all of which and many more French words have cousins in British Celtic languages. The French word for a church, *église*, derives from the Graeco/Latin noun for an assembly, *ecclesia*. That is remarkable only because it is therefore contiguous with the Welsh *eglwys* and the Gaelic *eaglais*, and because they are all a thousand miles from the equivalent English noun, church or kirk.

Such words, and their associated culture, drifted piecemeal into the British islands until, over a period of many centuries, they became hegemonic. Such vernacular and material connections point to a shared past between the insular Pritanoi and the people who emerged from central and western Europe to be called Celts by Herodotus and his contemporaries in the fifth century BC, and perhaps also by themselves. As the clock ticked down to Year Zero and the end of prehistory, the British Isles became a quarrelsome but stable Celtic society.

Then Jesus Christ was born and the Romans invaded, and everything changed.

3

Soldiers and Saints

> "The Picts and the Britons, who foolishly, in these two remote islands of the ocean, and only in part even of them, strive to oppose all the rest of the world."

SAMUEL JOHNSON visited Raasay in 1773 in the company of his friend and future biographer, James Boswell. As they landed at Churchton Bay in the south of the island, Boswell noticed "a cross, or rather the ruins of one, upon a rock, which had to me a pleasing vestige of religion".

The cross which took Boswell's eye was engraved on the flat front of a modest outcrop of gneiss hard by the landing area, much as many centuries later a printed wall poster might have been pasted there, where it would confront anybody and everybody who came ashore. At the time of Johnson and Boswell's visit it was roughly a thousand years old. Boswell was told that lairds of Raasay "in old times" used to pray before the inscribed rock face. "I could not but kneel upon the spot and gratefully remember the death of Christ, uttering a short prayer. This I did the morning I left Raasay, while the family [of the proprietor, MacLeod of Raasay] accompanied us to the shore; but nobody could imagine that I was doing anything more than attentively satisfying my curiosity."

The two men proceeded to Raasay House where they were entertained by John MacLeod, 11th of Raasay, and his family. The family included MacLeod's three sons, the oldest of whom, James, was twelve years old at the time and would inherit his insular estate upon the death of his father thirteen years later.

At some point between the year of his accession in 1786 and his own death in 1823, James MacLeod of Raasay set men to build a carriage road between the landing place and his big house, a distance of less than a quarter of a mile. While they were clearing the track the workmen uncovered, a hundred yards inland from the old rock face carving at the landing place, a free-standing, rectangular, dressed and engraved stone which measured four feet eight inches long, one foot nine inches across and six inches thick. James MacLeod instructed his men to transplant it upright by the side of the road behind his mansion, at the foot of a prominence known as Temptation Hill, where it remained.

The engravings on the stone and the rock face were virtually identical. They were faithfully reproduced Pictish symbols, carved with consummate skill in bas-relief. Their date of origin is not precisely known. They could have been carved as early as the sixth century AD and as late as the tenth. Their significance is not in doubt.

They are evidence of the arrival in Raasay of the island's two paramount cultural and spiritual influences in recorded history: Gaelic and Christianity.

The Romans who invaded south-eastern Britain in AD 43 were pagans, who discovered in the islands a comprehensible polytheistic society. They stayed for four centuries, in which period Rome itself became a Christian imperium and the new monotheism was permitted to leak into its westernmost province.

The Highlands and Islands of Scotland famously did not become part of Provincia Britannica. For most of their hegemony Roman forces occupied, more or less comfortably, the regions which would become the Scottish Borders and the Central Belt between Edinburgh and Glasgow. In the earliest years of their presence, their camps, garrisons and stores suffered periodic raids from the northern tribes. The Latins and Gauls of the legions identified those Highland tribes as Celts belonging to a dozen different clans. In AD 297 Eumenius, a Gallic-Roman writer of Greek descent who was born and raised in Lugdunum, modern Lyon, in the Celtica region of old France, named the indigenes of the British islands who had remained out of, and hostile to, the Roman Provincia Britannica as "Picti and Hiberni". Picts and Hibernians, to the north beyond the mountains and to the west beyond the Irish Sea.

Picti means painted in Latin. From his seat in the heart of Celtic France, Eumenius was probably referring to the tattoos of such northern British people as the Carnonacae, Decantae, Lugi, Epidii, Attacotti and Caledonii.

In AD 83 or 84 the Roman general Gnaeus Julius Agricola led a substantial army of legionary and auxiliary foot soldiers and cavalry on a punitive expedition north of the Firth of Forth and into the badlands of those tattooed tribes. Agricola's object was not to conquer but to deter the Picti from further forays into Roman comfort zones.

Six years earlier Agricola's daughter Julia had married a scion of the Roman upper middle class named Publius Cornelius Tacitus. The general's son-in-law would become a historian, and posterity's main source for accounts of the Battle of Mons Graupius.

The location of that engagement is unknown. It could have been anywhere between Fife and Moray. Tacitus recorded that Agricola sent his fleet up the east coast to provide naval support, and marched and rode along the North Sea littoral with as many as 30,000 men to meet a Pictish force of at least the same strength. To neutralise the Caledonian preference for guerilla strikes and tempt them onto an open battlefield, the Roman general approached his opponents' granaries with the clear intention of destroying their winter supplies.

It worked. The Picts assembled at the top of a hill, the Romans sent legions into their heart and deployed cavalry on the flanks, and the battle was won. Tacitus suggests that there were 10,000 Caledonian dead for the cost of just 360 of Agricola's men. Tacitus also gives us the figure of Calgacus, his possibly imaginary leader of the Picti. Calgacus' famous attack on Roman virtues following his defeat by Agricola – "To robbery, slaughter, plunder, they give the lying name of empire; they make a solitude and call it peace" – was almost certainly an invention of Tacitus. The phrase may have represented the historian's pacific republicanism; it may have been a swipe at his overbearing father-in-law. It may also have stemmed from his own paternity: in the alleys and the atria of Rome it was sometimes rumoured that Tacitus, whose origins north of the city were suspiciously obscure and who displayed an unRoman love of hyperbole, was in fact a Celt. The lines were certainly prescient. Calgacus' words would echo through much of the rest of Highland history.

Whatever the casualties, we know from its aftermath that Mons Graupius was a Roman success. Agricola returned south, ultimately to a triumph in Rome. The northern indigenes retreated to their far-flung brochs and crannogs, their clachans and their islands. For a century or two the incursions ceased, in both directions. Romans such as Agricola announced that there was nothing worth exploring or appropriating north of the Highland line – nothing, in fact, but a great Caledonian forest, sparse and wind-blasted and slowly turning to peat underfoot, and altogether unpromising to a man hoping to recreate Mediterranean comforts such a very long way from home. In places such as Raasay, the northern British retired to lead their insular lives, tell their tales and nurse their grievances, always aware of, but unmolested by, the global military power which loured just a couple of hundred miles to their south.

On at least one occasion they broke out. In the year 376, emboldened by signs of Roman retreat, a Pictish host rode south and rampaged through the Antonine Wall. Some war bands sailed down the coast and harassed Romano-British defences and settlements from the sea. The Romans retaliated, but it took two years for a new general and fresh legions to quell the rising, after which Roman troops largely confined themselves south of Hadrian's Wall, before leaving Britain for good thirty or forty years later.

Among the tribes involved in the assaults of 376 was a group known as the Attacotti. The origins of the Attacotti were obscure, even by Pictish standards. They were rumoured to come from the Hebridean islands or from Ireland. It is likely however that the Attacotti came from both Ireland and the Hebrides, as few people on the British mainland saw any difference between the two, and that they were an augur of the future.

If most of the northern mainland was chiefly Pictish and its people spoke a British Celtic dialect akin to Welsh, the western seaboard and archipelago were at least as closely linked to Irish Gaels. The Mull of Kintyre is 12 miles from Ulster and 200 miles from Edinburgh. Portpatrick in Galloway is 20 miles from the sea roads of Belfast and 100 miles from Glasgow. The southernmost large Hebridean island of Islay sits equidistant between Antrim and Argyll. To the seagoing people of all the Hebrides, Ireland and the Irish were and always had been vastly more accessible than the Pictish communities of Inverness or Aberdeen. In the millennia before the flags and borders of nation states, a symbiosis between the close neighbours of northern Ireland and western Scotland was inevitable.

Four centuries of Roman occupation atomised the British tribes. It prevented the evolution of mainland Britain as a single Celtic polity and civilisation. Following the first century AD, Celtic society was fragmented around the northern, western and southern peripheries of the archipelago. A network of neighbouring tribes became a diaspora of different subcultures. In the past the British people had offered at least moral support, sanctuary and a last resort to the resistance of their relatives and neighbours on the Continent to Roman imperialism. In the past, the Caledoni had been connected by language, culture and history, by occasional friendships, alliances and blood relationships, to those such as the Iceni of Boudicca in East Anglia, as well as to the people of Cumbria, Cymru and Kernow in their south-west. Borders and boundaries between the tribes and cultures were undefined and extremely porous. Raasay was one of many frontier communities, occupying the broad sweep of territory between island Gaelic and mainland Pictish civilisations, adopting the language of one and much of the culture and customs of the other.

Further south and east, the enormous and apparently indestructible bulwark of Roman Britain severed those ties. Only the sea to the west, across which the land of the Hiberni was often visible, remained an open Celtic thoroughfare.

The crosses and other motifs carved at Raasay's Churchton Bay landing rock face and on the nearby symbol stone are unusual. They are an amalgamation of the influences of different cultures which illustrate the syncretism of the early Celtic Church.

At the top are cross-of-arc and chi-rho designs. The cross-of-arc was created by describing on dressed stone, as if with a compass, four linked circles in a quadrate around a central fixed point. The resulting leaf pattern then forms the bars of a curved Maltese cross. Other identical, contemporaneous cross-of-arc crucifixes are found carved into stones in the island of the Hiberni, which would become Ireland. Ireland was of course not the home of Pictish, Brittanic Celtic culture, but of its Gaelic cousin.

Inside the Raasay cross-of-arc is inscribed a basic but enigmatic chi-rho, a common cipher among early Christians. It was nothing more complex than the superimposition of the first two letters in Greek Cyrillic of the name of Christ: χ-ρ, prounced "kee-row", so that the "χ" was overlaid with the "ρ".

Beneath those layered indicators of a Christian presence the sculptor laid what is usually described, because it looks exactly like one, as a tuning fork. It cannot however represent a modern tuning fork, as that device was not invented until AD 1711. It is a common Pictish emblem. The tuning fork is discovered, in various degrees of elaboration, on carved, dressed symbol stones most famously and explicitly at the old Pictish settlement of Aberfeldy in Perthshire and at Strathmiglo in Fife.

The Romans in Britain were particularly attached to the god Mithras, a Persian deity whose mystery flourished among the imperial legions between the first and fourth centuries annis domini. Mithraic temples have been excavated in London, below Hadrian's Wall and in East Lothian. Their rectangular design was idiosyncratic: two rows of congregants sat facing each other across a long narrow aisle which led from the entrance to an altar. The floor plans of mithraea looked rather like tuning forks, with the lines of seated initiates as the two tines of the fork and the altar as the handle.

Beneath the tuning fork on both the Raasay rock face and the dressed stand-alone stone is a decorated crescent transposed by a "v rod", as if a segment of orange was overlaid by a 45-degrees compass. It is among the most common symbols in the lexicon of Pictish design, and possibly translates as a broken arrow on a horizontal crescent moon, which in turn may symbolise death.

There is no reliable and comprehensive dictionary of Pictish symbols. But if they have a meaning, if they were signposts, if they told a story to visitors landing at Churchton Bay, it is possible to decipher the three motifs on the Raasay stones from top to bottom as "Christian", "Temple" and "Burial ground". That translation would be logical. A few hundred yards up the shore from the landing place at Churchton Bay stands the ruins of a chapel and graveyard dedicated to, and probably originally consecrated by, St Moluag.

Moluag was a muscular Christian missionary from the Dál nAraidi people of north-eastern Ireland. He was born in around AD 520 and some thirty years later he sailed with an entourage to Lismore, an island half the size of Raasay off the coast of Argyll.

In Lismore, at the same time as his famous contemporary Columba was establishing a headquarters in Iona, Moluag built his church and his base and set off to convert Scotland to Christianity.

Moluag lived to a good old age, dying in 592 among the Pictish communities of the north-east coast of Scotland. During four busy decades in the second half of the sixth century he evangelised across the world of the Picts. Following Moluag's work, and that of such Irish and British missionary co-religionists as Columba, Ninian and Maolrubha, it was possible to proclaim from pulpits across the north of Britain the arrival of Jesus Christ and the departure, after a thousand busy years, of the great pagan god Lugh.

Moluag's most celebrated accomplishments were in the populous east coast farmlands, but he consecrated a number of sites in the northern Hebrides. His name was left in the far north of the island of Lewis, at Europie in Ness where Teampall Mholuaidh still stands, and at Trotternish in Skye, where the township of Kilmaluag testifies to one of his churches. The tiny island of Pabay in Broadford Bay off the coast of southern Skye was probably given its name, which translates as Priest's Island, to mark the presence of Moluag or his followers. They were identifiable missionaries of the Celtic Church.

Unlike their Roman colleagues, their tonsures were not bald crowns surrounded by a halo of hair, but a punkish shaved strip running from ear to ear, leaving only the forelock and back tresses to grow free and long. More disturbingly in an international faith, they calculated the date of Easter in a different manner and therefore observed the commemorations of the resurrection of Jesus Christ on different days. That resulted, according to a contemporary account, in all of the rites of Easter being celebrated twice annually in at least one royal British household of mixed traditions. Those idiosyncrasies would be largely reconciled at the Synod of Whitby in AD 664, in favour of the established preferences of the Church of St Peter and St Paul in Italy, but during the lifetimes of Moluag and Columba they remained unapologetically distinct and obstinately separate.

The learned seventh-century abbot Wilfrid of Ripon in North Yorkshire expressed the frustrations of most of his contemporaries with the contrarians of the Celtic Church. Wilfrid at the Whitby synod, according to the Venerable Bede, announced: "The Easter which we keep, we saw celebrated by all at Rome, where the blessed Apostles, Peter and Paul, lived, taught, suffered, and were buried; we saw the same done by all in Italy and in Gaul, when we travelled through those countries for the purpose of study and prayer. We found it observed in Africa, Asia, Egypt, Greece, and all the world, wherever the Church of Christ is spread abroad, among divers nations and tongues, at one and the same time; save only among these and their accomplices in obstinacy, I mean the Picts and the Britons, who foolishly, in these two remote islands of the ocean, and only in part even of them, strive to oppose all the rest of the world."

"In these two remote islands of the ocean ..." The Celts of the British islands had something of a history with Rome. Wilfrid would not be the last southern theologian to express frustration with the singularities of Gaelic Christianity.

Since the early thirteenth century an elegant stone chapel has stood among the gravestones on Moluag's patch in Raasay. It almost certainly replaced an earlier construction, to which the inscribed rock face and freestanding waymarker stones may have drawn the attention of all who appeared on the island. The chapel, which was naturally dedicated to Moluag as Cille Moluag, which in turn was later corrupted to Kilmoluag, was described in 1563 by a former vicar of the parish of Raasay and Snizort in Skye as the only "paroche kirk, callit Killmolowocke" on the island. By the time of Boswell and Johnson's visit 200 years later, the Scottish Church had in most places moved away from Moluag's Catholicism, and Cille Moluag, the saint's Raasay shrine, had become the evocative little ruin which remains.

Moluag would have been taught to use Latin at the liturgy, but he was a demotic native speaker of sean-Ghaeilge, old Irish. He appeared in Pictish Scotland several centuries after the death of the common proto-Celtic language, if such a mother tongue ever existed, but was able to communicate with the users of Brittonic Celtic.

He possibly always had. We do not know exactly when people from Ireland first settled on the west coast of Scotland. Their proximity to each other suggests the existence for centuries of neighbouring families and communities who spoke different dialects, even different languages, without much antagonism. For perhaps 400 years the Gaels and the Picts shared at least their fear of – and consequent antipathy to – Roman Britain. Irish Gaelic will have been heard in Argyll before the assertion there of the post-Roman realm of Dal Riata in the fifth century. The Attacotti and those whom the Venerable Bede described in around AD 730 as "the Scots migrated from Ireland" had been around for centuries before, as Bede continued in his narrative, they had "either by friendship, or by force of arms, secured for themselves those settlements among the Picts which they still possess".

Things rarely happened quickly in antiquity. There were tensions and skirmishes between different clans. The historian Tim Clarkson suggests that Irish annals point to a fifty-year running conflict in Skye between established Pictish families and arriviste Dal Riatan Gaels at the end of the seventh century. If that was true it is certain to have involved, in some manner at some stage, the clerics and the lay people of Raasay. But there was no protracted war of conquest, no single invasion of Pictish territory by massed armies of the Scotti. The soft powers of religion, culture, language and sport were deployed. Gaelic culture, boosted enormously by its adoption of the powerful new creed of Christianity – a faith which along with its obvious virtues, was thoroughly modern and cosmopolitan – dominated and then assimilated its Pictish neighbour until only slabs of stone carved with mysterious and beautiful runes remained of the latter's identity, but the former was able to lend its tribal name to a new country.

Even though they shared its language and its religion, western islands such as Raasay would for several centuries have little or nothing to do with the new country of Scotland.

Medieval Raasay and Rona were, as they would remain until late in the twentieth century, self-contained. The islands' forty-three caves and rock shelters, seventeen of which in the twenty-first century still contained such evidence of prehistoric human habitation as middens and dry stone walls, had offered what they required to peripatetic hunter-gathers. They were likely to have been regarded communally, used and maintained by passing individuals and groups, like the bothies of much later times. But caves and rock shelters were unsatisfactory to more permanent residents. Settlements and steadings were established throughout the island, from Umachan in the north to Eyre in the south, with a concentration of activity on the hillsides of Fearns in the south-east. Early detached family homes were modest round-houses, or had long, narrow, low drystone walls with rounded gable ends and thatched roofs. They were often built down gentle slopes, to prevent rainfall from collecting within, and to drain away the effluent of animals sheltering in the lower quarters.

Much of the land was regarded as common property, held in trust by a family of hereditary leaders: an assumption which would survive more or less unchallenged until the nineteenth century, when it was summarily and traumatically removed. A couple of dozen families will have comfortably occupied Raasay, newly Christian families within the beneficence of the holy men at Cille Moluag. They were agricultural smallholders whose crops and beasts were supplemented by the excellent freshwater and saltwater fisheries for which Raasay would become celebrated; by wild herbs and by such other inheritances from their hunter-gatherer forebears as the collection of berries and nuts from the island's shrubbery, and the killing of deer and birds. They had learned to cut and dry slabs of peat from the bogs for household fuel, using a singular iron hoe with a long wooden handle which they came to call a *tairsgear*. Like their Stone Age ancestors, few of them lived past the age of forty years. It was a life not vastly different from, or envied by, most of the people in the rest of the British Isles. For that reason alone, they were largely left in peace until the men arrived by sea from the distant north.

4

The Summer Travellers

"Haakon's 1263 mission turned into a valedictory tour of the Suðreyjar. Collecting armed recruits and accumulating more ships as he went, the Viking emperor sailed through the Minch to the saltwater channels skirting Raasay."

FOR more than a thousand years, anybody in Raasay who was christened Tormod MacLèoid, Norman MacLeod in English translation – and there were many such men – assumed a fully Norse name.

By extension, as late as the twenty-first century a putative Ronald Nicolson of Arnish in Raasay carried a Norse identity in a Norse township in a Norse island – even though he, like Tormod MacLeoid – had never set foot in Scandinavia. The Christian name Ronald, Raghnall in Gaelic, derived from the Old Norse Rǫgnvaldr. Nicolson, which in Gaelic became Macneacail, was a variant of Nicolassen. Arnish derives from *orn-nes*, the Old Norse term for "eagle headland".

The precise etymology of the island of Raasay itself is more troublesome. The "ay" suffix certainly derives from the Norse "ey", meaning island, and its Gaelic transliterations are to be found throughout the Hebrides.

Early in the twentieth century the Skyeman Alexander Robert

Forbes, in his *Place-names of Skye*, registered the original of Raasay as "Roe-isle or roe-ridge-isle; 'raa', a roe, and 'ey', island, equal to 'ràr-àss-ey', roe-ridge-isle; in Norse 'rauneyja'."

Thormodus Torfæus was a seventeenth-century Icelandic alumnus of the University of Copenhagen who in 1682 was appointed Royal Historian of the Kingdom of Denmark-Norway, a union which between 1537 and 1814 included such remnants of the medieval Norse Empire as Iceland, Greenland and the Faroe Islands. Torfæus applied himself diligently. His native Icelandic language was closely related to Old Norse, and he used as historical sources a number of Norse saga manuscripts, which he rendered into Latin in his final copy.

Exploring the former overseas territories, Torfæus came across reference to the island that Alexander Forbes would dub "Roe-isle". He called it "Rosay". The Old Norse word "rá", as Forbes suggested, derived from the runic Proto-Norse ᚱᚨᛇᚺᚨᚾ, or raïhan, and was "akin to the English roe as in roe deer". It is in fact the origin of the English word "roe as in roe deer", and in some Norse dialects and traditions "rá" was pronounced "ro". The evidence suggests that Raasay was an island of roe deer, which in itself was useful knowledge for boatloads of hungry Norse seafarers. Samuel Johnson, who as a lexicographer felt obliged to test the theories, suggested delving into Icelandic to uncover "from 'ras' (Icel.), a course, or 'ra', a landmark, and 'ay' or 'ey', an island". His brief excursion down the rabbit holes of medieval Gaelic, Icelandic and Old Norse was soon abandoned.

"The name Raasay," wrote Alexander Forbes, "as may be surmised, appears in numerous documents and prints, etc., from at least 1549 onwards, and varies considerably from Raarsa to Ratharsair, etc., the late Dr. Norman Macleod (Caraid nan Gaidheal) spelling it Rathasa. In the Book of Clanranald, Macleod of Raasay is designed 'Eoin Garbh Mac Giolla Cholum Raarsaigh'."

Forbes listed 141 Raasay settlements, natural features and landmarks. The Hebridean ground rule of inland placenames being Gaelic, while the Norse christened the coast, broadly prevailed, despite the fact that very little of this long, narrow island is not adjacent to the sea.

So the central settlement was Bailemeanach, or Baile Meadhonach, which Forbes translated from Gaelic as "Mid or middle town or hamlet". He added, "This was of some importance once, as the ruins of a castle, dun, or fort, on a place called 'The Aird' here, and opposite the present clachan; a ferry from here to Skye used to exist."

In the south-west of the island the River Arish, Allt Arais, flows quickly into Churchton Bay, powering on its way a nineteenth-century watermill and a 21st-century hydroelectricity generator. It meets the sea at Inbhir Arais, or Inverarish, which has been a human settlement for centuries. In 1912 a workers' village was built from scratch on the naked hillside above the river to accommodate the labourers and management of an iron mine in the south of Raasay. The name Inverarish was promptly transferred from the river mouth to the new settlement. Raasay's biggest township had a new shape and a very old name.

Several places were named for their practical functions or idiosyncrasies. The Gaelic word "nigheadh" translates as "to wash", and so in the south-west of the island Loch na Nigheadh and Allt na Nigheadh signify the loch and river of washing. Alexander Forbes attached to Loch and Allt na Nigheadh the standard Celtic lore of "a mystical female who before a death occurs is seen washing the shroud of the doomed one".

A "cipean" in Gaelic is a stake or a peg or a tether-post. The small township of Baile nan cipean, anglicised as Balnakeepan, on the high cliffs of eastern Raasay, was named "from the necessity for tethering children, etc., out of doors to prevent them sliding or rolling off the hill-sides into the sea or pot- holes ..." Tethering toddlers and animals away from cliffsides was common practice on precarious parts of the Scottish coast into the twentieth century.

Fladda, the small, low-lying tidal island off the north-west coast of Raasay which was inhabited until the 1960s, is a straightforward Norse description of a flat ("flatr") island ("ey").

Rona, the larger but stony satellite which lies to its north, probably derives from the Norse Hraun-ey, or "Rough Island", although Forbes suggests the possibility of "ron-ey", from the Gaelic for a seal, and puts in a word for the long-odds possibility of St Ronan's Island. There were twelve early Irish saints of that name, several of whom spent time in Scotland.

Caisteil Bròchaill or Brochel, the fortress on the north-eastern coast which, from the fifteenth century onwards, commanded the Inner Sound of Raasay and the favoured sea lane between the island and the mainland, was built after the retreat of the Norse and seems to have been named for a broch which preceded it on the elevated site.

It is not known how the signature highest hill on the island, the 1,453 feet of Dun Cana or Caan, got its name. The seventeenth-century Skyeman Martin Martin recorded that it was "in form like the crown of a hat; it is called Dun-Cann, which the natives will needs have to be from one Canne, cousin to the king of Denmark". The Gaelic scholar and historian Dr John MacInnes suggested a possible link to "Cano … a petty king of Skye in the seventh century."

Dun Caan is easily accessible on foot and it has a flat summit. It is perfectly possible that it earned the "dun" prefix by being deployed as a defensive retreat, a central fortress in times of siege. Two centuries after Martin Martin, his fellow Skyeman Alexander Forbes suggested "Dun Caan. The white fort or hill, Latin canus" from the visual impact of the peak when covered in snow. Forbes added, "This hill also said to be named after some Danish Prince or other who built a fort thereon, but not known if any remains exist of such; it is the highest hill in Raasay … Sailors and others have dubbed it 'Raasay's Cap'."

Such names of people and places are the most obvious legacies of a Scandinavian ascendancy over the western islands which lasted for as long as 700 years. For almost 500 years after AD 800 the Norse had squatters' rights on Raasay and its neighbours, and for 200 years after that their successors ran, more or less unmolested, an autonomous insular principality. Their coastal placenames, scattered throughout the Hebrides and the mainland littoral, are the constructs of a seagoing people anxious to identify the silhouettes and natures of unfamiliar landfalls in hostile conditions.

The southernmost point of Raasay, the good, flat, accessible land with its antique dolmen, became Eyre because in Old Norse the word for a gravel beach was eyrie. Suisnish was a headland reaching into troubled water. Screapadal was a steading on a slope of rough scree.

Sorley, Somhairle, a forename which one of the island's most distinguished sons would make emblematic of Raasay, is from Sumarliði or Somerled, which in Old Norse signified a summer traveller. As well as MacLeods and Nicolsons, MacIvers, Macaskills, MacAulays and a dozen others, all told of Norse ancestry.

Aside from proper nouns there are surprisingly few everyday Norse loan words in Gaelic. English has many more. That will be partly because when the Norsemen first arrived Gaelic was already a functional, established language which had no need of new words for a house or a window, whereas English was a young, magpie vernacular, needing all the lexical help it could get. It may also suggest that while many of the Norse settled among the Gaels and Picts, they neither sought nor achieved cultural hegemony, being content to adopt their hosts' dialect as well as, ultimately, their religion. The phenomenon may also reflect the fact that languages are nurtured and disseminated chiefly by women, at the cradle and elsewhere, and almost all of the earlier Norse visitors were men. For at least a couple of centuries, many of those Norsemen in the British Isles were essentially freebooting pirates, and pirates leave little behind, certainly not their language.

The first recorded violent assault by the summer travellers occurred at Lindisfarne in AD 793 and sent shockwaves which never fully subsided throughout the north of the British Isles.

At the end of the eighth century, Lindisfarne in Northumbria had been for almost two centuries a southern outpost of the Celtic

Church to which Raasay, Iona and Lismore also subscribed. It was yet another small offshore island with its patch of consecrated land, its sacred site, its holy men and their gold and onyx chalices, their silver crucifixes, their exotic illuminated manuscripts, their ivory combs and their precious stones. To the pagan Norse it was little more than a poorly guarded treasury.

Seagoing people from Norway and Denmark will have beached on British shores for centuries. By the eighth century they were appearing frequently, in faster and more mobile ships, deploying advanced navigational techniques and motivated by acquisition as well as adventure.

Driven by land hunger, by a longing for concubines and other slaves, or simply by an infectious annual hunt for escapades, the Norse sailors reached and settled, albeit briefly, in Greenland and on the north-eastern seaboard of America.

They made more permanent homes in Iceland, which had previously been the province of a thin scattering of eremitic Gaelic holy men from the British Isles. They took their ships down rivers into modern Ukraine and Belarus. They became mercenary bodyguards to the Byzantine emperors in Constantinople. They raided Muslim Seville in the deep south of Spain. They walked through the souks of Baghdad.

In 1890 a native of Skye handed the procurator fiscal in Portree two obscure old silver coins which he had discovered near the prominent landscape feature of Bodach an Stoìr at the south of the Trotternish Ridge, just six miles due west across the sea from the Palaeolithic rock shelter at Loch a' Sguirr in Raasay, and close to Skye's Jurassic Age dinosaur footprints and its own Stone Age human settlements. The Sgitheanach had been trapping rabbits and found the silver pieces freshly scrabbled to the surface of a warren.

The Portree procurator fiscal duly passed the coins to George Frederick Pollock, a barrister who held the equally old and obscure legal position of Queen's Remembrancer and who was, in 1890, like many a British barrister before and since, enjoying a vacation in Skye. Pollock fortunately recognised his own professional and personal limitations and handed them to the antiquarian and archaeologist Joseph Anderson, the keeper of the National Museum of Antiquities in Scotland at Edinburgh.

Anderson saw their significance and launched a more detailed search in the vicinity of the Storr. That search yielded a further 110 coins, of which nineteen were dirhams from the Samanid caliphate, north of the Arabian Sea in Transoxiana. They were minted in the fabled Silk Road city of Samarkand between AD 895 and 942, and buried for safekeeping 4,500 miles away in the thin soil of northern Skye. There they lay unclaimed for perhaps a thousand years, until a crofter picked up and puzzled over two of them before dutifully handing them in to the office of the law.

The Storr Rock Hoard did not prove that whoever buried the coins had personally visited Samarkand. Writing early in the twentieth century, the Staffin schoolteacher William MacKenzie, who was an adult in the district when the hoard was discovered, suggested that according to local lore it had been the stolen property of a medieval "pirate robber" named Mac a' Choiteir, the Cottar's Son, and "What is likely is that Mac a' Choiteir, being hard pressed, hid his ill-gotten wealth and did not survive to reclaim it."

Nor should it be assumed that the coins were buried in Skye shortly after being minted in Samarkand. They could have changed hands many times over the centuries, anywhere between the Scottish Highlands and Transoxiana.

The hoard did however indicate that on the western edge of Eurasia, at points in their history the island of Skye and its satellites were occupied by some fairly wealthy cosmopolitans who dealt profitability in one way or another, at one remove or more, with their sophisticated peers in the eastern quarters of the known world.

The known world was more extensive to those seagoing cosmopolitans from Norway than to most other humans of their time. If they made deals with Byzantium and Baghdad, and created settlements in Greenland and North America, they treated the north-western British Isles as a home from home, as a mild, damp and fertile archipelago less than a week's straightforward sailing from harbour. The name of the northernmost county in mainland Britain famously derives its contrary name, Sutherland, directly from the Norse Suðrland, the southern lands, as they fondly referred to their holiday home in the sun.

For obvious geographic reasons most of the sailors to the east coast of England arrived from across the North Sea in Denmark, and most of the summer travellers to western Scotland and the Irish Sea came from across the North Atlantic Ocean on the west coast of Norway. The Old English term "wicing" is derived from the Old Norse "vikingr", which literally referred to people who came from bays and inlets. It was quickly deployed as shorthand for "pirates".

They were not known as wicing in the north-west of Scotland. The Gaelic equivalent was "lochlannaich", or people from the land of fjords. As lochlannaich they would sink into the folk memory, culture and lore of such islands as Raasay.

In 1098 the throne of Scotland acknowledged the status quo and officially ceded the Hebridean islands and fragments of the western mainland to the throne of Norway. There followed almost two centuries of less piratical and more routine colonial activity. The people who gave Screapadal and Hallaig on the east coast of Raasay their Norse names were probably settled there. They were equally probably Norse, or at least as Norse as the Bjorn who farmed at Bjørns dal, which would become Beàrnasdal, which in its turn would become Bernisdale – a township in northern Skye which should be twinned with Bjørndal in Norway and Björndal in Sweden.

We do not know how Bjorn and his contemporaries across the north of Scotland came to live there. It may or may not have been a peaceful process. Once established, however, they were woven into the cultural and social fabric.

Another prerequisite for turning aggressive Norse raiders of the Hebrides into diligent Norse colonial settlers in the Hebrides was their conversion to Christianity. Such a metamorphosis would at least insulate the holy places against further assault.

Columba's famous mission at Iona and Moluag's former headquarters at Lismore were both sacked early in the ninth century, and in 849 Columba's relics were removed from Iona for safekeeping. The Church could plainly not continue to accumulate spiritual and material wealth under the perennial threat of attack by bands of heavily armed young pagans. The trick was to get the pagans on their side and under their roof.

Scandinavia was slow to adopt Christianity. Most of the lochlannaich preferred the Æsir, the Norse pantheon of Odin and Thor, until well into the second millennium Anno Domini. The first Norwegian king to convert was baptised early in the eleventh century, shortly before the Hebrides officially became Norse territories.

In the second half of the twelfth century, an archdiocese was sanctioned by the pope at the Viking capital of Nidaros, as Trondheim was then known. The Archdiocese of Nidaros was established chiefly to confirm, consolidate and improve the Christian presence in Norway, but it echoed in the British Isles.

Among its ten far-flung suffragans, which spanned 1,700 miles of the North Atlantic Ocean from Greenland to Iceland, the Faroes and Shetland and Orkney, was the Diocese of Sodor.

Sodor was a corruption of Suðreyjar, or southern islands, by way of the Latin Sodoriensis. The Diocese of Sodor was formed and blessed by Rome in 1154. It contained all of the populated Hebridean Norse colonies, including Raasay, the Cowal and Kintyre peninsulas in Argyll, and the Isle of Man – in which island the Diocese of Sodor survived into the twenty-first century as a bishopric of the Church of England. Primarily an ecclesiastical administration, it was secondarily an acknowledgment by the Vatican of the extent of Norse sovereignty in the Middle Ages.

A century later that sovereignty was curtailed. King Haakon must have sailed past Raasay on his last voyage. Concerned that his hold on some of his British assets was slipping, in the summer of 1263 the fifty-nine-year-old Norse monarch Haakon IV Haakonsson voyaged south, at the head of a war fleet which was said to contain thousands of vessels, to reassert Scandinavian authority.

Haakon's 1263 mission turned into a valedictory tour of the Suðreyjar. Collecting armed recruits and accumulating more ships as he went, the Viking emperor sailed through the Minch to the saltwater channels skirting Raasay. He left his name on the settlement beside a narrow strait between south-east Skye and the mainland, where the kyle of Haakon would over the centuries be rendered as Caol Àcain and then Kyleakin. He voyaged south past the Small Isles, past Coll and Tiree and Mull, past Jura and Islay and the long finger of Kintyre, before doubling back north between Arran and the Ayrshire coast, where in October 1263 King Haakon engaged at Largs with the forces of the Scottish king Alexander III.

The Battle of Largs was closer to a series of unresolved skirmishes than a decisive military engagement. But the Norsemen were unaccustomed to unresolved skirmishes.

Haakon limped back north to Orkney to regroup and plan another campaign. With more significance than anything which took place at Largs, he died in Kirkwall in December. Three years later, at a conference and treaty in Perth in 1266, ownership and government of the Hebrides were given to Scotland.

Raasay and her cousins had been formally Norse for 168 years. That amounted in the Middle Ages to four or five lifetimes. They were preceded by a couple of centuries of Norse visits and assaults, and succeeded by a further few hundred years of devolved administration by local chieftains who were frequently of Norse heritage.

The question therefore remained, why was so little Norse culture, particularly its language, deposited in the islands?

Medieval inhabitants of Europe must often have been functionally multilingual. In the Scottish Hebrides they may have been cradle speakers of Gaelic, but will also have spoken as much of the other Celtic dialects of Pictish and Cymric, as well as such Latin and even early English as was necessary in a mixed society. In a pre-literate world, where most reading and writing was the preserve in Latin of holy men, that multilingualism may not have amounted to much of any single language. People other than those priests and monks and acknowledged seanachaidh, or tradition bearers, did not require big vocabularies or complex conjugations. Nobody cared much about the everyday demotic of ordinary people, so long as they could communicate and understand essential matters. There were no schools for the masses, and such states as the one that the Norse organised from Trondheim and Bergen did not consider language to be a political tool.

So the usage of different tongues was dictated by need. To most Hebrideans, of British or Norse descent, functional Gaelic was sufficient, augmented perhaps with a few useful Norse terms and phrases. When the Norse retreated after 1266 the people of the islands looked east again, in friendship or with suspicion, to a Gaelic-speaking Scottish throne and kingdom.

That language was suddenly more important than ever, while Norse rapidly became all but irrelevant. Only its proper nouns, the names of people and places, remained.

Among those placenames is an indication of at least one Norse tradition which stuck. The term Þingvöllr, or "thingwall", signified a meeting place, a point of assembly. It was most commonly an open space allocated to a gathering of representatives in a form of parliament. It has been sustained for a thousand years as the latter in the Isle of Man, where the legislative body in Douglas is still known as the High Court of Tynwald. Elsewhere, in Dingwall in the Scottish Highlands, Tingwall in Shetland and in Orkney, Thingwall on the Wirral in north-western England, Thingvellir in Iceland and Tingvoll in Norway, the origins of local councils are celebrated in their names.

Hebrideans did not disown or deny their Norse past, but they took a pace forward and away from the summer travellers. They were henceforth referred to as others, not as ours.

The "Norse watermills" which adorn the banks of fast-running burns in such islands as Lewis were almost wilfully labelled as foreign when they were built and used for centuries by Lewis men and women. The 120-metre-long man-made channel which connected a freshwater lochan harbour and boatyard to the sea at Rubha an Dùnain in the south-west of Skye could date from almost any age but was handily, and if carbon dating of recovered timbers is reliable, correctly dubbed a Viking canal. The carved walrus-ivory chess pieces discovered on the west side of Lewis and on the bed of a drained loch in Kilmuir in north Skye testified to the recreations as well as the artistry of the lochlannaich, but were never considered to be Celtic.

In the Gaelic world they left behind, the Norse frequently became a depository for the otherwise inexplicable. A huge cairn at the summit of a Skye mountain called Beinn na Caillich, or Hill of the Old Woman, became supposedly the burial chamber of a Norwegian princess. She may have been the same person referred to by the Inverness Member of Parliament Lord Malcolm Douglas-Hamilton in the House of Commons in 1950. "A thousand years ago," said Lord Malcolm, "a Viking princess lived in the castle the ruins of which still overlook the [Skye] ferry. I am told that she put a chain across the straits and used to obtain a toll from ships wanting to sail through them."

On the western slopes of Raasay, halfway between the north and south of the island, lie the remains of a small cairn known as Storab's Grave. Like most such Hebridean mysteries it is unexcavated. It probably dates to prehistory, but its legend is more recent. Storab, who is also commemorated nearby in Storab's Burn and Loch Storab, was supposedly a Norse visitor, some suggest a prince or even a king "of Denmark", who sought refuge, possibly from a shipwreck, in Raasay. Storab then fell out with his hosts and was chased up and down his eponymous freshwater stream and found temporary asylum in his namesake lochan before being summarily despatched with a knife and burned beneath a cairn. The surviving cairn stones, their name and the tale would inspire one of Raasay's distinguished twentieth-century residents to musical composition.

The Neolithic dolmen at Eyre in Raasay almost certainly prompted the Skye schoolmaster William MacKenzie to write early in the twentieth century that "There is another Leac Nighean Righ Lochlainn [Stone of the Daughter of the King of Norway] in … Raasay. The legend connected therewith is that the son of the Greek king eloped with Nighean Righ Lochlainn [the Daughter of the King of Norway]. They were followed, and the prince was killed. The princess caused a deep grave to be made. When her lover was put in the grave, she jumped in after him, and a *leac* (slab of rock) was placed over it."

As well as chessmen, placenames, coins and mythologies, the Scandinavians left behind their living bloodlines. Of the clans which formed the late medieval Lordship of the Isles, and would proceed to govern and populate most of the north and west of Scotland, half a dozen were of direct Norse ancestry.

They included the two biggest and most influential west Highland clans: the MacDonalds and the MacLeods. Clan Donald, the "children of Donald" (the MacDonalds), who would form one of the biggest diasporas in the English-speaking world, issued from Dòmhnall Mac Raghnuill, the twelfth-century son of an illustrious Hebridean line. He was a Norse-Gael: a Gaelic-speaking member of the Scandinavian ascendancy who built a strong local base on the island of Islay, a substantial and fertile estate which sat more or less centrally in the old Norse realms of the Isle of Man, the western shores of the Irish Sea and the remainder of the Hebrides. Following the Treaty of Perth in 1266, those realms became the autonomous Lordship of the Isles. Apocryphally, the victorious Scottish king Alexander asked Clan Donald to look after the islands for him, and received the haughty – and not entirely truthful – retort that in earlier, happier times MacDonald had never required the assent of Alexander's predecessor, the "king of Denmark", to assert dominion over the Hebrides.

Although Clan Donald was the largest, wealthiest and most powerful member, the Lordship of the Isles was a loose federation of kinships comprised of many of the popular Scottish surnames of following centuries. Three hundred sea miles to the north of Islay, for example, the third biggest island in the entire British archipelago, after Ireland and the mainland of Great Britain itself, was claimed by the sons of Leod.

The MacLeods of Lewis were if anything even more Norse than the MacDonalds of Islay, who at least boasted of their mixed Norse-Gaelic parentage. Óláfr Guðrøðarson, or Olaf the Black, a thirteenth-century Norse chieftain in Lewis, was supposedly the primogenitor of the Leod clan. The sons of Leod, the MacLeods, proceeded to fortify themselves in the north-west of Skye and in almost all of Lewis and Harris.

There are doubts and uncertainty about the medieval freehold of the west Highlands and Islands only partly because of an absence of documentation. The same doubts and uncertainties existed at the time. It was rarely clear exactly who owned what.

After the Treaty of Perth in 1266 the Diocese of Sodor fractured. Its southern reaches around the Isle of Man retained the original name and became a bishopric of the Church of England. In the north, from Islay to Lewis and Raasay, the Hebrides were assigned to a separate Scottish Diocese of the Isles.

The first seat of the Diocese of the Isles was at Snizort in northern Skye, a parish which had been paired with the island of Raasay. In 1526 a grandson of the Bishop of the Isles named Donald Munro was appointed to the vicarage of Snizort, Raasay and Kilmuir.

Almost forty years later Donald Munro who was by then a dean of the Church, would write that Raasay was "perteining to M'Gyllychallan of Raarsay be the sword, and to the bishope of the iles by heritage. This same M'Gyllychallan shuld obey M'Cloyd of the Lewis." With almost identical phrasing and resentment,

Munro reported that the small island of Rona at the north of Raasay "perteins to M.' Gillychallan of Raarsay by force, and to the bishope of the iles be heritage".

There is much to unpack from those few sentences. Before Munro's time in north Skye and Raasay no clan chief laid particular claim to Raasay. Various clan members used the island for its strategic position overlooking two busy and relatively sheltered seaways, and for its comparative anonymity.

Two medieval fortresses were constructed, "the castle of Killmorocht and the castle of Brolokit". Brochel was at the north of the island overlooking the Inner Sound of Raasay, Applecross and the Wester Ross mainland; Kilmoluag was close to the chapel in the south, commanding the Sound of Raasay and the eastern coast of Skye.

We do not know who built them. The Clan MacSween, a perennially martial brood, is sometimes suggested and was certainly in the vicinity. Long after their clan superiors had retired to Ireland in the fifteenth century, MacSweens and their homophonic cousins, MacQueens and MacSwans, remained in Raasay and Rona.

Of the two fortresses, only the vestiges of Brochel Castle survive. It was a sophisticated construction. Planted with elegant ease almost by the shore at sea level, atop a small but precipitous plug of volcanic magma, the fort's gate was accessible from the land by a stepped pathway cut into the side of the magma cliff. Its curtain wall surrounded a courtyard. Four different towers, three of them castellated, rose from each corner, containing a kitchen, a hall and sleeping quarters. Its surrounding turf machair was farmed and cultivated to offer provisions to the occupants of Brochel Castle. It looked across the busy seaway of the Inner Sound of Raasay at the vast bulk of the Applecross peninsula and was inhabited for only a couple of centuries, being abandoned by 1671.

In May 2016 a visitor from Skye discovered a strange artifact in the thin soil beside Brochel Castle. It was a lead pencil inside a beautifully elaborate decorated holder. The holder, it was quickly established, came from India, and it must therefore have belonged to William Daniell.

William Daniell was an English artist who, at the age of sixteen in 1784, accompanied his uncle and adoptive father, the landscape painter Thomas Daniell, to British India. Thomas made prints and aquatints of the cities and countryside of the subcontinent, which the two men sold to the expatriate communities of Calcutta, Madras and Bombay. William quickly progressed from his uncle's assistant to Thomas's collaborator. After ten successful years, in 1794 the Daniells returned to London. Before they left, he recorded in his diary that his Indian lover, a Hindu woman, had commissioned from local workmen and presented to William Daniell an exquisitely crafted pencil holder. Poignantly, it depicted a Hindu bride.

In 1813, as an established artist in his own right, William Daniell planned his masterpiece, *A Voyage Round Great Britain*. His crusade to show the British people their own momentous coastline in 308 aquatints took Daniell on six separate expeditions between 1813 and 1823. He arrived in Raasay in "sultry" weather on 20 July 1815, and he stayed for two days.

His method was to make detailed pencil drawings of his subjects, and recreate them as aquatints back at his London studio. He made preparatory sketches of the two main buildings: the deserted Brochel Castle and the busy and thriving mansion home of his host, James MacLeod, 12th of Raasay, with which he was impressed.

At Brochel, after twenty-one years in which he had carried the exotic keepsake from his Indian lover halfway around the world, William Daniell somehow spilled it onto the ground in the north of the island of Raasay. It was never retrieved by Daniell. Two hundred and one years later, the pencil point protruding from the grazed turf was spotted by a passerby, and it was finally recovered.

Daniell's representation was the last image of Brochel Castle in a state approaching grace. Shortly after his visit the main, north-eastern tower fell, and its dissolution was almost complete.

Kilmoluag Castle in the south-west of Raasay, of which little or nothing has remained since 1746, will have been as impressive and arguably more comfortable: until it was burned to the ground that building was the residential seat of the island's superiors. We know from Donald Munro that in 1563 Kilmoluag, which was also situated on good low ground, and Brochel, were served by "twa fair orchards".

Donald Munro also wrote in 1563 of An Acarsaid Mhòr, the big harbour in Rona, as "ane havin for heiland galeys in the middis of it, and the same havein is guyed for fostering of theives, ruggairs, and reivairs, till a nail, upon the peilling and spulzeing [plundering and pillaging] of poure pepill".

If Rona was a buccaneers' den in 1563, it will have been so for centuries. "Broken men" were a phenomenon of the time.

They were freebooting outlaws, divorced from the protection and semi-respectability of the main body of their clans owing to their own criminality or serious misfortune. In the words of Richard Sharpe, their "occupation was largely piracy, which remained a popular pursuit for several centuries". Rona and Raasay were, and remained, safe havens to such people. Even into the twenty-first century there was no permanent police presence in the islands, and as late as the twentieth century the authorities refused to send officers to Raasay to enforce the law, or even to deliver summonses. The reasons in modern times were the same as in the Middle Ages: on their own familiar, inscrutable land and sea, in their cliffhangs, caves, woodlands and tidal races, local transgressors who did not want to be found, would not be found. They could easily evade pursuers from such alien places as Skye and the western seaboard.

An edict from that Hammer of the Hebrides King James VI in 1598 accused many such "brokin men", as well as virtually every clan which had been involved in the Lordship of the Isles, including the MacDonalds and MacLeods, of "thift, reif, oppressioun, and sorning". Sorning was effectively sponging on the goodwill of other people, by force or persuasion, an abuse of hospitality which was particularly grave in the Scottish Gaidhealtachd.

The "poure pepill" who, according to a former vicar of the islands, were plundered, exploited and despoiled by such itinerant thieves, rogues, robbers and reivers, were the ordinary, year-round settled populations of Rona and Raasay.

There were in the Middle Ages about 300 of them, capable of raising a respectably sized war band of between 60 and 100 teenaged and adult men. They were practised seafarers. The archipelago of the medieval British Isles contained some 400 inhabited islands, and a quarter of those, including, in Lewis and Skye, two of the largest, were claimed by the Lordship of the Isles. They were all, by tradition and necessity, populated by seagoing people. The Norse conquest had delivered better boats and advanced marine technology. The Hebrides had probably always bred the best sailors in Britain; from the Middle Ages onwards they were also the best equipped. No mainland fleet could approach them, and for several centuries none bothered to try.

The obvious peaceful way to exploit their mastery of the sea was to fish. But fishing was hard and dirty work which brought little material reward. To a young Ratharsach, as to any other Hebridean, the appeal of a freebooter's life was obvious. Preying off stray cargo vessels and skirmishing with the crews of other islands and mainland clans brought thrills, spills, cash and the opportunity to see the world – or at least, to see the north-western seaboard of Scotland. To such people, summer wandering and summer raiding was part of a substantial Norse heritage.

It may have suited a vicar of their church to describe the crews of the "heiland galeys" which wintered in their deep anchorages as marauding brutes who exploited the defenceless locals; in reality the relationship had to be more accommodating. Whatever they told the visiting priest from Skye, the people of Raasay and Rona spent hundreds of years hand in glove with seagoing thieves and reivers. They would often have been indistinguishable. Piracy presented, if not an attractive career path, a useful summer occupation before settling down in Hallaig with a family and some cattle and a nostalgic view of the flat open sea between Raasay and Applecross.

That state of affairs – of skilled seafarers in fast and manoeuvrable little warships making hay all down the west coast of Scotland, raiding and fighting with impunity and even claiming the mantle of an autonomous lordship – was always intolerable to the Scottish Crown, as it would have been to any state emerging from the Middle Ages into the early modern period. It had nonetheless to be tolerated until the mainland authorities were in a position to do anything about it.

In view of what would happen three centuries later, it is ironic that it fell to the Stuart dynasty to pull down the shutters on the Lordship of the Isles. The Stuarts were of an Anglo-Norman line which had claimed most of mainland Scotland since 1371, and who would be propelled for centuries from one throne to another by an unshakeable belief in their own divine right to rule.

The tipping edge was reached in the second half of the fifteenth century. In 1462 John MacDonald of Islay committed the Lordship of the Isles to its most ambitious adventure. The Treaty of Westminster and Ardtornish, which was signed in London and Morvern in late 1461 and early 1462, effectively allied the Hebrides with England in the event of a future invasion and occupation of Scotland. Should such an occupation succeed, the Lordship of the Isles was guaranteed by treaty to inherit half of the Scottish mainland which lay north of the Firth of Forth. The Lords of the Isles would then become regents of a very large portion of Scotland.

That arrangement was unlikely to charm the reigning Stuart monarchs of mainland Scotland.

5

Taking Shape

"Raasay measures fourteen miles by between two and three miles; Manhattan measures thirteen miles by between two and three miles. Manhattan contains almost twenty-three square miles of dry land; Raasay twenty-four square miles."

THE monarchs who ended the last autonomous Gaelic Hebridean polity, were also the last rulers of Scotland who could have conducted an everyday conversion in their native language with the people of Raasay, or any of the other western islands.

James IV and his son James V were the last two Stuart kings to speak Gaelic. Neither of them was born into the language – James IV had a Danish mother and an English wife – but both of them learned at least some of it as a matter of kingly duty and convenience. In the sixteenth century, Gaelic was still the first, if not the only, language of perhaps half of their 600,000 to 700,000 subjects.

The Treaty of Westminster–Ardtornish, between the Lordship of the Isles and the English Crown, had been signed for twenty-six years when James IV acceded to the Scottish throne in 1488. It was then, and later, described as a treasonous attempt to "stab Scotland in the back with a Celtic dirk".

But the treaty was, as would have been recognised by both the English and Scottish Crowns if not by the islanders, seriously impractical. The prospect of the Hebridean Norse-Gaels holding and militarily defending fully half of central, eastern and northern Scotland might have appealed to John MacDonald of Islay, Lord of the Isles and Earl of Ross, but it was, by the later fifteenth century, fanciful. Even in its fourteenth-century heyday the lordship had been a scattered, loose and often internally feuding coalition of different islands and clans. By the fifteenth century their single shared heritage as former colonies of the Norse Empire in Scotland was losing its grip, and their nominal Norse identity was fading fast. Their military strength was almost entirely seaborne, and their small fleets were more comfortable with close-range smash-and-grab raids on their neighbours than with any notion of an extended conflict.

Objectively, the Treaty of Westminster–Ardtornish certainly was treasonous. The Hebrides had been part of the Scottish kingdom, albeit without their consent, since the Norse concessions in the Treaty of Perth in 1266. Whatever autonomy the Stirling court might have allowed its new western provinces, which were strung out like worry beads across a couple of hundred miles of the North Atlantic Ocean, they could not extend to making a military alliance with the most powerful nation in the immediate vicinity, especially when that alliance was specifically addressed to abolishing the Scottish Crown and carving up its state.

Subjectively, the treaty was more of a statement than a threat. It is unlikely that more than a very few of the clan chiefs and buccaneer skippers who considered themselves still affiliated to the Lordship of the Isles seriously thought that they would soon add hundreds of square miles of the Scottish mainland to their estates – although Alexander MacDonald of Lochalsh, a pretender to the Lordship of the Isles, had put matters to the test in 1491 by invading the east coast town of Inverness and briefly garrisoning Inverness Castle before being driven back west.

What they really wanted was a continuation of the status quo, with leeway for future strategic expansion, without interference from mainland monarchs. Their heritage and identity should not entirely be discounted. By the end of the fifteenth century they saw the Gaelic regions of mainland Scotland, which had two and three centuries earlier been extremely strong and widespread, slipping away from them. The Hebrides and the north-western seaboard were on their way to becoming a discrete Gaidhealtachd with a substantial mountainous buffer zone on the western littoral. If they wished to retain their culture undiluted, as well as their regional power, they might be advised to seek alliances beyond the Scottish central belt.

From the perspective of that central belt, the Treaty of Westminster–Ardtornish and the raid on Inverness elevated the Lordship of the Isles from being an ungovernable haven of piracy and other outlawed activity, to being an intolerable threat to the integrity of the Scottish state. A response was essential, and only one would be sufficient.

In May 1493, the title and possessions of John MacDonald of Islay, Lord of the Isles, were declared forfeit to the Scottish Crown. According to the mainland authorities, 200 years of official Hebridean semi-independence were over.

Three months later, in August 1493, James IV and his most powerful ministers made their first excursion to the west Highlands. In Dunstaffnage Castle, a loyal stronghold north of Oban on the Argyllshire mainland which was held by Clan Campbell, they received submissions of loyalty from two previously powerful local lieutenants of the Lordship of the Isles: John Maclean of Lochbuie in Mull and John MacDonald of Ardnamurchan. John MacDonald of Islay then arrived at Dunstaffnage to offer obeisance to the Stuart throne. His surrender was accepted. He was taken back to Stirling for safekeeping and put on a pension of £133 6s 8d a year. He never again saw the Minch or the Sea of the Hebrides. Ten years later, in 1503, the last true Lord of the Isles died in the east coast port of Dundee.

The transition from island lordship to Scottish kingdom was far from smooth. James IV built up a Scottish royal navy partly with his western approaches in mind. Within twenty years of the submissions at Dunstaffnage, rebellions in Kintyre, Mull and Lewis sent those ships of the line north and west, occasionally with James IV on board. Whether they were bombarding the defences of the recalcitrant Torquil MacLeod at Stornoway in Lewis, or anchoring relatively peacefully in Portree Bay in Skye, within clear view of Raasay, the ships of James IV made statements on behalf of the Scottish Crown. Only one future was henceforth open to the Hebrides, and it would be dictated, chiefly in the English language, from Stirling and Edinburgh.

In August 1609 nine west coast clan chiefs gathered on the consecrated island of Iona in the presence of Bishop Andrew Knox. A century had passed since the dissolution of the Lordship of the Isles. In 1567 the one-year-old grandson of James IV had succeeded to the Scottish throne as King James VI. In 1603 the thirty-six-year-old James VI ascended to the Westminster throne as King James I of England, or James VI and I of the United Kingdom of Great Britain and Ireland.

Unlike his grandfather and great-grandfather, James VI and I had no time or affection to spare for either the people or the language of the Scottish Gaidhealtachd. "As for the Highlanders," he announced while monarch of Scotland alone, "I see two kinds: the ones who live on the mainland are barbaric, but a little bit civilised; the others who live in the islands are totally barbaric."

The crusade of James VI against Hebridean barbarians would on at least one occasion directly involve Raasay. "James VI," writes Dr Aonghas MacCoinnich of Glasgow University, "ruling in his own right, sought, in 1587, to curb what he perceived as the excesses of Gaelic chiefs and exert more control over the Gàidhealtachd. Over 100 landowners from all areas of the Highlands & Islands were named in a parliamentary roll, with the intent of making them answerable for the behaviour of their followers." The list included the MacLeod chieftain of Raasay, MacGilleChaluim Garbh.

In 1599 James VI's Edinburgh parliament sent eleven "Gentleman Adventurers" from Fife and other parts of the Central Belt at the head of 600 privately commissioned and armed men to invade, subdue and colonise the "totally barbaric" island of Lewis. The local feudal lords, MacLeods of Lewis, mounted a stern but costly resistance. Unfortunately for them, James VI had a long memory and many years still to reign.

In 1608 the monarch of Great Britain and Ireland invited Andrew Knox, a muscular Protestant clergyman who was also Bishop of the Isles, to devise fresh means of integrating the Hebrides with the rest of the kingdom. After a couple of routinely unsatisfactory military expeditions to the islands of Mull and Islay, Knox established a commission which would meet clan chiefs in Iona and thrash out agreements which could then be passed into statute law.

The nine included five big hitters – Angus Macdonald of Dunivaig in Islay, Hector Maclean of Duart in Mull, Donald Gorm Macdonald of Sleat in Skye, Donald Macdonald, the head of Clanranald in Moidart and Rory Macleod of Harris – and four lesser chieftains in Lauchlan Maclean of Lochbuy in Mull, Rory MacKinnon of Strathordaill in Skye, Lauchlan MacLean of Coll and Gillespie MacQuarrie of Ulva.

More than a century had passed since the great-grandparents of those men had seen their privileges and powers revoked by the great-grandfather of King James VI and I. It had been a century of upheaval and uncertainty which the seventeenth-century clansmen were anxious to escape.

There was no representation from Lewis in Iona. The MacLeods of that island were still dealing with the repercussions from the invasion of the Fife Adventurers, lengthy and exhausting repercussions which would soon see the fall of MacLeod Lewis, not to the knights and landowners of Fife, but to the MacKenzies of Kintail on the western mainland – who would continue to hold that largest Hebridean island until the middle of the nineteenth century – and would also see Niall MacLeod, one of the most militant defenders of his clan's rights to Lewis, hanged in Edinburgh in 1613 following a summary trial for "fire-raising, murder, theft and piracy".

So nobody from Lewis was invited to Bishop Andrew Knox's conference in Iona in August 1609, but the shadow of events on that island hung over the debates. Bishop Knox had assured the assembly of "all kynd of hostilitie yf thay continue rebellious and dissobedyent". Hebridean estates were being forfeited and Hebridean chieftains imprisoned and executed.

There was credible rumour of planned Lewis-style invasions of the islands of Uist and the peninsula of Kintyre. They would not occur, but the largest and most consequential of King James's signature policy of internal colonisation would. The plantation in the traditional Gaeltacht, Catholic properties of clan chiefs in the north of Ireland, of tens of thousands of Anglophone, Protestant, Lowland Scots and English people, was officially launched in 1609, the summer of the Iona convention.

The Hebridean generation of 1609 was not the generation of 1493. Many of them, certainly not all but many of them, were prepared to be tempted by the prospect of an easier life, and were already seduced by the riches and luxuries of the south.

They did not regard Andrew Knox as an enemy, despite his adoption of the Bishopric of the Isles, the paramount ecclesiastical position of their ancestors' long-lost mini state. The fact of their attendance at Iona indicated their willingness to move along from being "rebellious and dissobedyent".

As he knew, Bishop Knox held the cards, and he played them ruthlessly. Both he and his monarch identified the chief obstacles to the absorption of Scotland's Gaels into the mainstream of Scottish and British society: their language, their Catholic faith where it still endured and their cultural identity.

Before they sailed from Iona back to their home ports, the nine Hebrideans had signed up to sending their own children, and those of their richer yeoman tenants, to southern schools where they "may be found able sufficiently to speik, reid and wryte Englische". They would appoint Protestant ministers in all of their parishes. They would no longer carry pistols or arquebuses outdoors. Bards and seanachaidh, Gaelic tradition bearers, and anybody else "pretending libertie to baird and flattir", would be outlawed. Fugitives from the officers of the Crown would no longer be given safe harbour. In an echo of the Scottish parliament's edict of 1587, chiefs would accept responsibility for the subversive or otherwise criminal activities of members of their clan.

Several clan chiefs signed several clauses with the fingers of their left hands crossed behind their backs. Clanranald, for instance, had no intention of promoting Protestant ministers, and nobody seriously intended to persecute their bards and seanachaidh. They would continue to shoot with pistols and arquebuses whichever birds and hares were unlucky enough to cross their paths, and the petitions of human fugitives would be considered according to the person and their circumstances.

The significance of the statutes was nonetheless clear. They were a step taken voluntarily in the direction of assimilating the old Norse-Gaelic fiefdoms of its north-western shoulder with the rest of the United Kingdom. The island of Raasay was not represented at Iona. That was only partly because it was small and relatively insignificant.

In 1609 Raasay had been for a hundred years the property of a sept of the MacLeods of Lewis. The written record of Raasay does not go back very far, and it fails to establish any MacSween possession of the island, which is testified in local oral history. Brochel Castle was certainly built before the arrival of the Lewis MacLeods. The local historian and genealogist Norma MacLeod suggests that it is possible to consider a cohabitation of Raasay between MacSweens and MacLeods, with the former dominating the north and the latter settling in the south, before MacLeod hegemony established itself, in Donald Munro's words, "be the sword". Accounts began to be made in the sixteenth century, and between them they establish a MacLeod proprietorship which began in the first decade of the century, possibly around 1510, with the stewardship of the second son of Calum MacLeod of Lewis, Calum "Garbh" MacLeod, when the boy was just seven years old.

A Hebridean legend, which was as apocryphal as any other and reflected the spirit if not the historical detail of the time, has it that Calum MacLeod inherited Raasay following a typical piece of medieval skullduggery by his grandfather.

Roderick MacLeod of Lewis had a large house on the tiny island of Isay in the mouth of Loch Dunvegan off the north-west coast of Skye. Early in the sixteenth century Roderick invited the other claimants to the apparently vacant property of the Raasay islands to a feast in Isay. During the festivities he invited his guests to a private audience on the shore outside. Once there, he killed them. Young Calum subsequently enjoyed unchallenged access to his new properties.

As well as the Raasay islands, Calum Garbh laid claim to, and was shortly granted by royal charter, "3 merklands" at "Snizort in Trotternish" in Skye. It was a substantial plot of land in the neighbouring island – the whole of Raasay itself was at that time estimated to be eight *merklands*. It covered land north of Portree on the Uig road, at the foot of the Trotternish peninsula, east of the head of Loch Snizort, including the Skye townships of Romesdal, Eyre and Snizort. It was broadly contiguous with the old parish of Snizort, which had also included Raasay and was the ecclesiastical base of Dean Donald Munro. The Raasay MacLeods kept their Skye properties for at least two centuries, and possibly more – the Snizort *merklands* were still referenced in estate documents early in the eighteenth century.

In the chaos of the eighteenth and nineteenth centuries, Raasay's Skye colony slipped out of touch. When the Napier Commission visited Raasay in 1883, the distinguished commissioners, some of whom were themselves Highland landowners, repeatedly asked local crofters, "Do you know anything about the mainland part of Skye that belonged to the MacLeods of Raasay?" They were told bluntly, “No”. As the land in question was by then part of the large Skye estate of Macdonald of Sleat, who was a perennial friend and ally of MacLeod of Raasay, it is possible that at some stage, perhaps in the uncertain days after the 1745 Jacobite Rising, Snizort was informally transferred to the care of the Macdonalds and simply never returned.

Calum Garbh, the first MacLeod of Raasay, had a respectable medieval lifespan, reaching his fifty-seventh birthday before giving up his life and his heritable properties in 1560. His longevity cemented the foundations of the MacLeod patrimony of Raasay, Fladda and Rona. It also established Calum Garbh, under his familiar byname of MacGilleChaluim Garbh (which broadly translates as “portly son of St Columba’s pageboy” and is the origin of the later Scottish surname MacCallum), as a fixed character in the western Gaidhealtachd’s pantheon of personalities. He was Donald Munro’s “same M’Gyllychallan [who] shuld obey M’Cloyd of the Lewis”.

MacGilleChaluim’s descendants inherited the MacGilleChaluim Garbh soubriquet. Their possession of Raasay long outlived their MacLeod relatives’ proprietorship of Lewis. The first MacGilleChaluim Garbh was succeeded by son after son after son until John, 13th MacLeod of Raasay, found himself financially embarrassed in 1843, sold the island and emigrated to Australia. The islanders’ ties to the island of Lewis were, however, never completely severed. Into the twenty-first century, even in Tasmania the MacLeods of Raasay laid claim to the chieftaincy of Lewis, despite claims from the larger island that it still resided in Swordale in Point.

For all the exigencies of the Statutes of Iona, the lives of MacGilleChaluim’s tenantry passed more or less undisturbed. The 300–400 people in Raasay in the sixteenth and seventeenth centuries found themselves in a comfortable oasis whose natural assets furnished most of their daily needs.

Donald Munro probably wrote the final draft of his account of the Raasay archipelago in the early 1560s, but he had first visited it as a young clergyman in the middle of the 1520s, just a decade into MacGilleChaluim's dominion. He was able then to admire an admirable estate, "with pairt of birkin woodis, maney deires, pairt of profitable landes, inhabit and manurit … with twa fair orchards … of freestanes and guid quarelles. It is excellent for fishing."

The birchwoods provided timber; the many "deires", for which the Norse had named the island, gave up venison; the surrounding sea and inland lochs were alive with fish; the inhabited, manured and well worked land and cultivated orchards were profitable in domestic produce and exported income; the scattered freestones and good quarries gave the resident population the means to build sturdy homes, and nurtured a long and proud Raasay tradition of skilled masonry.

A born and bred Skyeman, Martin Martin, described the ample fisheries available to his family and neighbours in the seventeenth century. They would have been much the same in neighbouring Raasay. As well as salmon runs, there were apparently inexhaustible shoals containing

> great quantities of herring … This sort of fish is commonly seen without the bays, and on the coast all the summer. All other fish follow the herring and their fry, from the whale to the least fish that swims; the biggest still destroying the lesser …
>
> The natives preserve and dry their herring without salt, for the space of eight months, provided they be taken after the tenth of September, they use no other art in it but take out their guts, and then tying a rush about their necks, hang them by pairs upon a rope made of heath cross a house; and they eat well, and free from putrefaction, after eight months keeping in this manner. Cod, ling, herring, mackerel, haddock, whiting, turbot, together with all other fish that are in the Scots seas, abound on the coasts of this island.

Fish, even deep sea saltwater fish, were caught by "angle fishing", or angling with baited hooks on short lines or longlines – a sustainable practice which would continue in the Hebrides well into the twentieth century, and put local fishermen at serious disadvantage from the rapacious trawlers and drifters of Lancashire and north-eastern Scotland.

> The best time of taking fish within angle is in warm weather, which disposes them to come near the surface of the water; whereas in cold weather, or rain, they go to the bottom. The best bait for cod and ling is a piece of herring, whiting, thornback, haddock, or eel.
>
> The grey-lord, *alias* black-mouth [grey mullet or rock cod], a fish of the size and shape of a salmon, takes the limpet for bait. There is another way of angling for this fish, by fastening a short white down of a goose behind the hook; and the boat being continually rowed, the fish run greedily after the down, and are easily caught. The grey-lord swims in the surface of the water, and then is caught with a spear; a rope being tied to the further end of it, and secured in the fisherman's hand.
>
> All the bays and places of anchorage here abound with most kinds of shell-fish. The Kyle of Scalpa affords oysters in such plenty that commonly a spring tide of ebb leaves fifteen, sometimes twenty, horse load of them on the sands.

Infant mortality was high by later standards. But men and women who made it to their tenth birthdays often passed three-score years and ten. Octogenarians were not uncommon, centenarians were known, and most people expected to keep themselves reasonably fit and productively occupied until the white shores of Avalon were clearly in view. As they drifted out of the Middle Ages, most Hebrideans could hope for little more.

We know how those Hebrideans dressed and looked. In 1964 two men cutting peat on Arnish Moor in Lewis exposed the remains of a murder victim. It was soon established that he was a man of between twenty and twenty-five years, five foot five inches tall, who had been killed in the early 1700s by a blow to the back of his head.

His clothes had been remarkably well preserved in the peat. He had sported a blue knitted bonnet, similar to a large beret. Above a long ragged patchwork vest he wore a "stylish but longer-length shirt, made in a more finely woven material of a similar light brown colour. It may have been made by a tailor, its buttonholes being neatly stitched, and the cuffs and collar lined." On top of them was a woven woollen jacket "flared out from the waist, with a central back seam, and a vent … It is likely that the cloth had been produced locally, even possibly by the man's own family. The jacket was fastened with eleven cloth ball buttons running from the standing collar at his neck to his waist. Further buttons secured his cuffs and the one large pocket on the left hand side."

Arnish Man walked in knee-length woven woollen leggings. Any plaid, drawers or footwear had been removed before his interment or had, unlike the other clothes and accessories, rotted completely away. He was carrying a striped woven bag which contained a birchwood comb, a horn spoon and two quill pens.

Our seventeenth century Skyeman would write of Arnish Man's mother and sisters:

> The ancient dress wore by the women, and which is yet wore by some of the vulgar, called *Arisad*, is a white plaid, having a few small stripes of black, blue and red; it reached from the neck to the heels, and was tied before on the breast with a buckle of silver or brass, according to the quality of the person. I have seen some of the former of an hundred marks value; it was broad as any ordinary pewter plate, the whole curiously engraven with various animals etc. There was a lesser buckle, which was wore in the middle of the larger, and above two ounces weight; it had in the centre a large piece of crystal, or some finer stone,

> and this was set all around with several finer stones of a lesser size.
>
> The plaid being pleated all round, was tied with a belt below the breast; the belt was of leather, and several pieces of silver intermixed with the leather like a chain. The lower end of the belt has a piece of plate about eight inches long, and three in breadth, curiously engraven; the end of which was adorned with fine stones, or pieces of red coral.
>
> They wore sleeves of scarlet cloth, closed at the end as men's vests, with gold lace round them, having plate buttons set with fine stones. The head dress was a fine kerchief of linen strait [wrapped tightly] about the head, hanging down the back taper-wise; a large lock of hair hangs down their cheeks above their breast, the lower end tied with a knot of ribbands.

There were few further written examinations of the islands of the Hebrides until the tumultuous eighteenth century. Those that appeared drew heavily from the well of Donald Munro, who had at least spent time in Raasay and Skye.

In the year of his death, 1582, the scholar and Edinburgh intellectual George Buchanan completed his *Rerum Scoticarum Historia*, or *History of Scottish Affairs*. Buchanan was the son of a Highland man and a Gaelic speaker who nonetheless spent most of his long adult life in western and southern Europe and the Lothians. His account of Raasay and its vicinity suggests an extreme reliance on Donald Munro:

> *Scalpa octo millia ad aestivum occidentem sita. Praeter alia commoda magnos cervorum gregesin silvis alit. Inter ostium Caronis sinus et Raarsam iacet Crusinga, statio navibus tuta.*
>
> *Et a Scalpa duo millia in septentriones porrigitur Raarsa septem millia longa, dua lata. Silvas habet betuleas, et in eis cervos. Quingentos ab ea passus est Rona silvis et erica operta. Portum in intimo sinu habet latrociniis infestum*

> *praetereuntibus, insidiis tegendis aptum, et in sinus (qui a brevitate Gerloch vocatur) ore est eius nominis insula.*

> Scalpa is situated eight miles to the west ... Besides other advantages, it feeds large herds of deer in its forests. Between the mouth of the Gulf of Caron and Raarsam lies Crusinga, a safe station for ships.
>
> And two miles north of Scalpa extends Raarsam, seven miles long and two wide. It has birch forests, and in them deer. Five hundred metres from it is Rona, covered with woods and heather. It has a harbor in an inner bay, infested with robbers passing by, suitable for hiding ambushes, and at the mouth of the bay (which is called Gerloch from its brevity) is the island of that name.

Crusinga was probably the Crowlin Islands, which lie between the mouth of Loch Carron and the south end of Raasay and which are separated by a narrow, sheltered channel of sea which has been for millennia "a safe station for ships". Buchanan's portrait of Rona as "infested with robbers" suggests that Munro's earlier narrative was still considered to be accurate and would continue to haunt that island.

In the last quarter of the sixteenth century – Professor Richard Sharpe, an authority on first-source material, estimated its dates to be between 1577 and 1595 – the Scottish Crown of James VI compiled a survey of the Hebridean islands "to bring the Highlands under control and strengthen the royal revenues in the area". That survey saw the light of day fully 300 years later, when William Forbes Skene reproduced it in his 1880 study *Celtic Scotland: a History of Ancient Alban.*

In the late sixteenth century, we learn,

> The haill Iles of Scotland were devidit in four pairts of auld, viz. Lewis, Sky, Mule, and Yla, and the remanent haill Iles were reknit but as pertinents and pendicles of the

> said four Iles, and were devidit amangis thir four Iles and annext thairto in this manner. First to the Ile of Lewis wes annext the Iles of Wist, Barra, Harragis, Ronalewis, Pabla in Harreik, Helsker, Collismown, and Iit.
>
> To the Ile of Sky were annext Raarsa, Eg, Romb, Canna, Ellan na muck, and Scalpa …
>
> Raarsa is ane Ile of five mile lang and thrie mile braid, perteining to the Bischop of the Iles; but it is occupiet and possest be ane gentleman of McCloyd Lewis kin, callit Gillechallum Raarsa. "His offspring bruikis the same yit, and are callit Clan Gillehallum of Raarsa. He hes ane strange little castell in this Ile, biggit on the heid of ane heich craig, and is callit Prokill. It is but 8 merk land, and will raise 80 men. It payis yeirlie to the bischop 16 merks, but to the capitaine thairof it payis of sundrie tributes better nor 500 merks. Thair is na woods, but great heich craigis in this Ile. It is commodious for corn and all kinds of bestiall, and chieflie horses.

A *merkland* or markland was a piece of agricultural property measured by its productivity rather than its size. In Hebridean terms, "8 merk land" was relatively affluent – although it is significant that the whole island paid just 16 merks annual rental to its nominal owner, the Bishop of the Isles, and more than 500 merks a year to the heirs of MacGilleChaluim.

The "commodious" grain fields, horses and other domesticated animals held real value. We must dismiss as an oversight the assertion that there were "na woods" in Raasay just a few years after Donald Munro noted "birkin woodis".

The claim that Raasay could "raise 80 men" for military duty was repeated for the English Lord Treasurer, and central figure in the Elizabethan court, William Cecil. In 1593 Cecil was informed, probably by way of the Scottish court's recent survey, that "Raarsay, possest be McGilliCallum of Raarsaye of the Cl[a]nLewyd of the Lewes, will rayse LXXX men."

It was not merely a notional militia. The Scottish parliament and William Cecil in London were chiefly interested in how many men MacGilleChaluim could raise for his monarch, but the MacGilleChaluims themselves found ample use for their little army. On at least one occasion early in 1589, "Gilcalme, Laird of Rasey" helped to lead an armed raid on Caithness as far north as Wick, in which "there were up to 300 people slain in one day". Eight years later, in 1597, the younger brother of MacGilleChaluim, Iain MacLeod, was slaughtered in a Dingwall merchant's shop by an heir to the Torridon estates, "striking him in the head with a two-handed sword, without giving him the least advertisement".

That killing led to MacGilleChaluim's Raasay forces, supported by some mainland allies, laying waste to much of north-west Ross. Their violent retribution in its turn brought legal charges two years later, in 1599, against "Gillichalume Rasey of that eilk & Gillechallum Rasay apeirand thairof" and "Murdo mcAne Cheill in Torridon, Alexr Geir mc Rore wc Ane, Ewir mc Connill wc keill thair, Donald mc Tormat wc Ane Roy in Rasay, Alester mc Tormod his brother thair [Raasay], John Mc miller skreuche, there, Donald mc Tormod there, Donald Bane mc Neill thair, Angus mc Donald wic Pherson there, his brother Gillichallum Neill thair, Donald and John mc Neills his brothers thair, Angus Pyper there, Murche mc Ane Dowe, Androwe Le, and Alexr Ley his brother, Donald Bane mc Ane vc rore, Alexr mc Ane vc Rore, Jon Baloche and Wa Roay, Kennoch Roy in Torridon, Jon Keill mc Ane wic Thomas mc Angus vc rioche, Dod Dow mc Rore in Garloche and Johne Helmoche his brother thair …"

As Dr Aonghas MacCoinnich writes, "This shows the support the Gillechaluim Garbh drew not only from his own island but [also] … his interconnectedness with the lands and people of Torridon and Gairloch." The presence of such surnames as MacNeil in the larger Raasay contingent also suggests a human legacy from the Lordship of the Isles in the form of Outer Hebridean immigrants to MacGilleChaluim's sheltered estate.

They seem, as might be expected, to have fought with their Lewis relatives against the invasion of the Fife Adventurers. Only one piece of writing attests to Ratharsaich making the voyage due north to take their place in the defence of Stornoway, but it is convincing. One of the Fife gentlemen, Thomas Cunningham of Crail, accused Coinneach MacKenzie of Kintail of joining the Lewis conflict on the islanders' side, and thereafter of orchestrating "… grit oppressionis, invasionnes, depredationes, slaughteris, & mo[r]theris at divers tymes committit be the inhabitants of the Lewis againis him …" and his fellow Fifers. Cunningham seems to have presented in support of his case against MacKenzie of Kintail the names of "Gillechrist mc Gillecallum Rasa, Murdo mc Gillicallum and Donald mc Gillechallum his twa sonis", as members of the Hebridean defensive coalition. MacKenzie replied that it might well have been the case that the Raasay men had shown up in Lewis and unleashed slaughter and murder on the Lowland invaders – but that could hardly be blamed on him, "seing they duell [dwell] not upoun ony of McKainzies lands, nather in Loch Brume, nor Assent, bot duells in Rasa …"

It is possible that as well as the Ross-shire allies, Raasay's potential fighting force was swollen by conscripts from Rona, from the subsidiary Snizort lands, and even from the littoral of eastern Skye. But wherever they called home, eighty men was a substantial platoon for the chieftain of a small Hebridean island to command. By the usual algorithm, it indicated an overall population of between 300 and 400 men, women and children, the calculation being that children under sixteen years, who made up half the population, would not be called upon to fight, and that of the 50 per cent of people in the adult population, only men would bear arms.

There were some fighting women in the Scottish Gaidhealtachd, and the idea that teenaged, pubescent boys stayed obediently at home with the cattle is an unwise presumption to make of semi-martial societies, but those flawed suppositions may be balanced by the similarly erroneous surmise that all senior men were fit enough and willing to go to war.

So we conclude with the received wisdom that 25 per cent of the tenantry of sixteenth-century Raasay was potential soldiery. It is probably an underestimate, in which case as the fifteenth century turned into the sixteenth, the island had a population of around 400 souls.

After the fall of the MacLeods of Lewis, early in 1608 the MacGilleChalums diplomatically accepted the superiority of the MacKenzies. Henceforth they would supposedly be vassal rulers of Raasay – an arrangement which nine years earlier might have given Thomas Cunningham of Crail a valid case to present against MacKenzie of Kintail. In a deed issued from Eilean Donan Castle on 21 August 1610, the MacGilleChalum of the day would be obliged to attend to his MacKenzie superior "and his lieutenants quhen thai sall happin to repair to the Yllis with ane birling of tuelve oares and, lykewyse, ansueiring in quhatsowver the said superior [directs in] his reichte effaires within the Yllis …"

We do not know on how many occasions the mainland MacKenzies of Kintail called upon the MacLeods of Raasay to provide a twelve-oared birlinn as a water taxi when MacKenzie wished to visit his new island properties. The terms of vassalage, as well as the MacKenzie mainland stronghold of Eilean Donan Castle, would shortly be overtaken by climactic events.

★

Martin Martin was born in north Skye in around 1660. His upbringing and heritage as well as his keen intelligence (Martin graduated Master of Arts from Edinburgh University, and later as Doctor of Medicine at Leiden University in Holland) made him comfortably the best chronicler of the western islands since Donald Munro.

Towards the end of the seventeenth century, Martin was persuaded by his contemporary Hans Sloane, the naturalist and Ulster-Scot secretary of the Royal Society in London, to prepare a published *Description of the Western Islands of Scotland.*

Martin crossed the Minch to research the Outer Hebridean islands in 1697 and 1699, but he had been unwittingly preparing the Skye and Raasay chapters since his birth.

Raasay in the seventeenth century, wrote Martin Martin, was

> seven miles in length, and three in breadth, sloping on the west and east sides; it has some wood on all the quarters of it, the whole is fitter for pasturage than cultivation, the ground being generally very unequal, but very well watered with rivulets and springs. There is a spring running down the face of a high rock on the east side of the isle; it petrifies into a white substance, of which very fine lime is made, and there is a great quantity of it. There is a quarry of good stone on the same side of the isle; there is abundance of caves on the west side, which serve to lodge several families, who for their convenience in grazing, fishing, &c., resort thither in the summer. On the west side, particularly near to the village *Clachan*, the shore abounds with smooth stones of different sizes, variegated all over.
>
> The same cattle, fowl, and fish are produced here that are found in the isle of Skye. There is a law observed by the natives that all their fishing lines must be of equal length, for the longest is always supposed to have best access to the fish, which would prove a disadvantage to such as might have shorter ones.
>
> There are some forts in this isle, the highest is in the south end; it is a natural strength, and in form like the crown of a hat; it is called Dun-Cann, which the natives will needs have to be from one Canne, cousin to the king of Denmark. The other lies on the side, is an artificial fort, three stories high, and is called Castle Vreokle.
>
> The proprietor of the isle is Mr. MacLeod, a cadet of the family of that name; his seat is in the village Clachan. The inhabitants have as great veneration for him as any subjects can have for their king. They preserve the memory

> of the deceased ladies of the place by erecting a little pyramid of stone for each of them, with the lady's name. These pyramids are by them called crosses; several of them are built of stone and lime, and have three steps of gradual ascent to them. There are eight such crosses about the village, which is adorned with a little tower, and lesser houses, and an orchard with several sorts of berries, pot herbs, &c. The inhabitants are all Protestants, and use the same language, habit, and diet, with the natives of Skye.
>
> About a quarter of a mile further north lies the isle Rona, which is three miles in length; vessels pass through the narrow channel between Raasay and Rona. This little isle is the most unequal rocky piece of ground to be seen anywhere: there is but very few acres fit for digging, the whole is covered with long heath, *erica-baccifera, mertillus*, and some mixture of grass; it is reckoned very fruitful in pasturage: most of the rocks consist of the hectic stone, and a considerable part of them is of a red colour.
>
> There is a bay on the south-west end of the isle, with two entries, the one is on the west side, the other on the south, but the latter is only accessible; it has a rock within the entry, and a good fishing.

A portrait of the island in the seventeenth century emerges. It contained 400 Gaelic-speaking people, contented enough with their hereditary governors, the MacLeods of Raasay, or MacGilleChaluims, making a decent living from fishing, rearing cattle and hunting deer and game birds. They cultivated herb and berry orchards to augment wild produce. They grew and harvested grains and some garden vegetables. They standardised fishing lines so that nobody had an advantage at sea over his or her neighbour. They were almost entirely self-sufficient and lived more or less independently from whichever state the distant courts and parliaments had decided to own them in any given year.

Most of them lived on the east coast of Raasay, overlooking the Scottish mainland. A quarry and a lime deposit on that coast provided raw materials for the walls of the townships of Fearns, Leac, Balnakeepan, Screapadal and Hallaig. The west side of the island however was not uninhabited.

MacGilleChaluim had his tower house in the south-west, close to St Moluag's chapel and burial ground, and overlooking Clachan Bay and Skye. Brochel Castle in the north-east was abandoned and crumbling. There were several settlements to the north and south of Clachan, and the people of the precipitous east coast appeared to use the gentler contours of the west for transhumance, summering there with their cattle in rock-hang caves and other temporary shelters.

None of the early chroniclers could agree on the precise size of Raasay, and not one of them got close to its actual dimensions.

Donald Munro, and consequently George Buchanan, had it "seven mile lang from the south to the north … twa mile of breid …" William Skene suggested "five mile lang and three mile braid"; Martin Martin offered "seven miles in length, and three in breadth"; and in 1720 William Macfarlane's *Geographical Collections* hazarded "5 miles at length".

Raasay was and remained fourteen miles long, from Eyre in the south to Kyle Rona in the north. At its widest the island measures three miles across, from Leac in the east to Clachan in the west.

A comparison is useful which was not readily available to Munro, Skene and Martin. Raasay is almost exactly the same size and shape as the island of Manhattan. They face each other across the North Atlantic Ocean.

Raasay measures fourteen miles by between two and three miles; Manhattan measures thirteen miles by between two and three miles. Manhattan contains almost twenty-three square miles of dry land; Raasay twenty-four square miles.

They are not identical twins however. Although Manhattan, on the north-eastern seaboard of the United States of America, is 17 degrees closer to the equator than Raasay, the Hebridean island enjoys a more temperate climate. Manhattan has bitterly cold winters and unbearably hot summers. Raasay, which lies in the careless embrace of a far-flung arm of the Gulf Stream, rarely experiences ice or settling snow, and its summer months are wet and mild.

Despite those climatic contrasts, in the twenty-first century more people live in Manhattan than make their homes in Raasay. In a 2024 census estimate, Manhattan Island's twenty-three square miles contained 1,660,664 people. The Island of Raasay's twenty-four square miles held, in a 2021 census estimate, 187 inhabitants. Four hundred years earlier, in around 1600, when the MacGilleChaluims of Raasay were helping their Lewis relatives to fight off the Fife Adventurers, and the native people of Manhattan were selling their island to Dutch adventurers for goods worth sixty guilders, they had similar populations of a few hundred people.

Over the next four centuries their fortunes changed. Manhattan prospered as the gateway to a newly conquered continent. Raasay did not. Raasay's potential as an entrepôt and sheltered deep-sea anchorage on the western edge of Europe was not exploited. Manhattan's equivalent promise in the United States of America was. In liberal modern democracies, density of population is not automatically a comfort or a virtue. It is nonetheless a measure of comparative prosperity and stability. Barring calamities, Manhattan will not be depopulated at any time soon. Raasay, like many other small islands across the world, lived for several centuries in fear of the extinction of its several thousand years of continuous human settlement. In the middle of the eighteenth century, large parts of Raasay actually were consigned to fire.

6

The Pretender

"Raaza, tis true you cannot raise many men; but the men you have are good. You can easily raise an hundred, and I resolve to raise nine hundred, which will make out a thousand good stout fellows betwixt us: for I am not for having boys or superannuate men amongst them. These I would divide into two battalions, 500 in each; and as you are a man that one can confide in, I resolve to make you Colonel of one of the battalions."

THE Forty-five did not arrive, in Raasay or anywhere else in Britain, out of a clear blue sky. It had been heralded, and rehearsed, for decades.

It was provoked by the deposition of King James VII and II fifty-seven years earlier, in the "Glorious Revolution" of 1688. That dismissal of a reigning monarch was a *coup d'ètat* with many motives. It was a conclusion of the regicide and civil war of earlier in the century, and saw the British state finally shrug off the Stuart line. It asserted Protestantism over Catholicism. It established Parliamentary procedure over the divine rights of absolute monarchy – and therefore laid the foundations of what would become known as constitutional monarchy. And as King James VII and II was permitted to go into exile while his Protestant daughter Mary and her Dutch husband William III of Orange assumed the throne, it was accomplished without chopping off his head.

There followed almost sixty years of sporadic violent unrest, whose insinuation by both parties into the most placid and distant parts of the United Kingdom is best illustrated by the fact that they culminated with the sack of the island of Raasay.

The extended Jacobite insurgency was the result partly of Stuart entitlement, and partly because, in their own terms, for once they were right. Their entitlement after 1688 was well founded. By any objective application of the logic of hereditary monarchy, James VII and II and his heirs were entitled to the throne of the United Kingdom. They were robbed of their God-given dues by an establishment, a government, a parliament and a state apparatus which no longer believed in the divine right of monarchs and the authority of the Pope in Rome, and which no longer trusted the House of Stuart to preside over even the most perfunctory Protestant parliamentary democracy.

Most Europeans in the twenty-first century would sympathise with sedition in such a cause. Most people in the seventeenth century did not, which should have given the early Jacobites a large helping of public support and a fast track to the moral high ground, if they had only known how to occupy it.

The first Jacobite rising took place immediately after the coronation of William and Mary in 1689. It was almost entirely a west Highland revolt involving several Gaelic clans, including the Keppoch MacDonalds. Under the leadership of John Graham of Claverhouse, Viscount Dundee, the forces mustered in Lochaber. While James VII and II re-entered his former kingdom in Catholic Ireland and built an army there, his Scottish Gaelic supporters won a famous victory over superior government forces at the Pass of Killiecrankie in Highland Perthshire. But those original Jacobite rebels lost a third of their complement, including Claverhouse, in the battle, and were defeated at Dunkeld a month later. A year after that, in 1690, James himself was defeated in Ireland by William's army at the

Battle of the Boyne. At the age of fifty-seven years he returned to France, this time for good.

In 1701, James VII and II died in Paris. His son, James Francis Edward Stuart, the man who, despite being just thirteen years of age on the day of his father's death, became known as the Old Pretender, assumed the Stuart claim. In 1708 he sailed from Dunkirk to the Firth of Forth with 6,000 French troops in thirty French ships. They were met there by the Royal Navy and chased anticlockwise around the north of Scotland before limping back to France, having lost both men and ships but without having put a foot or fired a shot on British soil.

The third rising, in 1715, was launched in the north when James Francis Edward Stuart persuaded the Earl of Mar to raise sympathetic Highland clans again. Mar did so at first with some success, proclaiming James Francis Edward Stuart to be James VIII of Scotland and James III of England and Ireland, before marching a sizeable army unsatisfactorily on Stirling and then stuttering to a halt at the demoralising Battle of Sheriffmuir. James Francis Edward Stuart himself arrived in Scotland for the first and last time after Sheriffmuir. He quickly lost faith in his own chances of success and caught a boat back to France early in February 1716. He had spent just six weeks in the country.

In 1719, the French having lost patience with James Francis Edward Stuart, the Old Pretender persuaded Spanish ministers to send 5,000 soldiers on twenty-seven ships to invade England, and two ships with 300 marines simultaneously to raise the faithful clans once more in the north-west of Scotland. The larger invasion force was prevented by a storm off Cape Finisterre from getting within 500 miles of the English coast and went home. The two ships bound for the Scottish Highlands got through. Significantly, they went first to Stornoway in the island of Lewis, whose MacKenzie proprietors had remained faithful to Catholicism and had discovered Jacobitism.

The Spanish ships then sailed across the Minch, through Loch Alsh and into Loch Duich in Kintail, the heart of the ancestral lands of the MacKenzies and their MacRae associates. They anchored by the small fortress at Eilean Donan, where a century earlier MacKenzie had dictated the terms of his feudal superiority to MacGilleChaluim of Raasay. Augmented by a thousand Highlanders and Hebrideans who had joined them in Lewis, Lochalsh and Kintail – there is no evidence of a contingent from Raasay, where MacGilleChaluim had possibly decided to sit this one out – they then decided to pursue an original objective of taking Inverness, fifty miles to the east. The multinational, multilingual expeditionary force got twelve miles inland before being met in upper Glen Shiel by a numerically similar but better-organised and equipped unit of British Army infantry and dragoons which also included many Highlanders, and which more crucially deployed mortars. The Spaniards and their Highland auxiliaries were defeated, dispersed and captured.

It was William MacKenzie's second and last roll of the dice. As the 5th Earl of Seaforth – a title which had been assumed since 1623 by the MacKenzies to reflect their Lewis holdings, Loch Seaforth or Shiphoirt being a deep and imposing fjord which doglegs along the old border between Lewis and Harris – he had taken 3,000 men south in 1715 to join the rising which stalled at the Battle of Sheriffmuir.

He consequently lost his hereditary titles, and with them, as a purely secondary consequence, went any residual pretension to feudal superiority over the MacLeods of Raasay.

When the 1719 expedition was launched, Uilleam Dubh, Black William MacKenzie, joined it as a landless chieftain in control only of the loyalty of his people and his family's ambitions. He was wounded at the Battle of Glen Shiel, but was carried by his clansmen to a boat and sailed to safety, first in Lewis and then in France. He never regained his title, but was later discharged by the Hanoverian King George II of any penal consequences, which enabled him to retire to the island of Lewis, where he died and was buried in 1740.

Back down at the foot of the glen, while the main body of

armed men climbed to their nemesis in Glen Shiel, perched prettily on its offshore rock, Eilean Donan Castle had become the expedition's magazine and was garrisoned by "an Irishman, a captain, a Spanish lieutenant, a serjeant, one Scottish rebel and 39 Spanish soldiers". Inside the fortress was stored "343 barrels of powder and 52 barrels of musquet shot".

The two Spanish vessels having departed for less claustrophobic waters, three Royal Naval ships of the line appeared in Loch Duich and bombarded Eilean Donan Castle. The garrison surrendered to a shore party from the warships, and either deliberately or accidentally, the gunpowder was then exploded, blowing the building apart. It stood as a gaping ruin, and as a vivid metaphor of the collapse of the fortunes of the MacKenzies and MacRaes of Kintail, for two centuries before being comprehensively restored in the 1920s by Lieutenant Colonel John MacRae-Gilstrap, a British army officer of Kintail heritage who married into money.

After three failed attempts in eleven years, the Old Pretender gave up. His first son and heir was born in Rome to his new wife Maria Clementina Sobieska, a daughter of the Polish throne, in 1720. Pope Clement XI acknowledged James and Maria as the legitimate king and queen of Great Britain and Ireland. Upon his birth, Clement naturally also recognised Charles Edward Louis John Sylvester Maria Casimir Stuart as the rightful heir to his father's crown.

Charles Edward Stuart was raised in a city palazzo in the Papal States, with a Protestant Jacobite home governor and a Catholic home education. He became not entirely fluent and not entirely literate in English, French and Italian. His recreations were equestrian sports and the ballroom. Above all though, he was educated in the absolute certainty of his entitlement to the throne of Great Britain and Ireland.

Assiduously courted by the large numbers of Jacobite exiles and other sympathisers in the continental Catholic courts of eighteenth-century Europe, he was repeatedly convinced that his divine right to rule Great Britain was favoured by divine blessing of the inevitability of the final outcome. Eventually, a Stuart prince would regain that crown, and it may as well be Charles Edward, firstly as regent for his aging father, and then as the third King Charles of his line.

By the summer of 1745 the twenty-four-year-old Prince Charles had gathered enough money and support and confidence in his cause to set sail for the Hebrides on a recently commissioned 32-gun, 150-ton French slave ship called, after a Breton village, *Du Teillay*.

Charles wanted to restore the throne of Great Britain to his family, which in 1745 meant to his forty-four-year-old father. As he knew well, that throne could only be found in London, in the south-east of England. He landed in the north-west of Scotland partly as a nod to Stuart origins, partly because he had been given the false impression that almost all of the Highland clans were Jacobite sympathisers, and mainly because the north-western islands and seaboard were considered in time of war to be the soft underbelly of the kingdom. Throughout the long centuries when wars were decided at sea and on land, rather than in the air, up to and including the Second World War two centuries later, the region's deep, sheltered inlets, depopulated glens and abandoned archipelagos were considered to be ideal geographical locations for invasion or clandestine infiltration.

Charles Stuart also needed the momentum behind him of a successful campaign before entering England. Not even his most enthusiastic champion would pretend that England was populated by a Jacobite majority yearning to be liberated. Most English people were probably indifferent to the lineage of their monarchy, and the percentage of the citizenry which, as late as 1745, yearned for another Stuart restoration was in the low single figures. The Young Pretender required impetus. He would have to stimulate and fascinate his prospective subjects.

And so on 23 July 1745 Charles Edward Stuart and seven companions were put ashore on a white sand beach on the small island of Eriskay, which lay between the staunchly Roman Catholic islands of South Uist and Barra. After a mixed reception from the local gentry they proceeded to an especially lonely quarter of the western mainland and raised their standard. There began the epic romance of north-western Scotland, the Arthurian saga and chivalric quest of the Gaidhealtachd, the Highland *Iliad* and the Hebridean *Odyssey*.

He had been expected. Word swept swiftly across Scotland. Most clan chiefs had already determined whether or not to come out in support of the latest Stuart insurgency.

In Raasay, the current MacGilleChaluim, Malcolm, the 9th MacLeod of the island, decided that he was a Jacobite. Malcolm MacLeod had possibly been influenced by the tribulations of his friend and erstwhile feudal superior, Uilleam Dubh MacKenzie of Kintail and Lewis, in and after the risings of 1715 and 1719. The 9th MacGilleChaluim was certainly influenced by his Jacobite cousin and namesake, Captain Malcolm MacLeod, a tacksman in the central Raasay district of Brae, halfway up the west coast of the island, who would play a significant role in the Forty-five and, for the remainder of his eventful life, in everything else connected to Raasay.

Raasay was, as the MacLeods knew, almost unique. No organised clan force appeared on behalf of Charles from Skye or any other of the larger north-western islands. MacLeod of Dunvegan did come out, but on the side of the government. Norman MacLeod led five companies of 100 men each against a scratch Jacobite army in Aberdeenshire in December 1745. They were routed at Inverurie and their piper, Donald Ban MacCrimmon, was taken prisoner. MacLeod of Dunvegan's militias would subsequently play a role as Hanoverian enforcers in their region.

Macdonald of Sleat in Skye contented himself with furtive expressions of sympathy while sitting squarely on top of his locked armoury. Macdonald actually agreed for the duration of the conflict to hold Malcolm MacLeod's estate in trust for his oldest son, John, thus hopefully insulating the thirty-year-old Raasay heir, who stayed at home, as well as his rebellious father against forfeiture in the event of another Jacobite defeat. "There has been an ancient league between the families of Macdonald and Rasay," James Boswell was told by John MacLeod in 1773.

"Whenever the head of either family dies, his sword is given to the head of the other. The present Rasay has the late Sir James Macdonald's sword. Old Rasay joined the Highland army in 1745, but prudently guarded against a forfeiture, by previously conveying his estate to the present gentleman, his eldest son. On that occasion, Sir Alexander … was very friendly to his neighbour. 'Don't be afraid, Rasay,' said he; 'I'll use all my interest to keep you safe; and if your estate should be taken, I'll buy it for the family.' And he would have done it."

It could have been very different for Macdonald's Skye tenantry. On 21 September 1745 the army of Charles Edward Stuart fought and won its first serious engagement with British government forces, near Prestonpans in East Lothian. The victory, over numerically superior forces who were broken within thirty minutes by a Highland charge, secured Charles's occupation of Edinburgh, and provided a huge morale and propaganda boost to Jacobites all over Scotland and points further south.

Following Prestonpans, the influential and well-connected tacksman Captain MacLeod of Brae in Raasay arranged a meeting at a "publick house" at Sconser in Skye between his uncle, MacLeod of Raasay, Alexander MacDonald of Kingsburgh in north Skye, who would soon afterwards become the father-in-law of Flora MacDonald, and the MacDonald high chief, Baronet Alexander of Armadale in Sleat.

Both the senior MacDonalds were known to nurse Jacobite sympathies, and Captain Malcolm MacLeod of Brae in Raasay was a stylish, charming and persuasive man. MacLeod was, observed James Boswell twenty-eight years later when the Raasay man was sixty-two years old,

> quite the Highland gentleman; of a stout well-made person, well-proportioned; a manly countenance browned with

> the weather, but a ruddiness in his cheeks, a good way up which his rough beard extended; a quick lively eye, not fierce in his look, but firm and good-humoured.
>
> He had a pair of brogues, tartan hose which came up only near his knees and left them bare, a purple camblet kilt, a black waistcoat, a short cloth green coat bound with gold cord, a yellowish bushy wig, a large blue bonnet with a gold-thread button. I never saw a figure that was more perfectly a representative of a Highland gentleman. I wished much to have a picture of him just as he was. I found him frank and polite, in the true sense of the word.

Captain Malcolm had been born in 1711 in Rigg in north Skye, and although he was given tacks in Raasay he was probably a human vestige of the Raasay MacLeods' properties in Skye. Malcolm MacLeod was married to an equally formidable and long-suffering woman named Catherine Macqueen.

In the event, at that meeting in Sconser the "firm and good-humoured" Captain MacLeod did not need to persuade Macdonald of Sleat to throw his hat into the ring. The baronet declared himself to be already convinced. According to MacLeod, and never denied by Macdonald, Baronet Alexander announced that Prestonpans "was certainly a most remarkable and surprizing victory the Prince had obtained; that he doubted not now of the Prince's succeeding in the attempt; and that therefore every one should raise his men to assist him in the design".

Macdonald then turned to MacLeod of Raasay. "Raaza," he said, "tis true you cannot raise many men; but the men you have are good. You can easily raise an hundred, and I resolve to raise nine hundred, which will make out a thousand good stout fellows betwixt us: for I am not for having boys or superannuate men amongst them. These I would divide into two battalions, 500 in each; and as you are a man that one can confide in, I resolve to make you Colonel of one of the battalions."

His proposal was substantial. The victorious Jacobite army at

Prestonpans had numbered around 2,000 men. In a public house in Skye, Macdonald of Sleat was offering to increase it by half again.

MacLeod of Raasay "most cheerfully accepted of the offer, and heartily thanked Sir Alexander for the command he designed to honour him with." The two men then began to work out the logistics of their campaign. According to the Jacobite history *The Lyon in Mourning*:

> the marching off the men was laid down by Sir Alexander himself, that Raaza should go off with his battalion first, and that Sir Alexander should follow at the distance of a day's march; and the particular places for quartering on the march were condescended upon.
>
> They likewise agreed upon what number of cattle they should drive along with each battalion for provisions till they should come to the low country, where they would get plenty. In a word, all matters were most amicably and frankly resolved upon for joining the Prince's standard without loss of time, and the company were highly delighted with the interview.
>
> Sir Alexander stayed all that night in the same house, making very merry, and taking a hearty glass with the gentlemen.

As the Sconser meeting progressed, at the other side of the country and the opposite end of the debate, another gathering took place. Duncan Forbes, who as Lord President of the Court of Session was the senior legal officer in Scotland, entertained in his mansion at Culloden outside Inverness his old friend, the Member of Parliament for Inverness-shire, clan chief, and general of substantial Hanoverian forces, Norman MacLeod of Dunvegan.

Both Forbes and MacLeod of Dunvegan were committed Hanoverians, government supporters who were pledged to oppose the rising. MacLeod thought that he had already won the support for King George II of his Skye neighbour, Macdonald of Sleat, when he heard through the Highland bush telegraph of the meeting that night in Sconser. Duncan Forbes and Norman MacLeod sat down in Culloden, wrote letters to Baronet Alexander Macdonald, and directed them to be sent post-haste to the Sconser public house.

> [The following morning] brought letters to Sir Alexander from President Forbes and the Laird of MacLeod, then at Culloden, which were delivered to him in presence of the company.
>
> He stept aside to a window and read the letters by himself, not allowing the company to know anything of the contents. Immediately he left his former chearfulness and frankway, and was quite upon the grave and thoughtful. He spoke not one word more of the matter, and left the company soon like one in confusion.
>
> To the importunities of the President and MacLeod had Sir Alexander in an instant yielded himself up entirely, and dropt the declared resolution of his own mind.
>
> Just as Sir Alexander went away, Malcolm MacLeod asked Kingsburgh what was become of yester-night's resolution, for that he was much surprized at Sir Alexander's leaving them so abruptly and dryly. Kingsburgh said he knew as little what was become of that affair as Mr. MacLeod did, but he was afraid that there would be no more of it.

There was no more of it. Alexander Macdonald's two battalions, formed chiefly by 900 men of his own, disappeared with the whisky fumes of that September night in Sconser.

MacLeod of Raasay was nonetheless, as Macdonald of Sleat had asserted before his dramatic about-face, good for a hundred men, and MacGilleChaluim did not recant. The small Raasay company was assembled. The hundred men exercised and were reviewed on a flat tract of common grazing land appropriated for the purpose to the north of Dun Caan. But they were too late to travel south with Charles's army.

They missed the march to Derby, where senior Scottish commanders took notice of their soldiers' concerns and forced a retreat back north, to the dismay of Charles himself, who thought he saw the Palace of Westminster on the near horizon.

Back on home soil, in January 1746, the Jacobite force of some 8,000 men laid a lengthy and ultimately aborted siege of Stirling Castle. Outside the walls of Stirling they were reinforced by levies from northern Scotland, including the 100 Ratharsaich. When the siege was abandoned, the army of Prince Charles marched with its Raasay contingent towards Inverness.

With a British Army division under the command of William Augustus, Duke of Cumberland, King George II's youngest son, hard on their heels, the Jacobite units were running out of ground. North, west and east of Inverness there was little but sea, islands and the wintry Highland terrain. They were obliged to make a stand.

They famously did so close to Culloden estate, Duncan Forbes's cluster of tied cottages around a mansion and stables three miles east of Inverness. A further three miles east of Culloden House, on the bare brown heather of Drumossie Moor, shortly after noon on 16 April 1746 the two armies faced each other.

A reduced force of between 5,000 and 6,000 Jacobite irregulars faced 9,000 Hanoverians with cannons. It was over in an hour. The Raasay men were on the inside left of the Jacobite front line – among other Gaelic speakers of Glengarry's West Highland regiment – when it was exposed to vicious cannon fire, and they then took part in a last, tired, desperate Highland charge which was outnumbered and dispersed in hand-to-hand fighting. By 2 p.m. their MacLeod officers had surrendered on the terms offered by the Duke of Cumberland.

Three hundred British Army soldiers fell at Culloden, and 1,500 to 2,000 Jacobites were killed outright, or died from wounds, or were executed in the heather. Extrapolation from those figures suggests that between twenty and thirty Raasay men and boys may have been left on Drumossie Moor. Captain Malcolm MacLeod, "who was one of the officers that led them to the field", told James Boswell three decades later that, "They returned home all but about fourteen." More must have been injured, when even a graze could quickly become fatal, but we know only of a musket-ball wound to the shoulder of MacGilleChaluim's third son, Murdoch MacLeod, which the young man survived. "He told me," reported the Jacobite chronicler Robert Forbes, "that the bullet entred at the left shoulder, and lodged under the right shoulder blade, and that one Balfour, a surgeon, took the bullet out the day after the battle".

So eighty or ninety men and officers in various degrees of good health returned to Raasay after their first exposure to contemporary warfare. Many of them promptly left again to seek anonymity, at least until the storm blew over. The historian and genealogist of the Outer Isles, Bill Lawson, relates the tradition that some made their way to Tong and Point in the east of their old clan territory of the island of Lewis. They were known there as Sliochd a' Chaiptein, the people of the Captain. "We know that some families fled from Raasay and came to Lewis at this time," writes Bill Lawson, "and I suspect that Sliochd a' Chaiptein were followers of Captain Malcolm MacLeod … who had been deeply involved in the Rebellion, on behalf of his uncle, the MacLeod of Raasay … Garrabost [in Point] families include MacSweens, Montgomeries and MacLeods – Sliochd a' Chaiptein – all good Raasay names, which suggests that they were among the refugees from that island …"

Charles Edward Stuart was hurried from Drumossie Moor to safety. He found refuge at Gorthleck, Fort Augustus and Invergarry before heading into the Highland hills, and then the Outer Hebrides.

The Gaelic *Iliad* was over; the Gaelic *Odyssey* was about to begin.

The departure of the Ratharsaich to the Rising in 1745 had launched a wave of retributive action from Hanoverian forces back home. John Campbell, 4th Earl of Loudon, raised in 1745 at Perth and Inverness a regiment of over a thousand men to fight on the government's side. As Loudon's Highlanders, they became heavily involved in reprisals and punishment actions against communities which were perceived to be Jacobite.

Early in 1746, while the Raasay infantry was making its way from Stirling to Inverness with the rest of the Jacobite army, Loudon took his troops to Skye and established a base on flat and comfortable land at the head of Loch na Dal in the north-east of Lord Macdonald's peninsula of Sleat. From there he garrisoned the island of Raasay with a handful of men, who removed all but two boats from the island and sailed them in convoy through the Kyle narrows and down the Sound of Sleat to be anchored or pulled up at Kinloch na Dal. The two boats which were spared confiscation were "one small one that was left to young Rasay by Sir Alexander MacDonald's intercession with Lord Loudon, and another that Captain Malcolm MacLeod hid in a house". Other than stranding the remaining Ratharsaich in their island, Loudon's Highlanders "did no great harm till after the battle of Cullodin; only disarmed six of the men that came home before the rest, and robed them of their plaids".

Then came the fire. A calendar month after the Battle of Culloden, on 15 or 16 May 1746, the Royal Navy's 91-foot armed sloop HMS *Furnace*, accompanied by several tenders, anchored off Raasay. It had a ship's complement of sixty men and was captained by a thirty-eight-year-old "cruel and barbarous" Aberdonian named John Ferguson.

The Lyon in Mourning is an unashamedly Jacobite record of the 1745 Rising. It was nonetheless thoroughly and repetitively researched by the Episcopalian bishop Robert Forbes, "who made it his life's work to collect all the reminiscences of participants in the 1745–6 rising as he could", and conscientiously attributed, collected and transcribed from living witnesses within a few years of the conflict. According to *The Lyon in Mourning*, on around 16 May 1746 Captain John Ferguson of HMS *Furnace* ordered Lieutenant Dalrymple of the British Army to take ashore a detachment of "sailors, marines, and Campbell militia" and "execute his vengeance" on Raasay.

Dalrymple seems to have begun by burning "to ashes" the tower house at Clachan which had been MacGilleChaluim's family fortress and home for centuries. They then torched "the whole houses upon the island, excepting two small villages that escaped their sight, with all the poor people's furniture. The number of the houses brunt, according to a strict accompt taken of them, exceeded three hundred. They likewise found all Rasay's furniture and silver-plate hid in a cave about a quarter of a mile from the house, betrayed by a small boy belonging to the island." The cave used by MacLeod to hide his family silver was the prehistoric Uamh nan Ràmh.

Dalrymple ordered his men "to march in three bodys throw the island, two near the shore, and the third along the hill. They gathered what cattle was in their way, cows and horses, sheep and goats, and slaughtered numbers of all kinds, and left many of them dead both in the shores and hill. The people of the island were then pretty quiet, only that they were frequently importuned to surrender their arms, which they at last did ..."

Jacobite sources portrayed Armageddon: "the whole Island of Raaza had been plundered and pillaged to the utmost degree of severity, every house and hut being levelled with the ground; and there was not left in the whole island a four-footed beast, a hen or a chicken." MacGilleChaluim's old tower house was certainly torched to extinction, along with his family furniture, and the thatches of many common homes and outbuildings were fired. But far from every building was levelled. Robert Forbes, who collected first-hand information from the Raasay MacLeods, estimated a few years later the damage:

The exact accompt of the damages sustained in Rasay as

> nearly calculated as possible, and which may be depended upon, is as follows:
>
> The number of the cows slaughtered amounted in all to upwards of two hundred and eighty, the sheep upwards of seven hundred, the horses shot for pleasure did not exceed a score, and the boats destroyed during these troubles were thirty-two in number, small and great; and the houses burnt exceeded three hundred; the whole amount of the articles above, with their furniture, close, and all other necessarys lost, according to an exact calculation made as the one of them selves would sell to the other, exceeded twenty-four thousand merks Scots.
>
> Besides all this Rasay himself, including his house, his house furniture, cattle, and other things, values his loss above fifteen hundred pounds sterling more; besides the poor people are at as much loss again by the want entirely of the two last years' crops. Tho' the island is of some extent, ten miles long, three broad in some places, and not even a mile in some parts, yet the above losses was very great, and quite ruin'd many of the people.

Forbes was later assured by young John MacLeod of Raasay that 120 families lived on the island when Captain Ferguson dropped anchor offshore. The possession of "three or four cows" was judged by MacGilleChaluim to qualify a tenant to pay rent. Young Rona, as the heir was known in reference to the second largest island in the estate, knew from experience of his family's accounts that many Ratharsaich did not reach the three or four cow bar, "even before they suffered any losses" from Lieutenant Dalrymple's men. The damage done to the island's economy was clearly substantial.

Two small companies of MacLeod militia enlisted by Norman MacLeod of Dunvegan on the government's side, one commanded by MacLeod of Talisker and the other by MacLeod of Waterstein, were based in Braes and Portree overlooking Raasay. They frequently crossed to harass their neighbouring islanders. In the course of the series of occupations and raids in 1746, several men were badly beaten by government troops for information that they did not possess, and at least two women were raped. Nobody was killed outright, however. MacLeod of Raasay, who in the months after Culloden made himself scarce in the rough bounds of Knoydart on the western mainland facing Skye – a Scottish mainland which he and his Hebridean contemporaries referred to as "the continent" – lost neither his life nor his property, which was the fate of other leading lights of Charles Edward Stuart's rising.

Even accounting for Jacobite exaggeration, which was considerable, the picture remains horrifying. The only small Highland community to send a platoon comprised of virtually all of its fit adult men to fight a dynastical war, was burned out of house and home. A benign little island which had nurtured its inhabitants for millennia was left shrouded in smoke and the stench of domestic incineration; many of its cattle and sheep dead or dying on the hillsides and in the coastal shallows – the troops seem to have been comparatively lenient to the ponies – its people left drawn and devastated. They took the only available course. They gave thanks that it was springtime, the weather was mild, some crops were in the ground and winter was many months away. They slept under such roofs as remained intact, and outdoors in the fields, in the open air or beneath makeshift shelters. Grimly, steadily and swiftly, they rebuilt.

At the end of June 1746, Charles Edward Stuart was rowed across the Minch from the east coast of Benbecula in the Outer Isles to the north-west coast of Skye. He was dressed as a lady's maid and was addressed by his companions and his mistress, a young woman from South Uist named Flora MacDonald, as Betty Burke. He had spent the previous two-and-a-half months ducking and diving through most of the islands north of his point of arrival in Eriskay, from South Uist up to Lewis, searching in vain for friendly French ships and dodging government militias and anybody else interested in the £30,000 bounty put on his head by the British government.

Once in Skye, he said farewell to both Flora MacDonald and Betty Burke, and found himself in a public house which was run by a landlord named Charles MacNab in the small town of Portree. Charles was met there by Captain Malcolm MacLeod and Murdoch MacLeod, both of them Raasay men who had fought for him at Culloden. The heir to the Raasay estate, John MacLeod, Young Rona, having missed the earlier excitement at Culloden, was desperate to meet Charles and he approached the two others and asked for a place in the small boat that they were preparing to cross to Portree. *The Lyon in Mourning* recounts how Captain Malcolm sympathised with John, but advised continued discretion:

> [The tacksman] begged him to consider well what he was doing, that as he had not been out [at the Rising], he ought to run no risque for satisfying his desire, which at present could be of no real use or service, and therefore he suggested to him to act in this affair with the utmost prudence and caution. Meantime Malcolm could not help owning frankly that he himself heartily wished that his friend might see the Prince, provided he could do it with safety. But then he would leave it altogether to himself to determine on which side he should think fit to chuse.
>
> After thinking a while, young Raaza positively declared he was resolved to see the Prince if it should cost him the estate and the head.

So John MacLeod of Raasay joined his younger brother Murdoch and their cousin Captain Malcolm in the yawl, which in the short midsummer night of 30 June 1746 was rowed by two local men, John MacKenzie and Donald MacFrier, from the west coast of Raasay across the sound and into the broad expanse of Portree Bay. MacKenzie and MacFrier had both fought in the Raasay contingent at Culloden, MacKenzie as a sergeant and MacFrier as a private. Once they had tied up at the Skye town's slipway, Captain Malcolm and Murdoch MacLeod climbed the hill from the shore into the centre of the village, leaving John "Rona" MacLeod behind with the oarsmen.

"Upon meeting with the Prince they spent very little time at Pourttree," Captain MacLeod later told Robert Forbes, "but attended him soon to the same small boat; and the Captain did not introduce young Raaza to the Prince till they were in the boat."

It was raining heavily and, having eaten voraciously, Charles was reluctant to leave Portree that night. The Raasay men persuaded him of the urgency of their situation and finally, with four shirts, a cooked chicken in a napkin, a bottle of brandy and a bottle of whisky tied to his belt, the heir to the Jacobite throne of the United Kingdom made his way through the mud and the downpour to the shore of Portree Bay, where they joined John MacKenzie, Donald MacFrier and Young Rona. The yawl was launched and they set off across the Sound of Raasay.

In the early hours of 1 July the fugitive party arrived back in Raasay. Their boat put into one of the beaches below the settlement of Glam, halfway up the island and just north of Captain Malcolm's tack at Brae. The two boatmen were placed as lookouts on nearby vantage points. John MacLeod went for provisions – he returned carrying a butchered kid in his plaid, along with fresh cream and butter – while the other men set up camp in "a mean" shepherds' hut, "so low", wrote Captain Malcolm MacLeod later, "that he could neither sitt nor stand, but was obliged to lie on the bare ground, having only a bundle of heath for his pillow".

There was on the following day an oddly unnerving encounter. A man had recently appeared in Raasay "upon pretence of selling a roll of tobacco". Having quickly disposed of his goods "he continued strolling up and down the island in an idle way without anything to do, for no less than twelve or fourteen days, which made the people of the island suspect him to be a spy."

The oldest standing structure in Raasay: the neolithic menhir at Eyre.

The south end of the island under snow. The residual circular walls of Dun Borodale are on the hilltop at right/centre. (Photograph by Calum Gillies)

Above left: Uamh nan Ràmh at Clachan. A souterrain that saw practical use from prehistory into modern times.

Above right: The Pictish stone whose enigmatic ciphers were repeated on other stones and at the Clachan landing place.

Right: St Moluag's medieval and early modern chapels.

The medieval Brochel Castle, as observed by William Daniell in 1815.

Uamh an Fhuaimhaire, the Giant's Cave on the east coast of Rona, was sculpted into a rock chapel, with pews and an altar. (Photograph by Alan Rankin)

Thomas Rowlandson's cartoon of Boswell and Johnson's passage from Skye to Raasay in 1773. The four passengers represented Johnson, Boswell, Boswell's servant and the remarkable Captain Malcolm MacLeod.

The orphaned Eliza Ross, who, as a foster child in Raasay House between 1794 and 1813, compiled a precious volume of the island's songs and instrumental music.
(Courtesy of Taigh na Teud)

One of two stone mermaids commissioned early in the nineteenth century by James MacLeod of Raasay and banished to his battery above the Clachan landing place.

Left: William Daniell's pencil, a gift from his Indian lover, lost in Raasay in 1815 and rediscovered two centuries later.

Below: Charles D'Oyly's portrait of Raasay House, in 1825, swivelled on its axis to provide a better view than usual of the mountains of Skye.

The industrial revolution arrives. German prisoners of war, with state-of-the-art equipment, excavate Raasay's iron-ore reserves.

Prisoners of war at leisure in Inverarish.

Part of the purpose-built mining village of Inverarish.

The poet Somhairle MacGill-Eain.
(Photograph by Cailean Maclean)

Calum MacLeod of Anish with one of several wheelbarrows.

The Sabbath.

Rona and Raasay from north to south. (Photograph by Kevin Gray)

The steep and forbidding but fertile south-east of Raasay, once home to Hallaig and several other busy townships. (Photograph by Kevin Gray)

Inevitably, the tobacco seller sauntered in the direction of Glam. Huddled inside their hut, the three MacLeods debated his fate. Captain Malcolm was in favour of settling the matter once and for all by going outside and putting a bullet in his head. Charles demurred, pointing out that the interloper might be no worse than he suggested, an innocent man enjoying a few days of refuge in Raasay from the chaos of the west Highlands in 1746.

One of the boatmen, John MacKenzie, was standing outside the entrance to the hut. Overhearing Charles urging clemency, MacKenzie stage-muttered in Gaelic, "Well, well: he must be shot: you are the king, but we are the parliament, and will do what we choose." Inside the hut the three MacLeods smiled. Charles asked for a translation and laughed aloud when it was given.

The tobacco seller walked past and was spared. It was later attested that he had been a bona fide chapman, an itinerant retailer, who had possibly been in the Jacobite army at Culloden and in the paranoid Highland summer of 1746 was just another displaced, wandering soul.

With or without potential spies, Charles was uneasy in Raasay. It was a smaller and more vulnerable island than he had expected. The accommodation left much to be desired, and with many other buildings still roofless or reduced to ashes following the exertions of Lieutenant Dalrymple and Captain Ferguson six weeks earlier, there was little prospect of improvement. Charles asked about the condition of Raasay.

> Upon his being told of all the houses burnt, and of the other great depredations in the island to which the houses were but a trifle, he seem'd much affected, but at the same time told that instead of the hutts burnt he would yet build houses of stone.
>
> Afterwards walking on a narrow green near the cottage he said that this was a little hard life, but would rather live ten years in that way than be taken by his enemys, and seem'd a little surpriz'd himself how he did bear such

> fatigues. For, says he, since the battle of Culloden, I have endured more than would kill a hundred. Sure Providence does not design this for nothing. I'm certainly reserv'd for some good.
>
> Thus they pass'd the day, and after having taken some supper he went to rest with as great pleasure and in outward appearance as little concern'd as if in the greatest prosperity, after placing the two servants as centinels without, Murdoch, Rasay's [third] son, and Captain MacLeod lying by him in the hut, young Rasay retiring to his own sort of habitation for fear of any suspicion.

On the following day, 2 July, Charles reconfirmed his desire to return to Skye from Raasay, and from Skye to make his way to some mainland rendezvous with a vessel bound for France. It was by then difficult for his party to argue that a better future lay in a low shed in Glam, so arrangements were duly made. The yawl was again put in the water, the two oarsmen, Charles Edward Stuart and the three Raasay MacLeods climbed aboard and at 9 p.m. that evening they set course for the district of Scorrybreac, north of Portree.

They "went to sea with a pretty high wind, and a very rainy night. The boat being small and the wind still turning higher, [Charles] seem'd somewhat uneasie, and I enquired if there was any danger. Upon his being told not, he appeared very gay, desir'd the lads to pull hearty, and began himself to sing a Highland song. Afterwards among other things he said: Gentlemen, I hope to thank you for this trouble yet at [the London Royal Court of] St. James's."

Back in north Skye, Captain Malcolm MacLeod determined that it fell to him alone to escort Charles to Elgol in the deep south of Skye, where Captain Malcolm's brother-in-law, John MacKinnon, would introduce them to the staunchly Jacobite Iain "Dubh" MacKinnon of MacKinnon, the 29th chief of Clan MacKinnon, whose second and current wife, Janet MacLeod, was a daughter of MacGilleChaluim of Raasay.

It was time for the prince to become a servant again. On the evening of 3 July, MacLeod and Charles, now posing as a retainer of Captain Malcolm named Lewis Caw, but at least dressed down in men's clothes, said farewell to the two Raasay boatmen and the two Raasay brothers. They then hiked around the west of Portree, down the west side of Glen Varragill, skirted the head of Loch Sligachan, cut due south from Luib to the head of Loch Slapin and made their way through the black Cuillins to the tip of the Strathaird peninsula.

In the vicinity of Elgol, Captain Malcolm MacLeod of Brae in Raasay was relieved of his charge. Iain Dubh MacKinnon took over. Black John MacKinnon was sixty-four years old in 1746 and had been chief of his small clan since 1700. He had joined the 1715 Jacobite Rising, which cost him his estates through an Act of Attainder. They were restored several years later as he seemed unlikely to pose a future threat to the Hanoverian state. When the Forty-five began, MacKinnon raised 200 men, joined Charles in Edinburgh and marched behind him south to Derby and north again to Culloden.

In early July 1746, he was unlikely to shirk his responsibilities. The 29th MacKinnon organised a boat and four boatmen to take Charles along with himself and John MacKinnon from Elgol around the Point of Sleat to the village of Mallaig, where they rested for three days close to the spot where, a century later, a railway station would be built. The seven Strathaird men then made their way up Loch Nevis and, on 10 July, passed Charles on to the Morar landholder, MacDonald of Borodale. On the following day, Iain Dubh MacKinnon was arrested in Morar by government militia.

Captain Malcolm MacLeod had meantime walked back up Skye to find the north of the island teeming with government troops. The sensible response would have been to go to ground, or to keep on walking until he escaped the district entirely. But "my wife being on the island of Rasay, the old Laird, his son, the Doctor, and my brother, without any word, I could not help going to Rasay, tho' it wou'd cost my life."

He boarded a boat which was plying for trade off the coast of Skye. "I was not far from the shore when some soldiers cam to the shore side. They began to cry after uss. The people of the boat said they would turn. I told them I woud make use of my arms first. Then the soldier began to fire after us. I desir the men to go on."

Back in Raasay, Captain MacLeod sent a message to MacGilleChaluim, who had returned from Knoydart, "telling hime how it was, and to take good care of himself." He located his own family in the fields: "I had not a home. I cam where my wife was with some cows. It was night then. I got word that they saw ships at the other end of Rasay. I took little rest. At break of day I went to the top of the Island with my servantt and told nobody where I was going. When I came to the top what did I see but fourty redcoats very near me. I heard a shot nearer then that to me, then a soldier apeired to me and began to pursue me, and cryed to me to halt. I ran as fast as I could."

Captain Malcolm evaded the troops, but they caught his servant, Donald Nicolson, tied the man to a tree and interrogated him. Quickly realising that they thought his master was Charles Edward Stuart, Nicolson elected to say nothing at all. "They left him there for dead," MacLeod told Robert Forbes.

> He was a long time before he did recover it. Then I got another servantt, John Roy Montgumury.
>
> All that day there was not anywhere that I wou'd turn my face but a partty of rid coats would meet me. At last my servantt told me that he knew a rock [overhang cave] that no body woud find use. So I went with him to that rock and stayed there tow days and tow nights without meat or drink, seeing the soldiers passing and repassing every day.
>
> The third day we cam out of the rock, and my wife met me and told me she did not know if they left Rasay or not. Then I sent my servantt to a freind of my own, on Murdo

McLeod, tacksman of Brea [Brae]. Murdo sends me word all the soldiers wer away and left Rasay, that I might go to his house, and so I did, and got meat and drink, which I had need of."

After another three days of being hounded by MacLeod's Skye militia across Raasay, Captain Malcolm MacLeod of Brae was finally surrounded and forced at gunpoint to surrender. Characteristically, he told Lieutenant Donald MacLeod, the fellow clansman who was in charge of the successful party, that he was slightly mollified by being arrested by another MacLeod – "there was not any neame in Scotland wou'd take me prisoner but thairsalvies". On 19 July 1746, Captain Malcolm was handed over to the Aberdonian Captain John Ferguson on HMS *Furnace*. Three months later Ferguson delivered him with other Jacobite detainees to Tilbury Fort, an artillery battery and arsenal commanding the mouth of the River Thames in Essex. By the end of 1746 Tilbury Fort held 268 Jacobite prisoners in its gunpowder magazines, of whom forty-five died from typhus fever before they could be put on trial.

Malcolm MacLeod was spared by being quickly transferred to house arrest in the London home of a King's Messenger named William Dick.

Captain MacLeod stayed in William Dick's house arrest in London for eight months. On 4 July 1747 it was determined that he and his Raasay corps had surrendered "in terms of the Duke of Cumberland's proclamation after the battle of Culloden". He was cleared of any other offence, which considering Malcolm MacLeod's strenuous activities on behalf of Charles Edward Stuart in the early days of July 1746 displayed either inept gathering of information, remarkable leniency or perhaps a desire once and for all to forget the whole sorry business. He returned to Scotland from London in a post-chaise containing another released Jacobite prisoner: a certain Miss Flora MacDonald.

Iain Dubh MacKinnon was detained at Tilbury Fort and at trial was released in deference to his great old age of sixty-four years. He left behind, hanging in the air of the south-east of England, one of the greatest apocryphal Jacobite rejoinders. As they were leaving the courtroom, the Attorney General, Sir Dudley Ryder, who was a sprightly fifty-five years old, asked MacKinnon of MacKinnon, "If King George were in your power, as you have been in his, what would you do?"

Iain Dubh replied, "I would do to him, as he has this day done to me. I would send him back to his own country." He enjoyed a further ten years of uncontroversial retirement before dying at his Strathaird home in 1755.

In the early hours of 20 September 1746, the relay baton that had become the eminent body of Charles Edward Stuart was handed on to its final leg. The young man was picked up in the Sound of Arisaig between Morar and south Skye by a French vessel which then carried him to Roscoff in Brittany. Bliadhna Theàrlaich, the Year of Charlie, was over, and in mute reply to a dozen plaintive songs, he would never return.

Captain Malcolm MacLeod not only returned to his tack in central Raasay. He was still there twenty-six years later, as large as life and twice as dashing, to facilitate the next momentous intrusion from the wider world into his island.

7

Song and Dance

"More effectively than other Hebridean lairds, they [the MacLeods of Raasay] succeeded in transforming themselves in just a few generations from roving pirates to gentlemen of cultured taste."

TWENTY-SEVEN years after he escorted the fugitive Charles Edward Stuart from Skye to Raasay on a wet night in a small boat, Captain Malcolm MacLeod of Brae performed a similar service, in happier circumstances, to two other distinguished visitors.

On 8 September 1773 he met on the coast outside Broadford in southern Skye the sixty-three-year-old English polymath Samuel Johnson, his friend, the thirty-two-year-old Edinburgh advocate James Boswell, and Boswell's Bohemian manservant Joseph Ritter, "a fine stately fellow above six feet high, who had been over a great part of Europe, and spoke many languages".

The visit of Johnson and Boswell to the Scottish Gaidhealtachd was the earliest serious manifestation of the fascination of southern Britons with tribes of noble savages on or just off their own north-western shores, and the attendant anxiety of the leaders of those tribes to demonstrate that they might be noble but were not savages. Johnson and Boswell had been guests of Macdonald of Sleat in Armadale for fewer than twenty-four hours when they received an invitation from MacGilleChaluim to visit Raasay. "It is incredible," mused Johnson about the Highland bush telegraph, "how soon the account of any event is propagated in these narrow countries by the love of talk, which much leisure produces, and the relief given to the mind in the penury of insular conversation by a new topick. The arrival of strangers at a place so rarely visited, excites rumour, and quickens curiosity."

The three visitors met Malcolm MacLeod – "one of the Rasay family, celebrated in the year 1745–6" and "four stout rowers, particularly a Macleod, a robust, black-haired fellow, half naked, and bear-headed, something between a wild Indian and an English tar" at Skinadin Bay, a mile north-west of the market town of Broadford. They were put into "a good strong open boat made in Norway" and rowed through the Scalpay narrows into the open Sound of Raasay.

Old Malcolm MacLeod, 10th of Raasay, having died in 1761, Johnson and Boswell were greeted at the rocky Clachan landing place – close to the rock face with its Pictish hieroglyphics – by Young Rona, John MacLeod, who had become the 11th MacGilleChaluim. At the age of fifty-nine years, he was making the best of a diminished inheritance. Following the Forty-five, MacLeod of Raasay had been obliged to recognise as his feudal superior MacLeod of Dunvegan, whose posses of armed men had put the island under martial law and had hunted down and abused his tenants and relatives after Culloden. John MacLeod archly told Samuel Johnson that "his ancestors have formerly disputed the pre-eminence".

His powers had also been limited by three post-Culloden pieces of legislation which were specifically aimed at the morale and standing of Highland clan chiefs. The Heritable Jurisdictions (Scotland) Act of 1746 removed their right to appoint sheriffs on their estates, which through patronage had given them devolved judicial authority within their own parishes. MacLeod of Raasay told Johnson and Boswell that "taking away the heritable jurisdictions had not been of such service in the islands, as was imagined.

They had not authority enough in lieu of them. What could formerly have been settled at once, must now either take much time and trouble, or be neglected." His guests sympathised with a statement that others might have interpreted as proof that the Heritable Jurisdictions Act was working as intended.

The Act of Proscription, 1746, obliged residents of the Highland counties to give up their weapons, and the Dress Act, also of 1746, banned civilians from wearing "the clothes commonly called Highland clothes (that is to say) the Plaid, Philabeg, or little Kilt, Trowse, Shoulder-belts, or any part whatever of what peculiarly belongs to the Highland Garb".

The last two were both repealed in 1782, on the assumption that most muskets had by then been confiscated, and the tartan plaid was out of fashion. They may have been honoured more in the breach than the observance. Nine years before the repeal of the Act of Proscription, in 1773, James Boswell was taken out to hunt with guns for game birds in southern Raasay.

John MacLeod had busily restocked his island with domestic animals, bought new boats from Scandinavia and built an elegant Georgian mansion overlooking the Clachan landing place, close to the site of his family's incinerated tower house.

They landed at about 6 p.m. and made the short walk to aperitifs, dancing and a dinner for thirty-six settings – black cock, grey hen and dairy desserts – in the new manor house. Samuel Johnson appreciated the calm and hospitality of Raasay House, and was impressed by the island as a whole. He estimated, optimistically but according to his own idiosyncratic application of the military/civilian equation, a population of 900:

> The number of this little community has never been counted by its ruler, nor have I obtained any positive account, consistent with the result of political computation.
>
> Not many years ago, the late Laird led out one hundred men upon a military expedition. The sixth part of a people is supposed capable of bearing arms: Raasay had therefore

> six hundred inhabitants. But because it is not likely, that every man able to serve in the field would follow the summons, or that the chief would leave his lands totally defenceless, or take away all the hands qualified for labour, let it be supposed, that half as many might be permitted to stay at home.
>
> The whole number will then be nine hundred, or nine to a square mile; a degree of populousness greater than those tracts of desolation can often show. They are content with their country, and faithful to their chiefs, and yet uninfected with the fever of migration.

They believed Fladda to be unpopulated and Rona to be the haunt of a solitary herdsman and his 160 cattle. Peculiarly and uniquely, considering the main island's history and the etymology of its very name, both Johnson and Boswell reported that in 1773 the archipelago had "neither deer, hares, nor rabbits". If there were no deer or smaller edible mammals in Raasay in 1773, they might all have been killed and eaten after the 1746 reprisals had ravaged the domesticated herds of cattle and sheep – and for at least a few of the following years, the Act of Proscription took away the island's hunting guns, which were in the eighteenth century the preferred way of culling deer and rabbits for the pot. Within a few years of 1773 the herds, droves and colonies had been reintroduced – John MacLeod told Boswell without further explanation that he would shortly "get some" deer – or had reintroduced themselves from Scalpay or Skye, and as Boswell discovered, guns had also been restored.

James Boswell got along famously with Captain Malcolm MacLeod of Brae. They climbed Dun Caan together, dancing a jig on its small summit plateau, and as they passed a hill loch,

> Malcolm told me a strange fabulous tradition. He said, there was a wild beast in it, a sea-horse, which came and devoured a man's daughter; upon which the man lighted a

> great fire, and had a sow roasted at it, the smell of which attracted the monster. In the fire was put a spit. The man lay concealed behind a low wall of loose stones, and he had an avenue formed for the monster, with two rows of large flat stones, which extended from the fire over the summit of the hill, till it reached the side of the loch. The monster came, and the man with the red-hot spit destroyed it. Malcolm shewed me the little hiding-place, and the rows of stones. He did not laugh when he told this story.

Samuel Johnson took enormous pleasure from proclaiming the last word on anything. "Raasay," he decided, "has little that can detain a traveller, except the Laird and his family; but their power wants no auxiliaries. Such a seat of hospitality, amidst the winds and waters, fills the imagination with a delightful contrariety of images. Without is the rough ocean and the rocky land, the beating billows and the howling storm: within is plenty and elegance, beauty and gaiety, the song and the dance. In Raasay, if I could have found an Ulysses, I had fancied a Phœacia."

Samuel Johnson's and James Boswell's first impressions of Raasay were musical. In the open boat which carried them from Skye to Raasay, both men had been struck by song. Malcolm MacLeod "sung an Erse song, the chorus of which was 'Hatyin foam foam eri', with words of his own. The tune resembled 'Owr the muir amang the heather', the boatmen … chorused, and all went well … Dr Johnson observed, that naval musick was very ancient."

As they approached the Raasay shore they saw men and women harvesting on the raised beaches of the green littoral, and "the singing of our rowers was succeeded by that of reapers, who were busy at work, and who seemed to shout as much as to sing, while they worked with a bounding activity." Johnson would later write: "I saw the harvest of a small field. The women reaped the Corn, and the men bound up the sheaves. The strokes of the sickle were timed by the modulation of the harvest song, in which all their voices were united.

"They accompany in the Highlands every action, which can be done in equal time, with an appropriated strain, which has, they say, not much meaning; but its effects are regularity and cheerfulness. The ancient proceleusmatick song, by which the rowers of gallies were animated, may be supposed to have been of this kind. There is now an oar-song used by the Hebridians."

Inside Raasay House that evening, Johnson was captivated when, "After supper the ladies sung Erse songs, to which I listened as an English audience to an Italian opera, delighted with the sound of words which I did not understand.

I inquired the subjects of the songs, and was told of one, that it was a love song, and of another, that it was a farewell composed by one of the Islanders that was going, in this epidemical fury of emigration, to seek his fortune in America. What sentiments would arise, on such an occasion, in the heart of one who had not been taught to lament by precedent, I should gladly have known; but the lady, by whom I sat, thought herself not equal to the work of translating."

When the company danced to the tunes of a sole violinist, Samuel Johnson was entranced – "nor did ever fairies trip with greater alacrity". He was even persuaded by a waulking song – "Lady Rasay shewed him the operation of wawking cloth," observed Boswell, "that is, thickening it in the same manner as is done by a mill. Here it is performed by women, who kneel upon the ground, and rub it with both their hands, singing an Erse song all the time. He was asking questions while they were performing this operation, and, amidst their loud and wild howl, his voice was heard even in the room above."

Song and dance was commonplace throughout the Highlands. In Raasay, as they recognised, Samuel Johnson and James Boswell had stumbled into an especially rich and accomplished local tradition. Two decades after they left the convivial surroundings of Raasay House, Eliza Ross arrived there.

Elizabeth Jane Ross was born in colonial India in 1789. Her father was Thomas Ross, a Royal Artillery captain from Fort

William. Her mother, Isabella Rose MacLeod, was one of the nine daughters of John, the 11th MacGilleChaluim, the same MacLeod of Raasay who had welcomed Johnson and Boswell to the island, and his wife Jane MacQueen of Trotternish in Skye.

Even within the beauty pageant of the Georgian Raasay House, Eliza's mother, Isabella Rose MacLeod, was noted for her astonishing good looks. The poet Robert Burns, who met her at a recital in Edinburgh in 1787, was sufficiently enraptured to make her the subject of no fewer than four poems. He effused:

> The crimson blossom charms the bee,
> The summer sun the swallow;
> So dear this tuneful gift to me
> From lovely Isabella.

In 1894, when Eliza was five years old, her father died in Madras. Her mother packed up Eliza and her baby sister Isabella, and took ship back to Britain. Only the two girls disembarked. The exact fate of Isabella Rose MacLeod is not known, but it appears that she died on the voyage and was buried at sea. The orphaned sisters Eliza and Isabella were then adopted and shipped to the Hebrides by their uncle, James MacLeod, the 12th of Raasay, who had inherited the title upon the death of John in 1786.

Eliza may have had some Gaelic from her parents; she certainly refined it as a girl in Raasay. She may have been taught music at Mary Erskine School in Edinburgh; she certainly had an ear and an aptitude. As a young woman in her teens and early twenties, Eliza began to transcribe the songs, fiddle tunes, bagpipe and piano music which formed the soundtrack of life in early nineteenth-century Raasay, from the moment she got into an open boat in Skye to the hour that she drifted to sleep in Raasay House with the adults still singing and playing below.

Her maternal line was a musical family. James MacLeod, 12th of Raasay, was himself a musician. A contemporary described him as "a celebrated Dilletante, or gentleman performer. His subject is the violin, which he touches with great neatness & expression. He plays dancing measures, with spirit and execution, and blends his own fancies with the originals, so happily, that one is often at a loss to distinguish which is which." James's wife, Flora Ann MacLean of the small island of Muck, was "an excellent performer on the pianoforte and whose gentleness of manner is in fine harmony with the elegance of her form, and lovely countenance". Their tacksman cousin, Captain Malcolm MacLeod of Brae, as well as being in possession of a robust singing voice and a catalogue of Gaelic songs for most occasions, was also an enthusiastic piper.

She also shared Raasay with the island's notable MacKay piping family, one of whom, John MacKay, was her uncle's official piper. The most nationally celebrated of those men would be John's son Angus MacKay, who in 1843 became Queen Victoria's piper, and was consequently the first British "Piper to the Sovereign". Angus MacKay knew Eliza Ross and would say of her, "Her musical taste was remarkably good, and she was so fond of Pìobeareachd [bagpipes] that she acquired many of the longest pieces from the performance of the family piper and was accustomed to play them on the piano with much effect."

In 1813, Eliza Ross's life in Raasay was brought to an abrupt end. At the age of twenty-four years she and her sister Isabella were shipped back to India on what was known as the "fishing fleet" of passenger vessels containing British women angling for husbands in the Raj. The two girls disembarked with "their wedding trousseaus already packed" as wards of the new governor-general of British India, Francis Edward Rawdon-Hastings, 1st Marquess of Hastings. Those connections in high places were explained by the Raasay diaspora. The Marquess of Hastings was married to Flora Mure-Campbell, who was a daughter of the Earl of Loudoun and Flora MacLeod. Flora MacLeod had been in her turn the second daughter of John MacLeod of Raasay, 11th MacGilleChaluim, and his Skye wife Jane MacQueen.

The architectural historian Mary Miers suggests that, "More effectively than other Hebridean lairds, they [the MacLeods of Raasay] succeeded in transforming themselves in just a few generations from roving pirates to gentlemen of cultured taste." Young Rona, the man whose father, brothers and closest friends had fought at Culloden, who had himself given refuge to Charles Edward Stuart and been grateful for the opportunity, within a generation saw his children marry into the heart of the British aristocratic establishment. Eliza Ross, the orphaned girl with a passion for Raasay's music, was in 1813 a cousin by marriage of the governor-general of India – whose wife was a niece of the current MacGilleChaluim, James MacLeod, 12th of Raasay.

Isabella quickly married a young soldier who later became the distinguished General Walter Raleigh Gilbert. Eliza Ross met Charles D'Oyly, an Anglo-Indian aide to the governor-general in Calcutta, and the heir to a baronetcy. D'Orly's passion was for the visual arts. An early Orientalist, he caricatured both native Indian society and the Raj in vivid lithographs. He was charmed by Eliza's musical gifts, and by her own sketches and her excursions into poetry. The thirty-six-year-old Charles married twenty-eight-year-old Eliza in India in 1815. Three years later Charles D'Oyly inherited his title, and Elizabeth Jane Ross became a baroness.

In 1825 they visited Raasay together, possibly so that Eliza's adoptive family could meet her husband. We know that because Charles made a dramatic and imaginative oil painting of Raasay House following some of its more modest earlier pavilion extensions. In the background of his landscape, the mountain of Glamaig in Skye cuts into clouds, and the white-capped Sound of Raasay is alive with sailing ships. In the foreground, cattle graze by the shore of Clachan Bay. Raasay House itself stood at an impossible angle to D'Oyly's preferred perspective, so he swivelled it round to face his easel, with its back to Skye.

After two decades spent hosting a popular artistic household in British India, for the sake of his ailing health, Charles and Elizabeth D'Oyly returned to Europe for good. They retired to Italy, where Charles died in 1845. The fifty-six-year-old Elizabeth moved to Dorset where she saw out her long later years, writing

English and Gaelic poetry and very occasionally making the long journey north to Raasay, before dying in Dorset in 1875 at the age of eighty-six years.

Her collection of musical transcripts led a separate but equally extraordinary life. She left the handwritten papers behind in Raasay House. In the form of forty sheets of fragile, browning paper, they miraculously survived there, "among other books and materials" for a further 140 years.

In the early 1950s the collection was removed from Raasay. It was then spotted in the stock of an Edinburgh bookseller – with a price tag of four guineas – by the musicologist Francis Collinson, who in 1954 directed the papers to the new School of Scottish Studies. In the twenty-first century the heritage scholars at Musica Scotia assembled it into a volume titled *The Eliza Ross Collection: Original Highland Airs Collected on Raasay in 1812*, and the Skye music publisher Taigh na Teud gave it a wider audience. Its modern editors wrote in 2011:

> Elizabeth Ross's book is now very fragile, and consists of 38 (originally 40) sheets of paper (watermarked 1806) stitched into brown marbled card covers. The leaves have twice been numbered and the two missing sheets vanished subsequent to the later numbering. The book's pages had also been cropped when they were bound with the result that all or part of the topmost title on many leaves was cropped away. Like many manuscripts of this period the pages have now turned very brown, the stitched binding is breaking up and the ink has leeched through to the other side of the paper. While it was in the care of the School of Scottish Studies William Matheson consulted the manuscript and pencilled in some of the incomplete titles.

But it was alive. It had survived, and its 150 tunes and airs offer a window into "the wide-ranging musical repertory known to Gaelic-speaking inhabitants of one Hebridean island, Raasay" at the end of the eighteenth and the beginning of the nineteenth century.

Elizabeth Ross never forgot the MacKay piping family of Eyre at the southern tip of Raasay. While in India she commissioned a craftsman to make John MacKay a bespoke set of bagpipes, and MacKay in turn composed an air, "Fàilte Baintighearna D'Oyly", "Lady D'Oyly's Salute", in her honour.

They were a remarkable line. The patriarch John MacKay was born in Eyre in about 1767. Ninety years later his distinguished son, the Queen's piper Angus MacKay, jotted down in his diary a short account of his father's upbringing. He was "commonly called Iain Mac Ruairidh of Eyre in Ratharsair, Isle of Skye. He was, I believe, left an orphan with one sister …"

Young orphaned John was, said Angus, taken in and raised by Captain Malcolm MacLeod, the tacksman of both Brae and Eyre, or Aoighre, the friend and guide of Charles Edward Stuart and Boswell and Johnson, who was known as Fear Aoighre, "Man of Eyre".

Captain Malcolm deployed the youngster, recalled Angus, "as a herd boy &c. and in the house. Fir Aoighre played the Pipes and was teaching a[nother] young lad. My father used to overhear them and pick up his lesson, and play the same on the moor while herding, and that on a Feadan Seileastair." By a "feadan seileastair", Angus MacKay probably meant a rudimentary practice chanter fashioned from the stalk of a bog iris. "He was overheard by Fear Aoighre, who taught him and afterwards sent him to the College of the MacCrimmons."

The MacCrimmon reference is telling. It establishes the Raasay MacKay school of piping as the link between the canon and traditions of the middle ages and the modern day. By 1833 George Clayton Atkinson, an artist who visited the island, would confidently state that "Rasa is celebrated for its pipers, sending forth more good ones than any other part of Scotland. McKay is just now the celebrated name …"

The MacCrimmons of north-west Skye were hereditary pipers

to the MacLeods of Dunvegan from the sixteenth century until the first years of the nineteenth, when their power, influence and properties rapidly reduced. They had been granted extensive farmland and steadings at Boreraig, on the other side of Loch Dunvegan from MacLeod's castle. As their fame grew the steadings became a celebrated piping school and cultural centre.

Towards the end of the eighteenth century, in the spirit of the times, MacLeod of Dunvegan cut by half the MacCrimmon family assets at Boreraig and put the remainder under threat. It is popularly thought that the last great tutor, Iain Dubh – Black John – MacCrimmon considered emigrating to America in the 1770s, but changed his mind and saw out the last days of the family institution, which included tutoring young John MacKay of Eyre in Raasay, possibly with the help of a representative of another celebrated piping family, Iain Dall MacKay, the blind piper of Gairloch. Iain Dubh MacCrimmon died in 1822 at the age of ninety-one.

John MacKay became piper to James MacLeod of Raasay, and in 1792 he won the Highland Society of London competition. He married Margaret MacLean, and in a longhouse at Eyre they raised a family. Angus MacKay's synopsis of his siblings' nineteenth-century lives paints a miniature of Hebridean out-migration and the expansion of the diaspora:

> Katherine Mhòr, as child who died in infancy, Donald, Mary, Margaret, Cursty, Katherine Og, Roderick, Angus (self) and John.
>
> Katherine married Norman MacFhionghain [MacKinnon], now in Prince Edward Island & has a numerous family. Mary married John MacKenyie in Castle, Raasay; she died in Raasay and is buried there. Margaret married Wm Robertson of Badenoch and died there; the other left a family.
>
> Cursty married A Maclean, her cousin, and she has one daughter in Prince Edward Island. Kathy Og married John

> Munro and has one son, Duncan, alive at Kyleakin, Isle of Skye. Roderick married Elisa Gillies of Raasay; he died in Edinburgh in 1854, leaving 4 children. I, Angus, married Mary Johnston Russell and have 4 children alive. John died in London, England. Donald died in London leaving three orphans …

All four of John MacKay's sons became pipers. Donald succeeded his father as piper to MacLeod of Raasay, and then to HRH the Duke of Sussex, a son of King George III, who was also Earl of Inverness. Roderick became a merchant at Kyleakin in Skye, where he was considered to be "the best player of the four brothers". John became piper to a wealthy Invergarry man and competed throughout his short life.

Whatever the popular opinion in Kyleakin, out of the four boys, Angus MacKay enjoyed the most luminous career. The famous piping writer Archibald Campbell of Kilberry recorded that as a thirteen-year-old, Angus MacKay of Eyre in Raasay competed at the prestigious Highland Society Piping Competition in 1825 and 1826 (the dates of the competition having presumably been moved closer together, and consequently avoiding his fourteenth birthday).

In 1835 he competed again, wrote Archibald Campbell in 1950,

> and was first with *The Lament for the Union*, having played at the rehearsal *The Lament for the Viscount of Dundee*.
>
> Thereafter he became piper, first to Campbell of Islay and then to Queen Victoria. The Queen records in her "Leaves from the Journal of our Life in the Highlands" that he entered her service in 1843, on the recommendation of Lord Breadalbane, and that he was about the best piper in Scotland. The only piobaireachd which he is known to have composed (apart from the variations to *Colin Roy MacKenzie's Lament*) is called *Farewell to the Laird of Islay*, and is dated 1840.

He remained in the Queen's service until 1854, when
he developed mental trouble and became an inmate, first
of Bethlem Hospital, London, and later of the Crichton
Institute, Dumfries.

The madness of Angus MacKay could not eclipse his accomplishments, which included collaborating with the Highland Society of Inverness to publish his formidable *A Collection of Ancient Piobaireachd or Highland Pipe Music.* A hundred years after his death, the founder of the College of Piping and editor for half a century of *Piping Times* magazine, Seumas MacNeill, would write, "there is only one giant of piping, and he, by his efforts, has made the work of others seem puny, if not futile. That man is Angus MacKay of Raasay."

The official account of MacKay's death on 21 March 1859, is that he escaped from the Crichton Institute in Dumfries and was drowned when crossing the River Nith to elude pursuit. A tradition has it that he was playing the pipes on the riverbank during a lucid interval, and that he suddenly leapt a high hedge and disappeared into the water …

The line and the tradition were not entirely extinguished on that sad day in Dumfries. "Even before the death of the last MacCrimmon in 1822, Raasay had become the centre of the piping world," pronounced the *Piping Times* in 1958. "There went Archibald Munro and many other famous pipers to receive the MacCrimmon tradition from John MacKay. There too was brought up one who was later to become famous, Malcolm MacPherson, the son of Angus Cam, the ruins of whose home can still be seen beside the road in front of Suisnish House and about two miles from that of John MacKay."

When he died in Argyllshire in 1957 it was noted that Pipe Major William MacLean, a prodigy who had been competing at the age of twelve years in the 1880s, "was the son of Archibald MacLean, a native of Raasay and a relative of John and Angus MacKay. The people from whom he came were originally

MacLeans of Boreray, who settled in Raasay and of whom some intermarried with the MacKays. William's immediate relatives inherited in good measure the intelligence and musical ability of the MacKays, and many of them were good pipers freshly imbued in the MacKay tradition and keenly interested in all aspects of Gaelic love and music." A veteran of the First World War, William MacLean taught and adjudicated younger generations of pipers into his seventies, and a couple of years before his death at the age of eighty years he recorded some of his extensive historical repertoire for the School of Scottish Studies. He holidayed regularly in Raasay in the twentieth century and his compositions included the march "Raasay Highlanders".

"His life had an essential honesty of expression," said Reverend George Buchanan at William MacLean's funeral, "nothing was shoddy about him: with him there was no guile. A strong sweet simplicity pervaded his whole nature, and how helpful he was! Gladly he gave of himself, of the wisdom gathered through the years, of the specialist knowledge that was his of Scottish and particularly Highland history, customs and folk lore, of the music of the great pipe, of the language of the Gael and of his hobby, gardening. All who came into contact with him went away the better for having known him."

★

"I think that the first great artistic impact on me was my father's mother singing some of the very greatest of Gaelic songs, and all in her own traditional versions," said the twentieth-century poet, Sorley MacLean of Raasay.

MacLean's grandmother carried to Raasay a cultural realisation of the island's old political links with Kintail. She was Mary Matheson (Màiri 'ain 'ic Sheumais 'ic Dhòmhnaill Ruaidh). Her ancestors had moved to Skye from mainland Lochalsh in the eighteenth century after having been deprived of their lands in Glas na Muclach by the then Earl of Seaforth. "They had brought with them," recorded the National Library of Scotland's programme for an exhibition arranged to mark MacLean's seventieth birthday in 1981, "a wealth of traditional song from Lochalsh and Kintail, and she, in turn, had learnt many songs common to those areas of Skye where they had lived."

Sorley MacLean's grandmother lived with the family until her death in 1923 when the poet was twelve years old. He recalled in an interview with Donald Archie MacDonald in 1982 that she sang Kintail songs like "Crò Chinn t-Sàile", and those from Lower Trotternish which had come from her own mother's side of the family.

Another important musical figure in the poet's early years was his father's eldest sister Peggy, who lived in Glasgow but came to Raasay for a month every year. She was also "full of old songs", and her repertoire was, according to the poet, almost as extensive as his grandmother's. His father, Malcolm MacLean, was also a fine singer of whom the poet commented that "in some songs his timing and weight were such that I now find it difficult to listen to those songs from anyone else. He was especially striking with the Crò of Kintail, the lament for William Chisholm, and with William Ross."

Through one of his uncles on his mother's side, Calum Nicholson, the young Sorley was introduced to the songs of Mary MacPherson (Màiri Mhór nan Oran), the nineteenth-century Skye bard, whose songs and poems were written in the 1880s at the height of the land war, and of whose work Sorley MacLean was a lifelong admirer.

Raasay's musical gene adapted happily to changing times and circumstances. The island's influence on national musical tastes and trends continued throughout the twentieth century.

In the 1960s, the musician Peter Zinovieff was introduced to the island by the formidable Prunella Stack. Stack, a former head of the Women's League of Health and Beauty and board member of the Outward Bound Trust, discovered dilapidated houses at Fearns in southern Raasay, one of which she bought and had converted into a holiday home. Zinovieff, his wife Victoria and their young family followed her there.

The son of White Russian immigrants who had met in London, Zinovieff began working with computer synthesised music in the early 1960s. Although he had little interest in popular music, popular music soon took a great interest in Zinovieff and his synths, and in his electronic products and processes, which he developed in a shed at his London home, using a massive and massively expensive computer to control banks of oscillators and amplifiers.

Peter Zinovieff's synthesisers were used by Pink Floyd, Deep Purple, Todd Rundgren, David Bowie, Brian Eno and Jean-Michel Jarre, as well as Karlheinz Stockhausen and the BBC Radiophonic Workshop, who created the *Doctor Who* theme. Paul McCartney visited his studio shed in the 1960s, while The Beatles were still intact, and Zinovieff said once, "I taught Ringo [Starr] to play synth. He wasn't very good – but neither was I."

There was no mains electricity connection at Fearns, so he worked there from batteries powered by a windmill, and from a domestic generator. In the late 1960s Zinovieff began working with a young avant-garde composer from Lancashire called Harrison Birtwistle. It was therefore almost inevitable that Birtwistle would visit Raasay, where Zinovieff built him a workshed. It was perhaps less inevitable that in 1973 he also would go to live in the island, in a house by the shore at Eyre, directly below Fearns.

Harrison Birtwistle lived in Raasay for eight years. In that period he wrote large sections of *The Mask of Orpheus*, with his neighbour Peter Zinovieff contributing the libretto. Peter Zinovieff's son Leo recalls:

> The creation of *The Mask of Orpheus* took longer than was envisaged, and led to them falling out seriously and I'm pretty sure they never worked on anything together again.

> It's a dramatic and immensely long opera that is considered something of a masterpiece by the aficionados. Dad invented a language for it, the alphabet made up from the letters in names of Orpheus and Eurydice. They were both pretty prolific in their work, and dad in particular had a massive capacity and energy for everything he did.
>
> He had a particular aptitude for massive camping trips in storms on remote islands (Rona, Crowlin, Trodday, Soay, Eilean Taighe), several times there were close calls in small boats with the entire Zinovieff and Birtwistle family. I think Harry referred to one of these trips in an interview implying that a near death storm experience with dad was a pretty good metaphor for the person too, and I would agree.

Birtwistle was inspired by the fact that in Raasay, "there's a burn called Storab, a loch called Storab's Loch and a grave, Storab's Grave. Storab was a Viking. The legend is they chased him, and he went to the island in the loch. They couldn't swim, so they drained the loch, and he ran down the burn and they killed him. I wrote 'Duets for Storab', the idea of the outsider."

Despite insisting that "I never sat down to write a Raasay piece," Birtwistle also took the title of his quartet memorialising the clearances, "A Tree of Strings", from a Sorley MacLean line. "I still know every inch of that place," he would say many years after leaving for France and then Wiltshire. "I mean, the way of the land. I used to go fishing. I loved the east coast, where nobody ever went."

★

In 2006 three brothers, John William, Andrew and James Gillies, were gathering sheep in the depopulated far north-east of Raasay. They routinely started the gather at Umachan, an abandoned hamlet on the east coast shore.

"A shower came on or something," said James, "and we sheltered in a house there. I don't know how it happened, but while we were waiting Andrew must have spotted something above the fireplace, up the chimney. He put his hand up and brought down a white plastic bag with a collection of CDs inside it. They were by The Clash. I knew about The Clash, of course, and Joe Strummer, but I'm not sure we knew of any Raasay connection. Bradan, Cuddy and myself put the CDs back up the chimney and went on with the gather."

Chrissie Nicolson died at the age of ninety-four in 2009. Chrissie had been born in 1915 on the tidal islet of Eilean Taighe, just off the north coast of Raasay in the Sound of Rona. Eilean Taighe is two miles from Umachan, where The Clash CDs had been found up a cold chimney by those crofting brothers. In her native language, the name of Chrissie's birthplace is instructive. It means Island of the [Single] House.

Tigh is one of the essential root words which crop up in all of the detached Celtic languages. In Irish the word for a house is "teach", in Manx it is "thie", in Welsh, Cornish and Breton it is "ty". They are pronounced similarly. When an observer gets his or her eye in, they crop up everywhere. Avon is another one. The River Avon translates as River River in two languages, the words *abhainn* and *afon* meaning "river" in Gaelic and Welsh. The great romantic waterway of west-central England carries the DNA of Celtic Britain. From Naseby to the Severn it was once just the Afon – the River.

There are the ruins of a second house on the islet, named after a former inhabitant, Tigh Bellaig, but An Eilean Taighe is too small to sustain more than one family, and Chrissie Nicolson was born and brought up there speaking nothing but Gaelic. That fact alone told her exactly where she lived. To her north was Rona, which she knew as Eilean Ronaidh, the rough island. To her south was the large, green, wooded and altogether more promising island of Raasay, Eilean Ratharsair, the island of roe deer. To her east was tiny Eilean an Fhraoich, the island that was home only to heather and to the nesting seabirds whose eggs the people of Eilean Taighe would row over to collect. To her west was An t-Eilean Sgiathanach, the great winged island of Skye. Her language interpreted and illuminated her environment.

At Torran School in the north of Raasay in the 1920s, Chrissie Nicolson and her contemporaries were supposed to be educated out of Gaelic into English. Their schoolteacher, a former Customs and Excise officer from Skye named James MacKinnon, gave up trying.

Chrissie Nicolson received most of her schooling in her native language. "'Ginger James' … taught his pupils in Gaelic and had little time for English!", said one of Chrissie's contemporaries. MacKinnon's successor, another missionary to Raasay from Skye named Rita Campbell, discovered upon arriving when young Chrissie was thirteen years old that "children at the age of ten and over … had the barest knowledge of the English language".

So Chrissie Nicolson's first language, for much of her life her only language and for all of her life her preferred language, was Gaelic. She became fluent in English as a young woman, while working as a housemaid in Glasgow, but Gaelic remained what philologists call her default language. In the absence of pressure to do otherwise, she defaulted to Gaelic.

She was born with Gaelic and she died with Gaelic. She held that significant detail in common with all of the other native residents of Raasay north of Brochel Castle until the twenty-first century.

As the decades of the twentieth century came and went, Chrissie knew progressively fewer and fewer people with whom to converse in Gaelic. They died, or they went away and never returned, and they took the language with them, if only for a generation.

Chrissie Nicolson's mother's maiden name was Mary Gillies. Before marrying and moving to Eilean Taighe, in the 1890s Mary was brought up in a large family two miles away at Umachan. One of her sisters, Jane Gillies, married a man named MacKenzie and moved away from Raasay to live in Bonar Bridge in the eastern Scottish Highlands, on the border of the Gaidhealtachd with English-speaking Scotland.

That sister – Chrissie Nicolson's aunt Jane – gave birth in Bonar Bridge to a daughter named Anna.

As a young woman during the Second World War, Anna MacKenzie travelled to London from Bonar Bridge to work. She met and married a young Foreign Office diplomat called Ron Mellor, who was shortly afterwards posted to Turkey. Their son, John Graham Mellor, was consequently born in Ankara, the capital of Turkey, in 1952.

Gaelic probably did not leave the Gillies/MacKenzie/Mellor family until John Graham Mellor himself in the 1950s. Early in the twentieth century half of the small population of Bonar Bridge still spoke the language. Jane Gillies from Raasay certainly spoke it, so too, in all likelihood, did her MacKenzie husband, and they probably passed it on as a cradle language to their daughter Anna. If so, the first generation of their family not to speak Gaelic was the generation of Anna's son, John Graham Mellor, who was born in a British residency in Turkey with a Gaelic and English speaking mother but a father who spoke English and no Gaelic. That last eventuality alone precluded the use of Gaelic in John Graham Mellor's childhood home.

In his twenties, back in London in the 1970s, John Mellor formed a cult band called The 101ers and changed his name to Joe Strummer. In 1976 he became the co-founder, lyricist, rhythm guitarist and lead singer of The Clash.

That is why Joe Strummer was neither a Gaelic speaker nor a Gaelic bard. It was a close call. Strummer knew about his Highland family background, of course. He put seed money into the Future Forests plantation at Orbost in Skye, which following his premature death in 2002 was renamed Rebel's Wood in his honour.

Days before his death in Somerset, at the beginning of December 2002 Strummer attended a wedding at Bonar Bridge. He told one of his Gillies cousins there: "I've been a terrible

Scotsman, but I'm going to be better."

He met his cousin Chrissie Nicolson at the same wedding, and Strummer pencilled a visit to Raasay – his first visit to Raasay – into his diary for the summer of 2003. If he'd made it, he would have been surrounded by relatives. It was difficult to throw a stone in early 21st-century Raasay without hitting a descendant of the Gillieses of Umachan.

He didn't make it. Three weeks after that Bonar Bridge wedding, on 22 December 2002, Joe Strummer died suddenly of an undiagnosed congenital heart defect. He was fifty years old. In Raasay, Chrissie Nicolson heard of his death and felt sorrow; she was eighty-seven and had seven more busy years of life ahead of her in the south of the island

The village of Umachan was deserted in the 1910s, not long after Chrissie Nicolson's mother and Joe Strummer's grandmother left the place. In 2006, Strummer's bassist with The Clash, Paul Simonon, and Strummer's biographer, Chris Salewicz, visited the remnants of the small Raasay hamlet where it had all begun.

Simonon, an art school alumnus who had become an established visual artist, took along his canvas, easel and brushes. In the pouring rain at Umachan he made a portrait of the roofless old home of Jane and Mary Gillies. Salewicz watched astonished as Simonon strapped his canvas to the easel in the billowing wind and painted, standing upright, with rainwater running through the colours.

When he had finished, Joe Strummer's former bandmate put a set of CDs of The Clash performing in New York into the chimney place. He then wrote on the blank reverse of the painted canvas, "I'll be back. Paul," put the painting in beside the CDs, and the two men set off along the track back to southern Raasay and the ferry to Skye.

In 2003, the American cultural arbiter *Rolling Stone* magazine ranked Joe Strummer at number 125 on its list of the 200 Greatest Singers of All Time.

8

Disruptions

"It was the morning of the Monday after their last Sabbath, perhaps the day referred to by Sorley MacLean as the 'Sabbath of the dead'. On the following day thirty-seven of its people were shipped via Liverpool to Australia. The remainder, and their former neighbours from Eyre, Fearns, Leac and Screapadal, soon followed."

AT the National Census in 1841, the population of the Raasay islands was greater than it had ever been before or would be afterwards. There were 987 people recorded as living in 178 households in Raasay itself. Rona had 110 people in 20 dwellings, and Fladda contained 29 people in 6 thatched houses. Eilean Taighe was temporarily unoccupied.

That made a total in the archipelago of 1,126 inhabitants. They were evenly scattered in townships from coast to coast, from the north of Rona to the south of Raasay. The east coast was especially healthy.

In a survey published in 1824, the geologist John MacCulloch wrote:

> Nearly all the green and cultivated land of Rasay lies on the tops of the high eastern cliffs, which are everywhere

> covered with scattered farms, that form a striking contrast to the solitary brown waste of the western coast. As we rowed along beneath this lofty land, they appeared perched above our heads; often seeming to hang over the deep below, like birds' nests, and, in some places, so high as to be scarcely visible from the water. These cliffs reach from five or six hundred to a thousand feet in height, being formed of beautiful white sandstone, and the precipices being intermixed with grassy slopes and patches, and skirted at the foot by huge masses that have slid down from above, or by piles of enormous fragments, heaped in all the disorder of ruin.

In 1841 there were 178 men, women and children in the east coast settlement of Fearns, 30 in Eyre, 70 in Leac, 101 in Screapadal and 129 in Hallaig. The people in that small quarter of the island comprised a little more than half of the entire population of Raasay. They occupied a precipitously steep and apparently inhospitable district, but the twentieth-century ecologist and Highland farmer Frank Fraser Darling would identify the south-east as having the best and deepest soil in the island.

The census twenty years later, in 1861, showed seven people still living in Fearns, none in Eyre, none in Leac, none in Screapadal and none in Hallaig. The dramatic and well-populated east coast of Raasay, whose counter-intuitive combination of wildly forbidding landscape and busy human settlement had attracted the wondering eye of John MacCulloch, who came from the gentle, green island of Guernsey in the English Channel, had been comprehensively cleared of 500 settled inhabitants.

On a June afternoon in 2004 a small group of people stood among the ruins of Hallaig on what had become one of the loneliest coastlines in western Europe and heard a poem read aloud, firstly in its original Gaelic and then in English.

The English version was delivered in an educated Irish accent. "There was a tremendous, dignified sense of occasion," said its reader, the Nobel laureate Seamus Heaney, afterwards. "A sense of a circle being completed."

Many circles were completed that day at Hallaig. It was the 150th anniversary of the forced clearance of the township in 1854, and the 50th anniversary of the first publication of the Raasay poet Sorley MacLean's astonishing eponymous elegy to the ghosts of his forebears. It was the first time that Heaney – a friend and admirer of MacLean's who had made his own translation of "Hallaig" – had visited the place.

By the twenty-first century, Hallaig frequently echoed to the sound of living rather than sepulchral voices: the soft conversations of pilgrims drawn there by the great art which had been done in its name. Sorley MacLean's Raasay poem "Hallaig" had achieved a life of its own. In 2012 it would lend its title to a new lifeline car ferry between the island and Skye – a christening which was welcomed everywhere but among some members of the older generations in Raasay, to whom the word Hallaig summoned all of the bad luck associated with a cleared township and should therefore not be imposed on a boat. The rest of the world saw only, in both of Sorley MacLean's Gaelic and English renderings, the greatest Scottish poem of the twentieth century, and the ferry company Caledonian MacBrayne decided to pay homage to the words, and risk karma. On the dual anniversary in June 2004, the Irish poet convened with men and women from Raasay, Skye and elsewhere, to hear MacLean's verse evoke once more the mystery of Hallaig wood.

Seamus Heaney had first heard those words almost forty years earlier, in the sonorous tones of MacLean himself, at a reading in Dublin's Abbey Theatre. "MacLean's voice," he recalled, "had a certain bardic weirdness that sounded both stricken and enraptured. Whether you were listening to him or reading him on the page, you were led into an uncanny zone, somewhere between the land of heart's desire and a waste land created by history ..."

The lifetime's work of Sorley MacLean, who had died eight years earlier in 1996 at the age of eighty-five, created that zone in a variety of places, from the desert war in North Africa to the Cuillins of Skye. Inevitably, for he was the pre-eminent Highland writer of the twentieth century, it reached its most compelling pitch when dealing with the island that he left as a young man.

The son of a tailor in Oscaig, Sorley MacLean grew up in a family which was, as we have seen, unusually musical. It was also extraordinarily accomplished. John Nicolson, who moved to Oscaig from Torran in the late 1930s, described the tailor's children as "the MacLean scholars". Sorley had six siblings: his brother John was a piper and became the rector of Oban High School, his two younger sisters, Ishbel and Mary, both also became schoolteachers, Calum Iain was a noted folklorist in Ireland and Scotland, and Alasdair and Norman both became general practitioners. Alasdair was also a folklorist and the author and editor of several history books.

After departing for Edinburgh University in 1929, Sorley MacLean never again lived in Raasay. His profession as a teacher and headmaster took him all across the shrinking Scottish Gaidhealtachd.

After retiring from his last post as the rector of Plockton High School in Wester Ross, in 1972 he moved to live with his wife Renee in the township of Peinchorran in the parish of Braes, where he stayed until his death in 1996.

Peinchorran sits by a raised beach on the east coast of Skye. In almost all weathers it looks over to Raasay, virtually within shouting distance but separated by two stern miles of sea. In Peinchorran Sorley MacLean had his back to the Cuillin, rising steeply behind him "on the other side of sorrow", and his face to the woods of Raasay.

Even in childhood he had never experienced Hallaig as a living community. The settlement was largely emptied by the new landowner George Rainy on 5 June 1854. It was the morning of the Monday after their last Sabbath, perhaps the day referred to by Sorley MacLean as the "Sabbath of the dead". On the following day, thirty-seven of its people were shipped via Liverpool to Australia. The remainder, and their former neighbours from Eyre, Fearns, Leac and Screapadal, soon followed.

Thereafter George Rainy, the mainland sheep farmer Royston MacKenzie and their successors used the place as a sheep walk and a deer park. The village itself was never repopulated. In 1833 the people of Hallaig petitioned the Gaelic Schools Society for some educational provision, insisting that "no less than 60 Scholars could be got to attend School". Then came the eviction notices and the emigrant ship. Its placename did not even survive in everyday use for long enough to be mauled into phonetic English on Inverness Council's road signs – Hallaig remained Hallaig, in both languages.

Sorley MacLean was born in 1911 at Oscaig on the "solitary brown waste" of the western littoral of Raasay, into a family with typically long and vivid Highland memories. He must have heard of Hallaig, the Hallaig of "MacLeans and MacLeods, / all who were there in the time of Mac Gille Chaluim", before he ever saw the place. When he did see it, his imagination repopulated Hallaig despite itself.

Two people had a job to do on that Saturday in June 2004, in the drizzle among the hungry midges on the green clifftop overlooking the Inner Sound of Raasay. The poet and novelist Angus Peter Campbell read the fourteen stanzas of "Hallaig" in its, his and Sorley MacLean's native Gaelic.

Then Seamus Heaney opened his paperback of MacLean's collected work and presented the poet's own "scriptural" English rendering. "Tha tim, am fiadh, an coille Hallaig ... Time, the deer, is in the wood of Hallaig."

As moved as any deracinated Gael by the sound of his estranged language, Heaney described Angus Peter Campbell's as a "tremendous reading".

"I was thinking," he said later, "that poetry takes you into once-upon-a-time without betraying your own time – it moves you into two dimensions, and that is what it was like today. There was something about that gathering, something of total dignity without any hint of overstatement, which made it a once-in-a-lifetime experience."

Heaney was brought up as a monoglot English speaker in County Derry. Sorley MacLean's work in general, and "Hallaig" in particular, embraced him like a lost relative. Here was a Scottish Gael expressing in Scottish Gaelic the great symbols of dispossessed rural Gaelic Ireland. "As a youngster I grew up among lonely wallsteadings, empty houses, boarded windows. So knowing the poem, I felt entirely at home here. But the placenames, the Raasay placenames had extra resonance …"

The poem "Hallaig" deals not only with its township. It translates the rest of the small island of Raasay into a mythical universe. Locations such as Inver, Screapadal, Bailechuirn, Fearns, Clachan and Suisnish – some still inhabited, some as lonely as the night – and emblematic vistas like Dun Caan, the volcanic plug overlooking Raasay like a watchtower, were sewn into the tapestry of the narrative.

Many of those places are in western Raasay rather than the "green and cultivated land" of Hallaig and the east. The poem "Hallaig" and the place Hallaig spoke for them all, and for all of the hundreds of other cleared townships whose stone shells would litter the Highland landscape for centuries. Hallaig summoned in all its dimensions what Heaney called "the great absence that the Highland clearances represent in Scots Gaelic consciousness".

Before presenting his new translation of "Hallaig" at the Edinburgh Book Festival in 2002, Seamus Heaney described it as "at once historical and hallucinatory, a poem in which the deserted homesteads of a little settlement on the island of Raasay are repopulated by a vision of 'a fair field full of folk'. It arises out of Maclean's sense of belonging to a culture that is doomed but that he will never deny."

It was a final ironical closing circle of "Hallaig" that the verses written in 1954 to lament and reinvoke a lost civilisation, helped to enhance and extend its life. Among the ruins of Hallaig that day, Seamus Heaney was in the company of many Gaels speaking

Gaelic. He was at Hallaig on 5 June 2004 with Gillieses, Campbells and MacKays, MacDonalds and MacLeans, whose language, if it did not entirely revive, was given new vision, form, purpose, strength, and ultimately new life on that day in 1954 when Sorley MacLean sat down to write:

> Tha bùird is tàirnean air an uinneig
> troimh 'm faca mi an Aird an Iar ...
>
> The window is nailed and boarded
> through which I saw the West ...

★

When the seventeen-year-old John MacLeod assumed the title of the 13th of Raasay in 1823, he cannot have seen the world of misery which hovered like a barren planet just over the near horizon.

In 1823 the teenaged John will have had little idea that, while he would retain his title, his own stewardship would culminate in calamity in Raasay: in the collapse of its population and the beginning of an apparently inexorable millennial decline. Young John MacLeod cannot have imagined that he would be the last MacGilleChaluim.

He had been raised within, and had appeared to inherit, a blessed dominion. His tenantry was thriving and growing by the decade. His home in Raasay House itself reflected what appeared to be a golden age. To accommodate all of the guests attracted to that cultivated taste, and to provide a suitable home for such an elevated lineage, Raasay House was improved and rebuilt at regular intervals throughout the later eighteenth and nineteenth centuries. For all the island's abundance of excellent building stone, the costs were large.

The mansion had been expensively extended by John's late

father, James. Between 1796 and 1805 James MacLeod built an imposing seven-bay facade from large square-cut blocks of stone along the front of the mansion that his father had raised in 1761.

"James," wrote Calum MacLeod of Arnish in his twentieth-century account of *The Cruel Clearance of Raasay*, "lacked common sense and was most extravagant. First, he began enlarging his mansion till it resembled a palace, but being unwise, he did not consider the cost. The walls were far from complete before his funds were nearly exhausted, and so he obtained loans on credit from various persons. But before the walls attained the required height, his purse was practically empty."

During the Napoleonic Wars, in around 1809, he built a defensive battery on a hillock above the old landing place in Churchton Bay, below Raasay House, and placed six cannon within its battlements in case Bonaparte decided to invade. The cannon soon had company. James MacLeod commissioned from an Italian sculptor two large stone busts of mermaids to place in the porch of Raasay House. It appears that the sculptor neither visited Raasay, nor was he given the dimensions of the mansion's porch. When the mermaids were delivered by sea, they were far too big to sit inside the building. They were also formidably ugly.

James banished them to the battery. He then sued the Italian sculptor, who successfully defended the court case and edged the MacLeods of Raasay a little further into insolvency.

James MacLeod's extravagant investments certainly succeeded – as they were in large part intended to do – in impressing visitors from the south. In July 1815 the visiting artist William Daniell found that, "the general character of the island is not picturesque, but such parts as are capable of tillage bear an aspect of judicious and thriving cultivation, which evinces that the worthy proprietor has not confined his spirit of improvement to the mansion itself, and its pleasure grounds.

"At some distance on the left [of Raasay House] there are spacious outhouses, constructed for the purpose of drying the crops, an operation often rendered necessary by the prevalence of wet weather in this western region. Even at this pertion [in July] … the sky was frequently overcast, and afforded but faint hopes of a single day without rain."

In 1818, the geologist John MacCulloch visited for the first time. Having anchored in bad weather in Clachan Bay and finding himself unenchanted by the "brown, dreary, comfortless land" of western Raasay, MacCulloch,

> was shortly surprised by a visit from the friendly Laird himself, who insisted on taking me to his house … only imagine my utter confusion of mind and body, when I suddenly found and felt myself in an elegant drawing room, round which were arranged some twenty young ladies, with their white muslins, and feathers, and all other things befitting, like flowers in a green house, breathing sweets. To emerge from a coal pit into the sunshine, could not be more dazzling. Whenever you wish to enjoy afresh, the impressions long blunted by the crowds of Grosvenor or Portman square, come to Rasay: come in a black narrow ship, in a storm, anchor among the winds and the breakers, land your boat in the surf, ride to shore on the back of a Highlander, and, from a dark night of wind and rain, tumble headlong into the complexity of silks, and muslins, and beauty, and lights, and plenty, and elegance; into festivity and conversation, music and the dance. It seemed as if I had been destined to feel the full force of Dr Johnson's well-remembered remark, and that too in the very same place.
>
> I scarcely can tell you from how many lands the present party had been collected; as the term neighbour has, in this country, a signification not much less wide than in the Parable. Neighbourhood seems to extend from Barra to Stornoway, to Sky, Rasay, Coll, nay, to Inverness. And what is much more amusing, every one knows of his neighbour's

> births, whether of calves or children, and of his business, and of his wife's tea drinkings, for a hundred miles round; and a coterie in Sky or Mull discusses the ribbands, complexion, loves, and hatreds, of all the misses and masters whose mutuality of sentiment might be supposed diluted to nothing, before traversing distances, as remote and difficult of transit as those which lie between the Baltic and you.

It was the life of "of silks, and muslins … and plenty, and elegance … music and the dance" which had been known and treasured by the young, adopted orphans Eliza and Isabella Ross, who had been sent back to India on the fishing fleet five years earlier. Such extravagant, trans-Highland hospitality, offered freely to all-comers day after day, year after year, decade after decade, did not come cheaply to the MacLeods of Raasay. In common with so many of the southern British minor aristocracy whose existences they had chosen to emulate, the MacLeods had developed unsustainable lifestyles.

They had a real income from their growing population, and a potential income from their land. The clearances in Raasay began with the last two MacGilleChaluims clumsily and cruelly realising both of those revenue streams at the same time. "To supplement his master's income," wrote Calum MacLeod of Arnish, "and to meet expenses, his factor MacKinnon of Corry steadily increased rents till tenants were impoverished and obliged to quit their homes and lands. Not only that, but when the factor learned that sheep would pay better, he began forming a sheep farm by amalgamating vacant crofts, and then expelling the tenants of nearby crofts on the least pretence, and adding their lands to the project – a large sheep farm."

The seventy-four-year-old Alexander MacLennan of Fladda told the Napier Commission in 1883: "I was born in the south of Raasay. I was acquainted with the two last lairds, MacLeod of Raasay. When the first laird [James] got into difficulties, Mr

MacKinnon, Corrie, was factor, and the sheep began to come to this place. The place was getting into debt ever since then …

"I have one word to say for myself. I was at the quay when the people were sent off, and they were like lambs separated from their mothers. There was one old man there who said, 'Should I go to Australia I may die on my arrival, I should prefer remaining in Raasay, but I must go.'"

"So far as you are aware," Alexander MacLennan was then asked, "until the time of MacLeod who got into difficulties, were the lairds of Raasay minding their people, and were the people fairly comfortable?"

"Yes," MacLennan replied," they had the hill from the upper part of Raasay to Scribidale …"

"Are you aware that any people were sent away to America in the time of the MacLeods before Corrie became factor?"

"No, that was the first break that was made in the population of Raasay when Corrie became factor, and when MacLeod left Raasay the place was getting into debt."

John MacLeod became a British Army officer in the 78th Highlanders. His frequent absences led him to loan the use of Raasay House and some of the Home Farm to at least one old friend. He married Mary MacLeod, the daughter of an Indian Army officer from Skye. Their only child, a daughter, died at the age of three years in 1839. They buried her by St Moluag's chapel, and the unhappy couple began making plans to leave their gloomy inheritance far behind.

Having confirmed the Raasay islands on the course to ruin which had been set by his father, in 1843 John MacLeod, the thirty-seven-year-old 13th MacGilleChaluim emigrated to Tasmania. Two years later, in his absence, he was declared bankrupt. The estate was left with trustees, who sold it for £27,600 in 1846 at a London auction house.

The buyer, George Rainy, was born and raised in the parish of Creich in eastern Sutherland, the son of a Church of Scotland minister from Aberdeenshire. Relatives from both sides of his family drew the young George Rainy into the Demerara sugar plantations in Central America, where he made a fortune.

The Demerara plantations were driven by slaves. When slavery was abolished throughout its empire by the British Government, the middle-aged George Rainy owned 2,793 slaves in the British American colonies. He was duly rewarded with an additional £146,295 by the Slave Compensation Act of 1837. In the 1840s George Rainy found himself in possession of an even bigger fortune and a lot of spare time and energy. So he bought from the trustees of John MacLeod the inhabited islands of Raasay, Rona, Eilean Taighe and Fladda.

George Rainy returned to Scotland after three decades on the slave plantations of Demerara with fixed notions about the relationship between landowners and the labouring classes, and with a complicated domestic life. He brought from Central America to the United Kingdom two young daughters, who were of mixed race, but who, thanks to their father's largesse, were spared from heritable chattel slavery. Mary Augusta, who in 1841 was thirteen years old, and Elizabeth Jemima, who was eleven years old, were sent to a boarding school at Minchinhampton, a market town lost in the Gloucestershire Cotswold hills, a long way from Sutherland or Raasay, before being shipped away to see out their lives discreetly in Australia.

Rainy's intentions in the Hebrides were clear and cold. He would restore the Raasay estate to profitability by any means necessary. He could not have arrived at a more distressing time for the Ratharsaich.

In 1846, a potato blight of the same strain that ravaged rural Ireland arrived in the west Highlands. "The potato, as a field crop, had been common in England for many years," wrote the biographer and historian Florence MacAlister early in the twentieth century, "but it was not grown in Scotland, except as a rare garden vegetable, till after 1770. In the Highlands and islands, where the climate made cereal crops most uncertain and troublesome to harvest, the potato quickly became the chief food of the people."

The arrival of the blight was therefore as horrifying in Scotland as it was in Ireland. "It has been said that no one born since 1846," wrote Florence MacAlister, who was born in 1880, "has ever tasted a potato at its best, that the flavour has entirely changed, and though the disease-resisting potatoes now grown have almost restored the original plentifulness, still, we have little idea of what the loss of the abundant, easily-grown, floury, and delicious tuber meant to a people already in straitened circumstances, whose staple food it had been for seventy years. When the housewife went to dig a potful to boil for dinner, she found only rotten, uneatable roots, under a mass of blackened, evil-smelling shaws".

Food aid was, however, more quickly and easily despatched to the Scottish Highlands than to rural Ireland, wrote MacAlister:

> From 1846 to 1851 the public again responded splendidly to the cry of distress from the Highlands. Money was subscribed in Nova Scotia, New Brunswick, British Guiana, and other colonial possessions. London gave large sums, so that Mr. Skene, at the office of the Highland Destitution Committee in Edinburgh, was able to send thousands to the local clergy and others to distribute in the distressed parishes. The Parochial Boards were specially reminded that the law preventing able-bodied persons from receiving relief was so framed that in such exceptional circumstances the able-bodied could be temporarily relieved, and thus be prevented from becoming legally eligible through incapacity … For four years the relief continued, then the Highland Destitution Committee's funds were exhausted, and still the disease did not abate.
>
> At a meeting on 16th January, 1851, of the Board of Supervision it was decided that the time had come when the Government could advantageously take steps in regard to the existing destitution in the Highlands. It was arranged, with the Prime Minister [Lord John Russell's] and the Home Secretary [Sir George Grey's] approval,

> that Sir John McNeill should personally conduct a special inquiry in the districts principally affected. For this purpose he set out on 3rd February, and returned on 10th April, having investigated the condition of twenty-seven Highland parishes.

MacNeill was a Gaelic speaker and would insist that he spoke to all classes and occupations in those twenty-seven west Highland parishes – "crofters, cottars, ministers, factors, tacksmen …"

"The method of procedure was," he reported, "to call together the members of the Parochial Boards, which were generally composed of the most intelligent persons in the district, and to discuss the questions in public, other resident inhabitants usually being present. As great interest was taken in the matter, persons of all classes attended. The discussions were carried on partly in English and partly in Gaelic."

His intentions may have been pure, but they were not always practiced. Sir John MacNeill spoke to no crofters, cottars, ministers, factors or tacksmen in Raasay, because he did not visit the island. Instead he received – and entered as primary evidence in his report – a long dissertation from the new proprietor, George Rainy.

The Hebridean climate, the thin soil, the recent potato blight and the contemporary distaste of Lowland palates (and consequently of Lowland butchers) for Highland black cattle, argued Rainy, had all combined to make Raasay incapable of sustaining its thousand inhabitants.

The official welfare programmes and charitable relief schemes offered to hungry Highlanders by kindly southerners had, George Rainy told Sir John MacNeill, made matters even worse. Rainy wrote to MacNeill:

> The present apathetic state of the greater part of the people of these districts affords a melancholy instance of the injurious consequences of a system of eleemosynary

> aid, in undermining every feeling of independence, and any disposition to exertion. Accustomed for four successive years to a renewal of aid from a public fund, although told that each year was likely to be the last of being so helped, they have come to depend on it; and now that it has ceased in right earnest, they can scarcely be brought to believe that it is so, but entertain a confident belief that they will and must be helped from some quarter; and, consequently, a great number, who would otherwise have long ago made personal exertions to provide, in some way, for their families, now lounge about in listless idleness – their moral and physical energies alike paralysed – still confidently expecting that aid will arrive from government, or some other public source.

George Rainy's manifesto could not have been more contemptuous of his new tenantry, or made his plans for their future more obvious. The Ratharsaich needed, considered their proprietor, a short sharp shock, followed by as many more short sharp shocks as was necessary to get them aboard the emigrant hulks.

Unsurprisingly, for he was the son of the laird of Colonsay, MacNeill agreed wholeheartedly. He reported to the government: "In every parish, with one or two exceptions, men of all classes and denominations concur unanimously in declaring it to be impossible, by any application of existing resources, or by any remunerative application of extraneous resources, to provide for the permanent subsistence for the whole of the present inhabitants; and state their conviction that the population cannot be made self-sustaining, unless a portion removes from the parish. The signal failure of every attempt that has been made to provide for the population by the expenditure of capital on the improvement of land and the employment of the inhabitants, corroborates that opinion."

Having reached those conclusions, wrote his granddaughter sixty years later,

> Sir John McNeill could suggest but one remedy – a well-considered scheme of emigration. The drawbacks to this were twofold – first, the expense; and second, the great unwillingness on the part of the people to leave their native shores. The expense, he suggested, could be met possibly by Government loans; the unwillingness on the part of the people was slowly disappearing under pressure of increased poverty and the knowledge that the Relief Committee's funds were exhausted.
>
> One thing which the inquiry brought out most strongly was that the relief given throughout the Highlands and Islands had a very bad effect upon the character of the people. Formerly their pride led them to conceal poverty and value independence; now they were rapidly learning to parade and exaggerate their poverty, and to place no value upon independence.

Worse yet; they were drinking it: "In Mull the consumption of retailed whisky rose from 8,701 gallons in 1845 to 10,212 gallons in 1850; the sum spent upon ardent spirits alone in Mull in 1848 was £6,099 4s. In Skye also the consumption rose by 2,974 gallons, the sum of £7,454 being spent on whisky in 1850. 'I have had occasion to see,' said the great Disruption minister, Dr. Guthrie, 'that morally as well as physically a population exceeding the number who can find full and regular employment is a great evil.'"

"The habit of dependence on the proprietor," reported Sir John MacNeill himself to the British government in 1851, "on the destitution fund, on some one who is to think and provide for them, is one of the most serious impediments to a permanent amelioration in their condition; and one of the advantages of emigration to the colonies has been the effect of new circumstances counteracting this disposition."

Of his sample of twenty-seven west Highland parishes, "The population had decreased between 1841 and 1851 from 99,004 to 92,424, but a much larger exodus than this was necessary."

If the Raasay proprietor needed one, MacNeill's official blessing of his own unofficial conclusions gave a bright green light to George Rainy.

He set about reconfiguring the island of Raasay in a methodical manner. Only interested in the relatively fertile central and southern landmass, he had a stone wall built to head height across the isthmus at Tarbet, halfway between Brochel Castle and Arnish. Rainy's wall was both practical and symbolic. No crofter's livestock was to graze south of the wall, where the turf was reserved for estate sheep, deer and other game – all of which could of course venture north of the wall without sanction. The increasingly stony earth on the few acres of Raasay, Rona and Fladda north of the wall, was expected to cater for almost all of the remaining human population which had not gone to America or Australia. Rainy's wall represented autocracy, oppression, division and hardship.

In 1883, the seventy-eight-year-old Donald MacLeod, who had lived "all my days" in Kyle Rona, gave a statement to the Napier Commission: "I remember Mr Rainy about thirty years ago clearing fourteen townships, and he made them into a sheep farm which he had in his own hands."

'What became of the people?"

"They went to other kingdoms – some to America, some to Australia, and other places that they could think of."

"Will you give us a rough estimate of the population of the fourteen townships?"

"I cannot; there were a great number of people."

"Were they hundreds?"

"Yes, hundreds, young and old. I am sure there were about one hundred in each of two townships."

"Will you name the towns?"

"Castle, Screpidale, two Hallaigs, Ceancnock, Leachd, two Fearns, Eyre, Suisinish, Doirredomhain, Mainish."

"Was there a good deal of arable land upon these townships?"

"They were altogether arable land capable of being ploughed."

"Are these now altogether in the proprietor's hands?"

"Yes, indeed. The only occupants of that land today are rabbits and deer and sheep."

In 1850 George Rainy reached a deal with a thirty-eight-year-old sheep farmer from Assynt on the north-western mainland. Royston MacKenzie came from the sheep ranching township of Ledbeg, where his father had also farmed. In 1850 Rainy leased to MacKenzie for £250 per annum the land at Glam, Suisnish and Eyre as a sheep farm. MacKenzie familiarised himself with the island and its potential, and five years later in 1855 he agreed with George Rainy to lease the grazings of "Suishnish, Borodale, Eyre, Glam, Brae, Upper and Lower Fearns &c" for a valuer's rental of £641 17s 6d a year. The "&c" did a lot of work – it signified Hallaig, Screapadal, Leac and the other cleared south-eastern townships, as well as Castle and other smaller settlements. Royston MacKenzie, his wife Hughina, their two school-age children and two servants moved into a large new house in its own grounds set back from the shore at Suisnish.

While MacKenzie stocked Raasay with sheep, George Rainy continued to reduce the human population. "Mr Rainy enacted a rule," Donald MacLeod of Kyle Rona told Lord Napier, "that no one should marry in the island. There was one man there who married in spite of him, and because he did so, he put him out of his father's house, and that man went to a bothy – to a sheep cot. Mr Rainy then came and demolished the sheep cot upon him, and extinguished his fire, and neither friend nor any one else dared give him a night's shelter. He was not allowed entrance into any house."

The unfortunate man's name was John MacLeod and he came from Arnish. "John MacLeod was my great-grand-uncle," wrote Calum MacLeod of the same township in the following century. "I have his photograph and that of his wife and their baby (as an adult), and also pictures of their graves near by the Macquarrie River." The Macquarrie River is in New South Wales in Australia.

The clearances, the edict against marriage and a wearying succession of other depredations had a significant effect. Between

1841 and 1861 the population of Raasay fell from 987 to 387 people. The number of occupied households collapsed from 204 to 114.

As well as the desertion of Hallaig, Fearns, Eyre, Leac and Screapadal, Oscaig on the western coast was assumed into the estate's Home Farm, and its population in the same period fell from seventeen to seven people. Suisnish over those two mid-century decades was reduced from a population of thirty-six to the eight people who lived with Royston and Hughina MacKenzie at Suisnish House: their two children, two servants and a lodging shepherd and labourer who had been imported from Sutherland.

Brae, the eighteenth-century tack of Charles Edward Stuart's escort, Captain Malcolm MacLeod, lost all of its seven people, and Glam went from fourteen people in 1841 to none at all in 1861. Manish enumerated forty-one people in 1841, and none at all twenty years later. The community of Castle, which had thrived for centuries below its magnificent crumbling fortress, had sixty-nine people before Royston MacKenzie took over its lease, and just nine in 1861.

North of Rainy's wall, the picture was different. That small district and its offshore islands of Rona, Fladda and Eilean Taighe became a refuge for the few who managed to avoid the emigrant ships. As a result, the population, while not quite "packed like herring in a barrel", in Calum MacLeod's words, was certainly increased beyond a sustainable level, Most of the men could only feed their families and ease congestion by leaving for half of the year to work as fishers on mainland trawlers.

So between 1841 and 1861, while the rest of Raasay haemorrhaged its population, Arnish grew from forty to forty-five men, women and children, Umachan rose from twenty-two to thirty-four, Kyle Rona from fifty-five to sixty-six, and the little island of Fladda from twenty-nine to forty-five people. The situation on the island of Rona was most dramatic. There, 110 people in twenty households rose in just two decades to 147 people in twenty-six homes.

By 1891, there would be 181 people in Rona and 51 in Fladda: easily their largest populations in recorded history.

There was one compensation. Those transfers of population meant that quite suddenly, the demographic balance swung from the south to the far north of Raasay. In early 1883, a royal commission established by William Gladstone's Liberal government to look into the conditions of Scottish crofters and cottars planned its visit to Raasay. At any time previously – and in most times afterwards – such an august body would have sailed into Clachan Bay and conducted its business in the busy, cultivated south of the island. In 1883 it threw precedent to the winds, booked Torran schoolhouse for a week, and on 22 May 1883 a yacht carrying six commissioners, their clerks and crew, anchored in Loch Arnish. The commissioners then picked their way up a steep hillside to take their places in the school room and call witnesses from the surrounding townships.

They heard from the fifty-six-year-old Rona crofter and fisherman Roderick MacKay "how we are crowded upon each other, so that we cannot take a living out of it. There are some in our township who remember when there were only seven families in the township, and there are now fifteen families. Should they get the place for nothing, they would not make a living out of it. They would need to get another place."

Thirty-six-year-old John Nicolson of Rona told them:

> I make it out that should I be here from sunrise to sunset I could not fully disclose the poverty of Rona. It is a place in which no man need expect to make his living. We are working on sea and land, both summer, and winter, and spring – every quarter of the year – and after that we have only poverty … we will ever be poor as long as we are kept crowded in a place of which we cannot make use. I can say with truth that my skiff is my cart, and that the wives and the children are the horses, and there is truth in that, because it is the work of the horses which they perform.

> The creel is on their back continually, and after being worked so hard as that, they cannot make a living out of it.

Donald MacLeod, the septuagenarian from Kyle Rona, was asked by the landowner and Conservative Member of Parliament for Inverness-shire, Donald Cameron of Lochiel, "But don't you think it would be for the eventual good of the people if, when a man married he left the croft, and went elsewhere, rather than settle on the spot and render each croft too small to yield a living?"

"It would do good to the people," replied Donald, "if the man who married got land from the landlord, and left his father's holding."

★

In 1818 the travelling geologist John MacCulloch encountered discontent in Raasay at the absence of a functioning church building and a resident church minister. The Ratharsaich were congregationists of the Established Church of Scotland – there were, for the moment, few alternatives on offer to Hebridean Protestants – and the Church of Scotland in MacCulloch's time failed to install a minister in Raasay.

Instead, Raasay was combined with the Portree congregation and the Ratharsaich were supposed to cross over to Portree for liturgy. They were very occasionally allowed to collect the Portree minister from Skye and take him home again after worship in Raasay, often in stormy weather. "This is, seriously speaking," wrote MacCulloch, "an evil of no small magnitude in the islands in general. It is often partially remedied by stated visitations of the ministers of these insulated maritime parishes, or by assistants, or by missionaries, as they are here called; but why Rasay was to be neglected, I could not discover. I could only discover that there was a good deal of reasonable anger on the subject."

Early in the nineteenth century there was a religious revival in Skye and Raasay, as those missionaries knew well. One of them,

Alexander MacLeod, wrote of a visit on behalf of the Highland Missionary Society which began on 7 November 1833:

> I left home, taking a circuitous tour by the farthest bounds of the parish and island of Raasay, returning to my own home on the 30th. Although I met with outward difficulties, from coarse weather and bad roads I had to travel, I humbly desire to praise the Lord that I was not prevented from attending to the means of grace, for they very often were refreshing to my own mind. I always catechised and held two diets a day, with very few exceptions; and I may say three diets, for the night family worship would be always very throng, as many of the people followed from farm to farm. And I desire to cherish good hopes that the labours of your society will not be spent in vain on these poor benighted islands.

MacLeod returned to Raasay early in the New Year of 1834, "Taking a circuitous course round the east side of the Island of Raasay, all diets were throngly attended, and many followed from farm to farm. At Hallaig, on the Lord's Day, though the weather was exceedingly stormy, and the people's passage by sea to the place consequently rough, yet it appeared that no house on the farm could contain the people; we therefore retired to a large cave near the seaside, where a numerous congregation were sheltered from the storm."

Over the centuries, the Raasay islands' many caves were deployed as places of worship. Most famously, in the perennial absence of a church building on that island, on the east coast of Rona, Uamh an Fhuaimhaire, the Giant's Cave, was sculpted into a fully furnished rock chapel, with pews and an altar, possibly from the Middle Ages or earlier, until the first years of the twentieth century.

Uamh an Fhuaimhaire attracted some idiosyncratic visitors and even stranger theories. The eccentric English archaeologist and parapsychologist Thomas Lethbridge wrote in 1957:

> In 1950 I was at anchor in the harbour of South Rona, which must be surely one of the most beautiful in the world …
>
> Whilst we lay at anchor, my old friend John M. Robertson, who was then a very old man, remarked that there was something on the island which I ought to see. As his gnarled old hands were busy on a splice, he tried to remember what it was. At last it came back to him. It was "the Giant's cave". He had not seen it himself. It was somewhere on the opposite side of the island and it was very remarkable. Then I too remembered that some years before a friend had come to me in Cambridge with a story about a pagan temple he had seen on South Rona.
>
> It took my wife and myself a long time to find the cave, for the east side of the island is much broken up by gullies and the heather was long. It turned out to be one of a series of old sea caves on a raised beach, at the foot of what had once been a small headland. The roof was formed by a great arch of contorted rock and the entrance was masked by falls of stone. Inside it presented a remarkable appearance. Large stones had been arranged in neat rows like the seats in a lecture theatre. At the mouth, a great block appeared to have been roughly trimmed into a cube; while in front of the rows of seats, a ring of stones had been formed to catch a drip from the roof in a kind of basin. It was quite eerie to find such a place on a deserted island, with only the passing Stornoway mail boat to remind one that we were living in the present century. The place indeed suggested some kind of religious gathering; but when and for what purpose it had been made and used seemed impossible to guess.

Luckily Lethbridge was enough of an archaeologist to recognise and analyse a cave midden: "As it happened, there was no difficulty in obtaining some idea of its date. The stone seats were arranged on a hard layer of humus and sheep's dung, perhaps six inches thick. The rain had, however, washed away the outer edge of this and an extensive midden layer was exposed beneath it. This layer presumably represented the giant's rubbish heap. Red deer, sheep, pigs, seals, fishes and shell-fish, including oysters, had been cut up and opened with metal knives. A few small pieces of broken pottery were to be seen. This pottery was apparently of about the fifteenth century of our era. It was not prehistoric. It did not look as if our giant was of any very great antiquity."

The chapel cave at Hallaig was not so finished, probably because it had not been in use for as long as Uamh an Fhuaimhaire. By the nineteenth century there had after all been a stone church of some description, in some state of repair, in the mainland of Raasay for a thousand years. The utilisation for worship of a shallow shoreside cavern served to emphasise the fortitude and commitment of such missionaries, and contrast them with established ministers who would only bother to visit the island in the summer months when a boat was provided between Portree and Clachan – and back again.

Reverend Còll MacDonald was the Church of Scotland minister to the parish of Portree between 1811 and 1854. As one chronicler maintains, Coll MacDonald was not an evangelical, and he "showed little concern for either Raasay or Rona".

Nonetheless, in 1836, with money raised from public subscription, which included a donation from the hard-pressed MacLeod of Raasay, Coll MacDonald's Established Church of Scotland built an elegant chapel below the Iron Age broch in southern Raasay.

It was too late. For more than a century, dispute over patronage had threatened to sunder the Church of Scotland. The status quo had ruled for centuries that the "patron" of a parish had the power and right to appoint or dismiss its minister, and consequently also to dictate the spiritual as well as the lay direction of the district. In Scotland, and particularly in the Highlands, that patron was most usually the landowner. Radical evangelicals in the Church had argued for a long time that the right of patronage should be transferred to the congregation.

Matters came to a head in extraordinary circumstances. On 23 May 1843, an estimated 474 evangelical ministers walked out of their General Assembly, made their way to another hall in Edinburgh and there announced the formation of a Free Church of Scotland.

Curiously, the precise numbers of Church of Scotland ministers in 1843, and of those who left for the new Free Church, has not been agreed. The Established Church's bookkeeping had failed to keep pace. Some calculated that 470 of 1,195 Church of Scotland ministers seceded, and that shortly afterwards 800 Free Church congregations existed within Scotland, containing between 750,000 and 800,000 people. The figures remained approximations. Others offered 454 or 451 seceders out of 1,203 established ministers.

They were a large minority but still a minority. Give or take a few points, the seceders amounted to 40 per cent of the Church of Scotland's ordained clergy. What was more, the remaining Established Church held all of the cards, which is to say that it held the manses, the glebes, the bank accounts, the residual attachment of worshippers, the bibles and all the accumulated assets of a 300-year-old national institution – including of course the essential stone and mortar of the church buildings.

Except in Raasay. The Free Church of Scotland gained footholds throughout the country, but in several of the Protestant parishes of the Highlands and the Hebrides it made a clean sweep. Just three years after its dramatic events in Edinburgh, in 1846 the Free Church estimated that of 23,439 people in the largest Scottish island of Lewis, only 460 were not in the Free Church.

In the second largest island of Skye the Free Church gained ground in rural districts, while Reverend Coll MacDonald, a "moderate" who remained with the Church of Scotland, fought out a score draw in Portree. The seceding minister from Snizort and leading figure in the Disruption in Skye, Reverend Roderick

MacLeod, who took over as pastor to the new Portree Free Church congregation, estimated in 1847 that after the Disruption he catered for 1,100 souls in the parish out of a total population of 2,500, leaving 1,400 with Reverend Coll MacDonald.

Roderick MacLeod added that on the other side of the sea sound east of Portree Bay, "all the residents of Raasay, nearly another 1,000 folk" had gone over to the Free Church of Scotland. He was right, as he might well have been, for Reverend Roderick MacLeod was a grandson of James MacLeod of Raasay, the 12th MacGilleChaluim.

Raasay went wholesale for the Free Church, which was interesting not least because there was no seceding minister for the congregation to rally behind. The island's official minister, Reverend Coll MacDonald, was busier than ever in Skye, staying loyal to the Established Church and retaining as many of his parishioners as possible. The twentieth-century Free Church minister and historian of Skye evangelism, Roderick MacCowan from Braes, thought that in the absence of a shepherd, the Raasay flock had been steered towards secession by such evangelical missionaries as Alexander MacLeod who, in the absence of Coll MacDonald or any other minister, had traversed the island in the decades before 1843. The almost instant and unanimous adherence of the Raasay population to the Free Church was attributed by MacCowan to have been "the result of the instruction, on the principles at stake … disseminated by the 'men'". By the "men", MacCowan referred to "Na Daoine", as proselytising lay catechists were known in the Gaelic Highlands.

In short, Raasay seceded from the Established Church of Scotland because that Church left a vacuum in the island, which was readily filled by persuasive and passionate prayers and preaching by ordinary human beings who were prepared to tramp through violent winter weather for the privilege.

The Free Church in Raasay also, most unusually, enjoyed the support of the big house. The family of George Rainy in Sutherland and Aberdeenshire had been on the evangelical wing of the Church of Scotland. At the Disruption, the Rainys transferred instantly to the Free Church.

Ironically, the right of patronage which the Free Church was bound to abolish gave George Rainy, as the Raasay landowner, full control over the island's church below the broch which had been built for the Church of Scotland in 1836. Never shy of exercising power, Rainy deployed his right and in the words of Richard Sharpe he "reserved the use of the church in Raasay for the Free Church, the Established clergyman being refused admittance". A Free Church minister was not permanently called to that building until 1851, when Reverend William MacDougall from Argyllshire was ordained, but in the meantime no Established Church minister was allowed across its threshold.

There would be fifty years of Free Church hegemony in the Raasay islands. It was an eventful half-century. George Rainy died in London in 1863, having accomplished his aim of transforming the face and character of Raasay. His son, the eighteen-year-old George Haygarth Rainy, inherited the estate, apologised for his father's offences and gave assurances that, in the words of Calum MacLeod of Arnish, "he would undo this by returning the land to the crofters. Within nine years [George Haygarth] Rainy died, and things did not improve."

Following the young man's premature death in 1872, Raasay was sold to George Grant MacKay, a sheep farmer and land speculator from Inverness. According to the Free Church minister of the time, Reverend Angus Galbraith, MacKay's "chief aim appears to have been to make pecuniary gain by the purchase. Accordingly he set immediately about increasing the rents. Rents were imposed on a number who paid none, and the rents which were before, and which were considered high enough, were in some cases nearly doubled. Taking an average of the whole, the rise was nearly 50 per cent. The people at the time remonstrated, and were almost driven to open resistance."

After two years George Grant MacKay gave up on Raasay. He sold the islands in 1874 to William James Armitage of London, "a kind, gentlemanly man ... He only kept the place about eighteen months, and having spent but one summer in it, he did little in the way of giving employment to the people, and left things pretty much as he found them."

After his single summer in 1875, Armitage passed on the property for £65,000 in 1876 to Edward Herbert Wood, a pottery magnate of Sudbourne Hall in Suffolk. Edward Wood was chiefly interested in possession of a fashionable holiday sporting estate, and before his death at the age of thirty-nine in 1886, he went some way to creating one. Sheep in southern Raasay fell out of favour and were replaced by rabbits and other game.

There was much talk in the later nineteenth century of the number of good jobs offered to the locals by Highland sporting estates. In Raasay the Free Church minister Angus Galbraith tackled that claim head-on. If Edward Wood's estate claimed that "the number of people permanently employed in the place is about 94," wrote Galbraith to the Napier Commission in 1883, "I have taken some trouble to ascertain accurately who compose this permanent staff. I find that a goodly number are mansion-house servants, yachtsmen, gamekeepers, gardeners, shepherds, tradesmen of various kinds, salmon-fishers, farm-servants, &c. I find, further, that only about one-half of this permanent staff are natives, and fewer still – I would say not more than one-fourth – are in any way connected with the crofters. I do not say these things in the way of undervaluing the employment hitherto given by the proprietor, but simply to show that only a small portion of the sums expended really benefit the crofter population."

Wood left Raasay to his wife, Evelyn Anne Valiant, and their children. Their proprietorship, which would see out the nineteenth century, left a legacy chiefly in buildings. The Woods had a clock tower erected on the facade of the substantial stone dairy farm steading which had been built by James MacLeod, 12th MacGilleChaluim, early in the nineteenth century for the Home Farm, a quarter of a mile from Raasay House at Clachan. Small schools were opened from Rona to southern Raasay, in accordance with the Education (Scotland) Act of 1872, which obliged regional school boards to provide and enforce compulsory elementary education in English to all children aged between five and thirteen years. Sturdy estate workers' cottages were raised in stone at various locations in southern Raasay.

Raasay House itself had always been a work in progress: an indicator of how affluent was the proprietor, or of how wealthy the proprietor imagined himself to be. The original post-Culloden phoenix, the Georgian manor which rose from the flames of Captain Ferguson's and Lieutenant Dalrymple's retribution in 1746, was embellished and extended by successive landowners until the stylish country hall became a Victorian stately home, which could have been airlifted wholesale out of its Buckinghamshire parterres and ha-has, and deposited among the heather and the peat.

George Rainy had pulled down the two side pavilions built by James MacLeod and replaced them with roof-level wings at the east and west of the main building, with a billiard room in the east wing. The Woods added service quarters in the east wing and bay windows at both ends.

They also completed walling and creating hothouses in the fruit and vegetable garden, that last relic of the orchard noted by Dean Donald Munro in the sixteenth century, and which had been praised by Boswell in 1773 as "well stocked with kitchen stuff, gooseberries, raspberries, currants, strawberries, appletrees ..."

★

William MacDougall was the Free Church minister to Raasay for just four years, returning with his wife to Argyllshire in 1855. The congregation was catered to once more by missionaries and visiting ministers until April 1857, when the Ratharsaich called to Reverend James Kippen, who assumed the responsibility for ten years until 1867. A probationer from Perthshire, Kippen was the scholarly son of a merchant. "Mr. Kippen was eminently qualified by natural gifts," obituarised his prebytery at Arrochar when he died there in 1881, "high scholarship, and large experience to perform the duties of that peculiar charge. To the resident Gaelic-speaking portion of the congregation he was able with much acceptance, to preach the gospel in their native language … he was able to present his Master's message with rare felicity and power."

In 1867, James Kippen was replaced by the dominant Free Church minister of the nineteenth century in Raasay. Reverend Angus Galbraith was born in Kintyre in 1837. Following an extensive education and a period spent teaching in Skye, he was ordained to Raasay thirty years later. "The Raasay people took to him from the very beginning of his ministry," writes the presbyterian historian Roy Middleton. "His personality and his influence, alike as a minister and a counsellor, were a great moral and spiritual force and a power for good … his hearers used to remark, 'That man's preaching seems to stick to one.'"

Some of those hearers would walk a dozen miles from their homes in the north end to the church in the south to attend Angus Galbraith's Sabbath service, and every third Sunday he returned the compliment by preaching at a mission house in Torran, which was built with the help of Edward Wood.

> In order to intimate that Galbraith was to preach," writes Middleton, "the people were accustomed to light a fire the previous evening on a high spot, and in fine weather the congregation was swelled by boat loads of people from the neighbouring [mainland] parish of Applecross, who came across the inner sound …
>
> There was no public house on the island, and crime and the policeman were consequently unknown, while family worship was universal. Galbraith had many seals to his ministry, both in Raasay and in the other places throughout the country where he preached at communions. At the sacramental occasions on Raasay, crowds gathered from the

surrounding islands and from the mainland to the Gaelic services, which were held in the open air.

His lay advocacy was as powerful as his ministry. In Angus Galbraith's written testimony to the Napier Commission in 1883 we hear the authentic voice of the radical Free Church of Scotland. Reverend Angus Galbraith told Lord Napier and his commissioners:

> The crofts in general are too small, and the quality of their land very inferior. The greater part of the land held by them [the crofters] is scarcely fit for cultivation, or for sheep either. During the time of Mr Rainy, senior, the best part of the island – where the people should still be – was cleared of tenants to make room for a large sheep farm. I am told that between the years 1852 and 1854, the following twelve townships were completely desolated – viz., Suishnish, Eyre, Upper Fearns, Lower Feams, Leac, Upper Hallaig, North Screpadale, South Screpadale, Castle, Manish, Doiredomhain, and Lower Hallaig. The number of families removed from these townships is said to have been about 97. By far the greater number of these were sent away against their will, while a few left of their own accord.
>
> A few families, about nine or ten of that number, were allowed to remain on the estate, and were settled among the other townships, whose land was not thought sufficiently good to be added to the sheep farm. The crofters who remained were not therefore benefited by these extensive clearances. Instead of being increased, their holdings were in some cases diminished, to make room for those families settled among them …
>
> Some of the oldest inhabitants now alive – and I consider them trustworthy – have told me that in MacLeod's time the people were more comfortable than they are now …

> The able-bodied men *now*, as a rule, go to the East Coast and other fishings, and on these earnings they mainly depend for the payment of their rents, and the support of their families. In MacLeod's time no one, as a rule, left the island for work. The population then was much larger than now, but they had plenty of land, and between their crofts and the herring fishing about the island, they managed generally to pay their rents, and to live comfortably. Doubtless the failure of the potato crop had a good deal to do with the poverty of succeeding years.
>
> But now that the potato crop is again doing better, if they had more land of better quality than they have, I believe their circumstances would be considerably improved.

The Woods' sporting estate, said Angus Galbraith, had introduced 2,000 pheasants and countless rabbits to Raasay, all of which enjoyed protected status, while "Two young men who were last year at the fishing, died this summer of consumption – a disease which is on the increase, and which, I believe, in most cases is traceable to cold and poor feeding, when the men are from home at the East Coast and elsewhere. In order to save as much as possible, they live too cheaply for their comfort and health. I have no doubt that poverty has a good deal to do with most of the cases of sickness. A medical man of considerable experience, who spent a couple of years in the island lately, on being asked what the prevailing disease in the island was, replied – 'The prevailing disease is poverty, and the chief remedy is food.'"

★

The son and the daughter of the sheep farmer Royston MacKenzie and his wife Hughina both died young in the 1860s. MacKenzie himself, who in 1871 proudly laid claim to "7000 acres [in Raasay], of which 80 are arable, employing 5 labourers, six shepherds & 1 boy", died in 1873 following a stroke. Hughina went to her reward four years later. The age of sheep-ranching in Raasay died with them, but their bloodline continued.

Royston MacKenzie's niece Jemima Sutherland married Reverend Angus Galbraith and settled in Raasay. They raised two sons, the oldest of whom, James John Galbraith, became a distinguished doctor and, in his sixties, in the first years of the Second World War, he was made chief of the Gaelic Society of Inverness.

He owed his Gaelic not to his mother, who was a monoglot Anglophone from Tain in the north-east, but to Raasay. "Dr Galbraith received his early education in Raasay School, where Gaelic was the language of the playground," wrote the Gaelic Society in 1941. "Unlike his brother [Alexander], who, when little more than a child, developed a passion for Gaelic lore, Dr Galbraith's early interest in Gaelic was lackadaisical until physical chastisement from his teacher for speaking the language at school fired his Celtic ire and made him a red-hot Gaelic enthusiast."

In 1890 Angus Galbraith and his family left Raasay for the parish of Ferintosh in the Black Isle at the other side of Highland Scotland. Four years earlier a Crofters Act of Parliament, provoked by the findings of the Napier Commission, had given the people of Raasay almost exactly what Angus Galbraith had recommended to Napier – security of tenure and independently fixed fair rents.

After half a century of being thrown to the mercy of the free market, and the same half-century of Free Church ministry, as Galbraith also pointed out, they were worse off. The population of Raasay itself was, at 430 people, much less than half of its pre-Clearance total of 987 people. But 181 people now lived in Rona, 51 in Fladda, 8 in Eilean Taighe and more in the small townships of northern Raasay. Any land in the south which was made available by the "thinning" of the overall population had not been redistributed among the remaining crofters; it was rather turned over to the estate's Home Farm and shooting reserves. The protections of the 1886 Crofters Act were certainly welcome, but they did not overnight put right fifty years of wrong.

After twenty-three years of Angus Galbraith, the people of the Raasay islands would not blame the Free Church of Scotland for their land starvation. But they were still restless, still reasonably, rationally discontented, still open to notions of change in their public sphere.

In the last quarter of the nineteenth century, the Free Church had been exercised by a doctrinal dispute. The Westminster Confession of Faith had been a cornerstone of reformed Church theology throughout the United Kingdom since its articulation between 1643 and 1647, during the British Civil War. For two centuries, the Westminster Confession had been regarded by presbyterian evangelists as the immutable foundation of Church liturgy, discipline and government throughout England and Scotland.

In the later nineteenth century, moderates within the Free Church sought ways of loosening the Church's attachment to the Westminster Confession, not least because strict adherence weakened the case for absorption within the Free Church of other, smaller presbyterian confessions. That reforming group was led by one Robert Rainy, the principal of New College in Edinburgh, the Free Church's theological seminary, and the moderator of the Church's General Assembly in 1887. Robert Rainy was a nephew of George Rainy, the clearing Raasay landowner before his death in 1863. In 1891, Robert Rainy's faction passed a Declaratory Act at General Assembly, which effectively made the Westminster Confession a voluntary creed rather than a mandatory dogma.

In Raasay, Angus Galbraith was a supporter of the Westminster Confession and was opposed to the Declaratory Act. But Galbraith was a Free Church loyalist, and anyway he was leaving Raasay for Ferintosh. The Raasay congregation put out a call to a man from Uist.

Donald Macfarlane was fifty-nine years old in 1893. The son of a farm manager on South Uist Estate, with a mother from Trotterrnish in Skye, he had been born in North Uist and schooled in South Uist and Benbecula. His teacher in Benbecula,

Donald MacDonald, was just ten years older and would become his greatest friend and associate.

Macfarlane worked hard to pay for and then complete a divinity course at Trinity College, the Free Church academy in Glasgow, and was licensed by the Prebytery of Skye and Uist at the age of forty years in 1874. When he received the call from Raasay in the early 1890s he was the minister at Kilmallie in Lochaber. He was also known to be a Constitutionalist in the Free Church, devoted to the Westminster Confession and fiercely opposed to Robert Rainy's Declaratory Act. In this he had at least one west-coast ally. The minister at Shieldaig was his old teacher from Benbecula, Donald MacDonald. He quickly found another in his namesake, the Raasay schoolteacher Alexander Macfarlane (they were not closely related). Alexander Macfarlane, who had been the schoolteacher at Clachan since 1871 – and who therefore was the dominie who had boxed young James John Galbraith's ears for speaking in Gaelic in schooltime – was the son of a Gaelic Free Church catechist from Laxay in Lewis. Before accepting the position in Raasay he had taught in Portree and Braes. Alexander Macfarlane had also been an elder of Reverend Angus Galbraith's Raasay Free Church.

While he was still at Kilmallie in 1892, Donald Macfarlane, in the words of Dr James Tallach in 2001, "Immediately on hearing what had happened at the Assembly [the passing of the Declaratory Act], he called a Kirk Session meeting, which entered in their records a formal protest against the Declaratory Act. He was persuaded to stay on in the Free Church by the Constitutionalists as they were hopeful of having the Act rescinded at the 1893 Assembly."

In April 1893 Reverend Donald Macfarlane was inducted as the Free Church minister to Raasay and its offshore islands. Matters then moved quickly. Upon his induction he told his new presbytery and congregation "that he was not taking office as minister of Raasay under the Declaratory Act in any sense or degree".

A month later, in May, it became clear that the 1893 General Assembly of the Free Church of Scotland would not repeal the Declaratory Act. Donald Macfarlane, who was that year present in Edinburgh, walked up to the clerk's table and laid upon it a document in his own hand, the crucial part of which read, "I, the undersigned minister of the Free Church, in my own name, and in the name of all who may adhere to me, declare that, whatever I may subsequently do, neither my conscience nor my ordination vows allow me to act under what has been made law in this Church."

On that occasion, the Golden Jubilee of the birth of the Free Church, there was no mass walkout, as there had been fifty years earlier. Initially just two ministers, Macfarlane of Raasay and MacDonald of Shieldaig, strode away.

The second Sunday in June 1893 saw the start of Raasay Communion. Reverend Macfarlane took the opportunity to tell a large open-air gathering of 2,000 congregants and visitors of his reasons for leaving their Church. He asked everybody who agreed with him to stand up. "All present stood, apart from six."

In August, Reverends Macfarlane and MacDonald of Raasay and Shieldaig, and Alexander Macfarlane the Clachan schoolteacher, held in Portree the first local presbytery meeting of an entirely new denomination, the Free Presbyterian Church of Scotland, and passed a formal Deed of Separation from the Free Church.

Most of Raasay and all of Rona, Fladda and Eilean Taighe, followed their new pastor into his new Church. Far from fearing change, they welcomed it. Equally, the people of Raasay and Rona will have required little prompting to mistrust the words and deeds of a mainland Scot called Rainy. For those and for other convincing theological reasons they flocked willingly, and more or less unanimously, behind Reverend Donald Macfarlane and his new Free Presbyterian Church of Scotland.

Donald Macfarlane was at first denied by the Wood family not only a church building but also a place to live. Evelyn Wood retained the church below the broch for the vestigial minority Free Church congregation of Raasay. Reverend Macfarlane "was required to vacate his manse forthwith and for the next five years, until a manse was built, he lived in Broadford and crossed over the sound to supply Raasay every weekend. The main reason for the delay was the opposition of Mrs Wood, the proprietrix of Raasay, who at first refused to give ground to build on and then set very stringent conditions on her offer of ground at Holoman." Until 1898 he lodged in Broadford and sailed, or was rowed, weekly across the Sound of Raasay to pursue his ministry. In 1899 a Free Presbyterian Church, seating 200 worshippers, was raised and opened beside the manse at Holoman.

Raasay then settled down to 100 years as a model Free Presbyterian island. The Free Presbyterian Church adapted and thrived. A fine new roadside church was built on a hill overlooking Clachan Bay and Inverarish in 1929. Its roof timbers were taken from the first dedicated Free Presbyterian Church at Holoman.

The Free Presbyterian Church established congregations throughout the Highlands and Islands, Lowland Scotland and in England. The occasional visits to Raasay of elegant, beautifully dressed Africans testified to the existence since 1904 of a Zimbabwe Presbytery of the Free Presbyterian Church of Scotland. Its foundational evangelism also maintained an Asia Pacific Presbytery with congregations in Australia, New Zealand and Singapore. A Southern Presbytery covered its outposts in England, Ontario and Santa Fe in Texas. In 2002 the Church's Western and Skye Presbytery adopted a congregation in the city of Odesa, in the recently independent country of Ukraine. Following the Russian invasion of 2022, Reverend Dmytro Levytskyi reported that its small assembly still gathered. "When we had spent all our savings," he said, "help came. Prices in supermarkets and at petrol stations shot up. Still, several people from countries like Australia, Scotland and the United States give big donations to our congregation and others. May the Most High bless them a hundredfold.

"We have to use our main weapon, which is prayer. We must bring present circumstances before the throne of God's grace and plead with the Lord that this war will stop and not spread all over the continent."

Insulated from most of the rest of the outside world by the fact that no dedicated passenger or car ferry served Raasay until 1976, in the later twentieth century its Presbyterianism became as fundamental to the island's character as its Gaelic.

Their faith informs the nature of inhabited Hebridean islands. It is difficult to visualise Lewis without the Free Church, or South Uist without Catholicism. In Raasay, throughout the twentieth century, it was easy to discern what one observer described as a distinctively Edwardian courtesy, caution and reserve. Such qualities can as easily be symbiotic and transferred from the population to the host body. They can also be regional, albeit with different local emphases. Obstinacy and internally disciplined self-sufficiency are not unique assets, although it is worth noting what many visitors observed over time: that the authorities have never felt obliged to station a policeman in Raasay. Nor is a dry, wry, knowing wit the copyrighted property of any single Highland parish, let alone confession. Some are simply drier than others.

The epochal prose of the King James Bible may sometimes be heard in almost any Christian church. Only in the Free Presbyterian Church of Scotland has it been obligatory since 1961, when the Church synod decreed that no other version of God's word should be heard.

In 2001 Reverend James Tallach wrote in his history of the Raasay congregation that "When Mr Macfarlane separated from the Free Church [in 1893], he had a congregation of several hundred, including 34 members in full communion. Even within living memory, congregations of 250 on an ordinary Sabbath were common. Today there is an average attendance of around 30, and there are 9 members. Even allowing for the changes in society at large arising from the leaven of unbelief already noted, and the decline in the combined population of Raasay, Rona and Fladda … this constitutes a sharp decline in church attendance."

At his induction in 1983, Reverend Tallach had been called by 103 members and adherents. In 2001, he wrote, "there is an average attendance of around 30, and there are 9 members".

James Tallach may have suspected that he was to be the last Free Presbyterian minister in Raasay.

9

Industrial Revolution

"We will take the law into our own hands and make a general raid in both sheep and Home Farm in Raasay, which is for a number of years now let to [a] sporting English gentleman, who rears calves with the milk we should be getting to feed our little children".

IT had been known for millennia that Raasay's generous mineral deposits included large quantities of iron ore.

Iron ore was certainly dug out of the ground and then processed in parts of the medieval mainland Highlands. The 3,000-year-old spearhead which was found at Eyre early in the twentieth century may have been cast in the island as the late Bronze Age gave way to the early Iron Age.

Writing in 1936, the scholar, conscientious objector, amateur geologist and maternal uncle of the poet Sorley MacLean, Alexander Nicolson of Braes in Skye, described finding among the heather in the deep south of Raasay "the site of a bloomery, or furnace, used by early man". A bloomery was a clay, earth and stone-built smelting kiln, similar in the layman's eye to an outdoor pizza oven. "Its position," added Nicolson, "is now represented merely by a green mound and a few pieces of slag, practically all the material having been removed to repair the adjoining road."

In 1893 the geologist Henry Woodward published in the *Geological Magazine*, which he edited, the information that in a recent survey he had "discovered the outcrop of an oolitic ironstone at the base of the Upper Lias in the Island of Raasay". The Upper Lias signified strata of deposits from the Jurassic period; oolitic ironstone was usually rich in iron ore.

In 1909 Woodward drew the attention of the engineer and mine-owner Wallace Thorneycroft to his findings in Raasay. Thorneycroft set off that same summer to the Inner Hebrides:

> I had little difficulty in finding most of the outcrops seen by him, but without [Henry Woodward's geological map of Raasay] I should have walked over these outcrops without noticing anything in particular, for, as it happens, in several cases the top of the ironstone forms a ledge along which there has been a footpath for many generations, and the weathered surface looks like a softish green whinstone, especially when it is wet, as it generally is in these parts. Probably every visitor to the island for sport or otherwise walked over that footpath without noticing anything different from the common rocks of the country.
>
> Having made arrangements with the proprietrix of the island, I sent in April 1910 an expedition with two hand diamond drills and two sets of chisel drills, together with a number of men …

That expedition changed the face of twentieth-century Raasay. It discovered that beneath the surface of the moor east of Clachan Bay, beyond the River Arish in southern Raasay, there were layers of Jurassic rock, including strata of ironstone to an average of 2.5 metres and a maximum of 5.2 metres in thickness. Those seams clearly suggested substantial quantities of iron ore. Equally importantly, they promised the space available to tunnel and mine it.

William Baird & Company of Coatbridge in Lanarkshire was a 100-year-old mining enterprise which in the 1860s had become the largest single producer of pig iron in the world. Always hungry to expand, Baird jumped at the Raasay deposits.

The problem, as they knew, was that the landowner also possessed the mineral rights. So, in May 1911, with Wallace Thorneycroft acting as broker, Baird bought the Raasay islands estate from the Wood family.

It would turn into one of the biggest misadventures in British industrial history. The estate itself was not expensive – the Crofters Act of 1886 had reduced its potential for exploitation by sheep or game – but the building programme that was instantly pursued by Baird in southern Raasay was colossal. The Coatbridge ironmasters let out Raasay House to shooting tenants but had no interest in the rest of the island. A factor collected croft rents and issued shooting and some farming leases as well as the use of Raasay House, but Baird was altogether unconcerned by the well-being or otherwise of the Raasay estate's settled population of 500 people. So long as they did not obstruct the enterprise in the plump south of the island, they could live out their days in Kyle Rona, Kalgoorlie or Kentucky.

Raasay crofters were not expected to provide an iron mine's workforce or management. Those employees would almost all be imported, there would be a lot of them, and they would need accommodation. So William Baird & Company built a mining village in the Hebrides. Designed by the prolific architect James Grewar Falconer of Blairgowrie, Fort William and Oban – "the Christopher Wren of the Highlands" – it was situated on sloping land immediately to the east of the deep defile through which Allt Arais, the River Arish, ran past a superannuated watermill to the sea.

The village was built between 1912 and 1915 and would ultimately be composed of two rows of terraces containing a total of sixty-four cottages, each with a small back garden, facing one another across a central green with shared laundry- and wash-houses. Further uphill a shorter single row of slightly larger foremen's cottages was built: "a pretty terrace with bracketted eaves," writes Mary Miers, "piended dormer heads and gabled porches". At the western foot of the village a small recreation hall was added in 1918, like an afterthought. The new settlement was named for the mouth of the river, Inbhir Arais, or Inverarish. The sixty-four terraced homes would be labelled in the valuation rolls "Inverarish Houses", and the eight managerial dwellings "Inverarish Cottages". In the community they would thereafter be referred to as "the village" and "the cottages". Inverarish would have a brief but dramatic life as a home for iron miners and German captive labourers, and a much longer role as a foundation of continuing human life in twentieth-century Raasay.

The chief mining engineer, a man from Cumberland named David Todd Munro, doubled up as estate factor and was accommodated with his family by the shore in Royston MacKenzie's former home at Suisnish House. Baird's cashier and accountant was given the lodge at Borodale House outside Clachan, which had been built for their estate manager by the Wood family.

Outside on the hill, there began the serious work of creating the most ambitious industrial complex in the Highlands of Scotland. Only a small amount of Raasay ironstone could be reached opencast. Two long mine shafts were sunk with the help of an engineering wonder of the time: steam-powered draglines. The head of the first shaft was just "a few yards to the west" of the ancient bloomery spotted later by Alexander Nicolson.

An underground network of five miles of tunnels was excavated. Pit head buildings were erected by their entrances to contain offices, workshops and equipment houses. There would be no mains electricity supply to Raasay for a further forty years, so the mineworks generated its own. Railway tracks were laid across the hillside, which would transport trucks of iron ore hauled by steam-driven cable out of the shafts, across 1.5 miles of rough land and over viaducts, and then downhill by the pull of gravity to the shore at East Suisnish. There the ironstone would be calcinated and reduced in a row of five mammoth kilns, before being dumped in a concrete hopper the size of a small glen, and then funnelled down the 125 yards of a T-shaped pier, to be transferred to sea-going vessels and sailed to the Central Belt ironworks

The pier was no sooner completed than the First World War began in August 1914. Thirty-six Ratharsaich members of the local militia were called up, as was much of Baird's workforce.

More crucially, the quality of iron ore brought up in Raasay had been disappointing. Iron ore was considered useful if the ore was composed of between 50 and 60 per cent iron. Some prized ore was two-thirds iron. Any of the raw material which contained less than 30 per cent iron was considered to be commercially unviable. When it was brought up in bulk, Raasay iron ore was discovered to contain just 23 per cent iron, and it was being recovered from the ground at the most inaccessible mine in the British Isles.

William Baird decided to concentrate its remaining workers at its established plants in Lanarkshire rather than throw good men after bad into a Hebridean enterprise which might not bear ripe fruit. The war, after all, would be over by Christmas.

It was not, and Baird's Raasay operation did not resume until 1916. By that time, two years into the war, increased German U-boat activity was making deliveries of imported ore precarious. As neither William Baird & Company nor the British Government could do without processed pig iron in the middle of a global conflict, they reached an agreement. Baird would reopen in Raasay, with a workforce of German prisoners-of-war and a detachment of British soldiers to guard them.

They would be "Prisoners of War who were acquainted with mining", and Baird would require "about 100 miners to begin with, gradually working up to 200 in all in the island of Raasay".

For its part, the British Government would relax its standards, regarding both the quality of iron ore required, and its observance of those protocols of the Geneva Conventions which explicitly forbade a detaining power from working prisoners-of-war in its war effort.

"When it was agreed," wrote Laurence and Pamela Draper in the German mining history journal *Der Anschnitt* in 1999, "that prisoners would be employed on Raasay, a contingent of about a dozen troops under Captain K G MacLeod as Commanding Officer was despatched to the island."

They prepared to greet the first arrivals. The thirty-two terraced cottages in the upper, eastern half of Inverarish were fenced off with high curtains of barbed wire. Elevated guard platforms were erected at two diagonally opposite corners, and powerful arc-lights at the other two. The lights were charged by the large works generator in the industrial multiplex by the pier. The dozen troops who comprised the camp guard bunked down in the lower, western terraces outside the fence and in nearby estate cottages.

By June 1916 the first batch of eighteen prisoners-of-war were at work in the Raasay iron mine. Their numbers would grow until almost 300 men had passed through the island, perhaps no more than 250 or 260 at any one time. The ordinary soldier prisoners were squeezed into bunks on the floors of the thirty-two Inverarish cottages which had been repurposed as a PoW Camp. Their officers were permitted roomier conditions in the foremens' dwellings further up the hill. That row of slightly larger buildings acquired a certain distinction. John Nicolson of Oscaig would recall that in the late 1930s, "'The Cottages' … were regarded as rather prestigious residences – the 'Milngavie' of the island."

The older, stone-built, lower thirty-two houses in Inverarish accommodated, as well as the military detachment, up to sixty British trained miners, most of whom were imported from the south and who did not, of course, sleep behind barbed wire.

William Baird's initial request for qualified German miners was not strictly met. In Germany as in Great Britain, most deep mining was during wartime a reserved occupation. There was therefore little chance of fit, experienced miners putting on uniforms, let alone being captured. It was also true that much of the work was outside the shafts, and that use could always be made of joiners, electricians, carpenters, masons and cooks. One man, who was always recalled "with affection" by the young daughters of Baird's chief engineer and the estate factor, David Munro, "was an accomplished musician who was first violinist in the Kaiser's orchestra! He played at concerts in the Mining Engineer's home accompanied by other members of the Engineer's family and friends."

Baird also opened the door to sailors as well as soldiers, and it seems that some survivors of at least one sunk German cruiser were sent to Raasay. That invitation was quickly withdrawn when Baird and the Ministry of Munitions realised that sailors could more easily sail away than could their colleagues in field grey.

Some did try to escape. The prisoners were obviously not told exactly where they were being taken, and probably not even that they were on an island. Those secrets would not, however, have long survived any amiable contact with Ratharsaich civilians, British workers and soldiers. Laurence and Pamela Draper wrote:

> Half a dozen of them stole a dinghy one night and rowed out to Baird's motor boat (a converted fishing boat which also had sails). They were unable to start the engine because the boat's engineman habitually took the magneto home to keep it dry. As it was a choppy night, some of them became so seasick that they all returned ashore in the dinghy and landed below the school house, from whence they must have walked to Inbhire, 5 kilometres to the north. They were recaptured by two crofters from nearby Balachuirn, who saw smoke from a fire lit to roast a rabbit which the escapees had caught. Seven or eight other men escaped while cutting timber but all except one were found in Borodale woods, and he later surrendered. Two men escaped while working in the ore-crusher and one walked as far as Fearns, 3 kilometres to the east, where he was caught by a gamekeeper; the other was caught elsewhere.

None of the few who made a run for it got off Raasay. Upon recapture they were transferred to a hard labour camp in Surrey.

There is no record of violence from any of the parties in those unconvincing escape attempts. On the contrary, the prisoners developed good relations with the locals, with their British co-workers and with their military guards. The people of Raasay were not expected to produce sufficient food for 300 young working men. Basic provisions were sent across country from Inverness to the railhead at Kyle of Lochalsh, from where they were shipped to Baird's pier at Raasay. However,

> The prisoners received poor rations, but such were the friendly relationships between prisoners and British workers that bread and oats were smuggled to the prisoners in false pockets sewn into trousers, and extra sandwiches were taken to work and given to prisoners to combat their hunger …
>
> Dr Sorley MacLean, the distinguished Gaelic poet, used to be thrilled as a small boy [of five to eight years old] to be invited by one of the prisoners to ride on a farm cart which he was driving. John MacLeod [a Ratharsach who worked at the plant] recalls that one German corporal was much more strict with his countrymen than were the British, but in general they behaved very reasonably, although one report did refer to fighting between prisoners, which is hardly surprising when a large number of men are confined for long periods in a small space …
>
> Several of the prisoners were able to equip themselves with musical instruments, but it is not known whether they were sent from home, or the men acquired them or, as is quite possible, built them themselves; they also obtained or made Tyrolean clothes. Such was the friendly relationship between many prisoners and the British workers that many wooden toys, including simple mechanical ones, were made by the prisoners and given to local children; they also made cigar and cigarette boxes which they gave to British workers, including one inlaid under the lid with "POW

> 1919" which they gave to the Mining Engineer. They also presented him with a beautifully-made small table inlaid with hardwood, all presumably constructed from scrap material; it is still a cherished piece of furniture today.

"You see, they were very skilled craftsmen, the Germans," the Ratharsach John Ferguson told the *Sunday Herald* journalist Torcuil Crichton in 2004. "They were chosen for the work because of their trades. They could make anything from a needle to an anchor, and I've seen both on this island."

They also, he continued, made exquisite lacquered wooden jewel boxes. "And they made the jewellery to go inside them. From a sovereign they could make a ring that would fit your finger beautifully."

"One Scot, Alex Fisher," wrote Laurence and Pamela Draper in 1999,

> was a poetic man with a compassionate personality who had been a Fireman but was rejected by the Army on medical grounds. Being Fireman was an important job as it meant that he was responsible for mine safety and entailed checking for gas, water and roof falls. Without his certificate each day the mine could not operate. He pleaded with the authorities to use him somehow, and as he spoke fluent German learned at night school, he was sent to Raasay where he could be an interpreter as well as Fireman. He built up an extremely good relationship with the Germans and arranged that his wife should give him extra rations so that he could pass some on to the prisoners. The sandwiches had to be shown to the camp guards, so he could not take in too much. He had two thick slices each with a fried egg and another slice with jam, and gave away one egg "piece", usually to one particular German, who occasionally insisted on handing over his 2-shilling pay to protect his sense of independence.

"All that generation worked with the Germans," John Ferguson told Torcuil Crichton in 2004. "My father got on with them very well and he could speak German until his dying day. I think he looked on them as elder brothers."

One of John Ferguson's uncles was a prisoner-of-war in Germany. Because of that, said John, his mother, John Ferguson's redoubtable grandmother Jessie, was determined to keep the German boys on her doorstep alive.

Jessie Ferguson came originally to Raasay from Applecross. A widow with seven children when the war began, she had lost a young daughter to appendicitis, and her two oldest sons went to war in 1914. Kenneth and Fergie were with the Broadford and Raasay B company of the Camerons infantry regiment.

For three years Fergie Ferguson was in a German prison camp, during which time his mother in Raasay made a point of feeding German prisoners, and hoping that someone would offer the same charity to her son.

"Everyone was living with the stress of waiting for a telegram coming through the door," said John Ferguson. "She got sneers that she was feeding these dirty Germans, and she put up with a lot, but she always used to say these are some mother's children, and so I hope that someone will be looking after mine."

Between the summer of 1916 and the end of British involvement in the First World War in November 1918, the Raasay iron mine delivered 168,032 tons of iron ore to be processed in Lanarkshire for the Ministry of Munitions. Almost all of it was retrieved from the maze of underground shafts which were approached through the entrance to Mine Number One.

Nothing came out of Mine Number Two, "because of severe faulting," according to the Drapers, "… which must have been an expensive white elephant considering the cost of constructing the high viaduct, hauler house and other mine-head buildings." The amount of iron ore scraped out of the open cast seam, even with the assistance of the state-of-the-art American steam dragline digger which arrived in 1917, totalled 12,000 tons between 1916 and 1919.

The total, 168,000 tons, was a lot of iron to issue from the small island of Raasay, but it amounted to less than half of 1 per cent of the United Kingdom's national requirements during the First World War.

The agreement between William Baird & Company and the British Government concerning the latter's staffing of the Raasay iron mine with prisoners-of-war, and guaranteed purchase of its produce, came to an end on 30 April 1919, five months after the Armistice was signed. Production had already collapsed, from 88,000 tons in the whole of 1918 to just 4,000 tons in the first four months of peacetime. As the prisoners were repatriated to Germany, and the British workforce to the Scottish Lowlands and to England, Baird put the mine into the care and maintenance of five Ratharsaich. They looked after the huge, sprawling plant diligently, keeping the machinery oiled and ready for re-use at any time of national emergency until 1941, when Baird recognised that not even a Second World War, which had been raging for eighteen months, would bring it back to life, and the Lanarkshire ironmasters gave up completely on their Hebridean enterprise.

It had been a failure of unimaginable proportions, an apparent neglect of due diligence which, despite the cheap labour and guaranteed income of wartime, must have cost William Baird & Company millions of Edwardian pounds sterling, amounting to billions a century later.

Writing after the war, in 1920, the eminent geologist and mining engineer Frederick Henry Hatch was dismissive of the Raasay seams. F. H. Hatch was well qualified to pass objective judgement on the past exploitation and future potential of the island's iron ore deposits. During the conflict he had served on the Iron and Steel Production Department of the Ministry of Munitions, with responsibility for ensuring a sufficient home-production of ferrous ores. Following the Armistice, he was appointed Director of the Mineral Resources Development Branch of the Board of Trade.

As part of his responsibility for assessing wartime supplies of iron, early in 1917 F. H. Hatch reported of the Raasay iron mine, "of which the output was then about 1,300 tons a week ...", that production on the island "could not be increased materially on account of the limitations to its use for making basic pig on account of its low iron and high sulphur content, and inferior physical condition when calcined".

Laurence and Pamela Draper point out, "By 1912 Baird's must have had the borehole samples analysed and known the true iron content, although none of these figures has survived. It must have appeared to have been a viable proposition at the time, but it can now be only a matter of conjecture as to whether or not someone in Baird's was gambling on the imminence of a large-scale war."

If it was such a gamble, it should have paid off, for in 1914, within three years of Baird buying the Raasay estate, the United Kingdom had involved itself in the largest and most industrialised war in the nation's history. But the Raasay iron mine cannot have recouped its parent company's investment. History might be better advised to look at vaunting imperial ambition and simple incompetence.

Two prisoners-of-war died while working in Raasay, one in 1916 and one in 1917. They were buried in the island's cemetery beneath a large tombstone sculpted by their colleagues. In July 1967 their remains, along with those of the twelve prisoners who succumbed to the Spanish flu epidemic in 1918 and 1919 and had been laid to rest beneath modest flat stones, were transferred to the Deutscher Soldatenfriedhof, the German Military Cemetery at Cannock Chase in the English Midlands.

Twenty-two Ratharsaich fell in the First World War, from a population in all the Raasay islands of 500 people. It was a fatality rate of more than 4 per cent, which was more than twice the national average of under 2 per cent. In April 1920, a memorial of their names was unveiled by the shore at Suisnish by Baird's factor, David Todd Munro, who would not finally leave Raasay until 1930. It was "enthusiastically subscribed by the inhabitants of Raasay and Rona". Twenty-six years later it would be augmented by the fallen of the Second World War.

★

One March morning in 1921 a small boat named *Speedwell* set sail from Acarsaid Thioram on the west coast of Rona. The skiff went more or less due south, into the Inner Sound of Raasay, with Applecross in the distance on its port bow and the empty townships of North and South Screapadal lowering above its starboard gunwales. The seven men aboard continued southerly down that ghostly coastline, past the broken stone remains of Hallaig and Leac, until they reached the accessible shore at Eyre. There they beached the boat.

In the thirty-eight years since the Napier Commission had heard of hunger and overcrowding in Rona, conditions in the island had not improved. Alistair Macleod, a son of one of the men in the boat, recalled how "The crofters managed to grow potatoes there by using their open rowing boats to collect the seaweed at low tide and fill the boats with it. The boat was then, at high tide, beached and emptied. This was done by the men and women who packed up their home-made creels and carried the seaweed to the small plots where they grew their potatoes. Digging was done by a 'Cas Chrom' [a home-made hand plough]."

Duncan MacSwan, who was born and raised in Rona at the end of the nineteenth century, would write that "Earning a living on Rona was not an easy task. The ground was difficult to work and in Spring and Harvest especially life was hard, but the people worked together, helping each other as much as they could, and this, and the friendliness which existed between everyone, made things easier. Owing to the lay-out of the crofts, it was not possible to use horses and so cultivation was done manually, and hard work it was too."

In Rona, as around the rest of the coast of the Raasay islands, fish was fortunately still plentiful in the first decades of the twentieth century, and as it had in the Neolithic era it sustained human life. In his own old age, Alistair Macleod wrote:

We used to take our rowing boat out at sunset, with our four fishing rods and come home with plenty of fresh fish.

No one bought fishing rods. We did buy the fishing lines, guts and hooks. We would find a suitable long thin branch, usually about 10ft long, and this was then chipped down with a sharp knife and it would be tapered from about 2 inches to about an inch.

The line would be fastened about the middle of the rod and again fastened at the point. It was then cut and attached to the gut and the hook. It would be the same length as the rod. The hook was fitted with a fly made of sheep wool and the finished fly and hook was shaped thus. When a mackerel, saith or lythe caught the hook the fisherman gently lifted the fish out of the water and then into the boat.

In normal circumstances four people would go fishing. Two would row the boat and two would fish. A plank of wood was placed across the stern of the boat and when the fishermen sat on it, the rods were placed over the stern of the boat and the end placed under the seat. In this way, one person could operate two rods and if there was only three people in the boat, one person would attend to the four rods while the other two did the rowing.

It was quite common to come home after one hour of fishing in the gloaming with one hundred fish. In dividing the fish, one share was usually given to the boat owner and one share to each person. This was not always the done thing, but it was a fair way of compensating the boat owner.

If a village had some person who was old or infirm or a widow, a share would be given to such persons. If we had more fish than we could use we could boil it and use it with oatmeal to feed the dogs and hens or sometimes ducks. We did salt fish and provided that the fish were properly prepared and given plenty of salt the fish would

> keep very well. The salt fish would be soaked and boiled and then served with potatoes and probably a glass of fresh milk.
>
> Most crofters had a couple of herring nets and when herring was in season it was again salted and it made a very nice meal. With all the clever equipment now available there is very little fish left in the sea where we used to fish. Father had told me that when he was young there was so many boats fishing in the sound between Raasay and the mainland that one could about walk from boat to boat on the boats that were fishing.

By the start of the 1920s a new generation had been raised in Rona, and its patience had worn thin. Duncan MacSwan, who was of that generation, wrote:

> The Board of Agriculture often sent its representatives to the Island. I have seen them there many times, and they always promised the people that soon they would let them have land, and a few houses, on the south end of Raasay. But they never did keep their word.
>
> In 1914 the war broke out. Many of the young lads were called to the Colours, including the writer, but when we returned after the war the Board of Agriculture had still not fulfilled their promise. Life on the Island had not got any easier, so, in March 1921 under the guidance of John M. MacLeod, now residing at Clachan, Raasay, seven men from Acarsaid Thioram raided the land on the south end of Raasay …

John M. MacLeod, An Greusaiche or "the shoemaker", had been born in Rona but moved south to Clachan in Raasay, from where this formidable self-educated man was elected to Inverness County Council and became a member of the council of the Highland Land League. An Greusaiche would play a crucial role as a supporter of, counsellor to, and agitator on behalf of all that followed.

The shoemaker's election to the county council for the ward of Portree East in 1914 was celebrated with rejoicings at Clachan, writes John Ferguson,

> where he was symbolically carried shoulder high by his supporters – an act signifying he was viewed as a "deliverer" rather than just a representative.
>
> Addressing the crowd, MacLeod's attitude towards Rona (where he was born) was one of fierce advocacy … He highlighted the "unspeakable privations" of the people there, noting that paupers on Rona received a pittance that forced them to "fast on Sabbath days", and condemned the roads in the north end of Raasay as "a disgrace to civilisation" where one had to "jump across the bogs" to pass. His platform was a direct challenge to this neglect, demanding that the "dispossessed be seen" and reconnected to the world.
>
> The irony of their situation on Rona was sharp. During the Great War the British government had suddenly found Rona strategically important. A telephone link was established to the mainland – not to help the starving crofters, but to facilitate the mobilization of men for the Navy and Army. The men of Rona served with distinction. But when the guns fell silent, the telephone wire was dismantled, and the island was plunged back into silence.
>
> By 1920, the conditions on Rona had devolved from difficult to "miserable in the extreme". The Land Court reported housing conditions that shocked even those hardened to Highland poverty. The island lacked a doctor or a nurse. During the winter storms, the community could be cut off for five weeks at a time, subsisting entirely on potatoes while their children cried for milk …
>
> On 19 February 1920, a group of residents from Rona

sent a strongly worded ultimatum to BoAS [the Scottish Board of Agriculture] regarding their stalled applications for small holdings on Raasay.

Highlighting the stark contrast between their impoverished conditions – described as unfit even for goats – and the fertile land on Raasay reserved for sport, the writers invoked their service in the First World War to justify their demand for a decent livelihood. They concluded with a stern warning that if the Board did not grant them access to the land by spring, sheer necessity would force them to "take the law into our own hands" and occupy the land to ensure their families' survival.

The disquiet about Raasay's future as a fertile but depopulated island, owned by a multinational ironmaster but without so much as an iron mine, was not confined to Rona.

In John Ferguson's account,

In March 1920, a group of [Raasay] locals – distinct from the Rona men – led by Donald MacLeod of Mill Place, conducted a "constitutional raid" on the Raasay Home Farm. They staked out land and wrote polite letters to the Parish Council announcing their intent to plant crops.

The legal system crushed them swiftly. On April 16, 1920, Sheriff Substitute Simpson granted an interim interdict. When the men failed to appear in court, they were saddled with nearly £20 in legal expenses and a perpetual interdict. They eventually withdrew, trusting in the Board's vague assurances of future settlement – assurances that evaporated as soon as they left the land. The "official" negotiations between the Board and Baird & Co. stalled over price and mineral rights.

Behind the scenes, officials were eager to delegitimise the movement by pinning it on a single agitator. In a secret report dated May 1920, Thomas Wilson of BoAS identified John M. Macleod as the "author of the raid" and the true "promoter of the trouble". To BoAS, these were not starving crofters with a just cause, but "utterly unreasonable" tenants led astray by a hostile ringleader.

In a letter dated May 15, 1920, John M. Macleod, wrote to the Secretary for Scotland, Robert Munro, stating that "unless the requests for holdings are granted immediately there will be forcible possession taken of all the available land in the islands". He denounced BoAS as an "incompetent body" whose "criminal negligence" was responsible for the unrest.

For the men watching from the rocks of Rona, the lesson was clear: polite protest and reliance on the Board yielded nothing but debt and hunger.

So the seven men sailed south, they went ashore, and on the old sites at Eyre and Fearns, which seventy years previously had been among the most populous parts of Raasay, "they lodged with local sympathisers and prepared for their permanent return by partially rebuilding the walls of a ruined house near Ferns to serve as a future shelter".

Recounting his father's memories, Alistair Macleod wrote:

> They brought some tools with them and were in breach of the law when they cut down some trees to make rafters to build a roof over this ruined house that had been set alight when their forefathers were removed.
>
> The wall was rebuilt to about six feet. The rafters made from the trees were fitted and on top with sods of peat. Then they found some rushes to make the roof watertight. They had nothing to make a door from but by searching the shore at high tide, they came across a ship-wrecked boat and from this they made a door. Father said that in those days there were so many boats fishing in the inner sound of Raasay that the place was like a regatta at the Isle of Wight.

What were they going to sleep on? Well they found some branches from the trees they had cut for the roof and made them into a mattress. Then, they cut some rushes, dried them, and then placed them on top. The ladies provided their men with warm under clothing.

The wool from the blackfaced sheep on Rona had been spun on their spinning wheel and then knitted into vest and long underpants. This helped to keep the cold out.

Making plans for more permanent homes, they began to stake out the soft land.

The Raasay Raids, as the Raasay Raiders knew well, were not unique. All across the Hebrides, in Uist, Harris, Skye and Lewis, returned servicemen had by 1920 and 1921 run out of patience. Before the war they had been assured of new crofts, during the war the survivors among them were promised homes fit for heroes, but after the war they came back from Flanders and the North Atlantic Ocean to the familiar status quo of poverty, disease and land hunger. Whatever had prompted their twenty-two fellow Ratharsaich to give up their lives, it was not that.

The Scottish Land Court had been established in 1912 partly in response to rural unrest in the north-west Highlands and Islands in the later nineteenth century and before the First World War. Despite being headquartered in Edinburgh, the court never entirely forgot its origins. It celebrated its centenary in 2012 by taking a pilgrimage to Braes in Skye, the site of a celebrated land battle in 1882, and acknowledging in a statement that 21st-century members of the Scottish Land Court "stand on the shoulders" of the nineteenth-century Braes crofters who fought the Macdonald Estate, its factor and their company police from Inverness.

The deputy chair of the Land Court at the time of the 2012 visit was Roderick John MacLeod, Lord Minginish, a Skyeman who later chaired the Land Court for eight years before staying on as its compulsory Gaelic-speaking member.

In 1919, having heard appeals from afar, the Land Court visited

Rona. After a quick look around, the judiciaries slashed the Rona rents, which were still being paid to David Todd Munro on behalf of William Baird & Company, and reported that the island was "entirely unsuited for a settlement of smallholders ... [it is] suitable for nothing else than grazing for a very limited number of sheep".

When the *Speedwell* set sail in 1921, the Board of Agriculture in Edinburgh, was warned that following angry public meetings in Rona and northern Raasay, "we will take the law into our own hands and make a general raid in both sheep and Home Farm in Raasay, which is for a number of years now let to [a] sporting English gentleman, who rears calves with the milk we should be getting to feed our little children".

That "sporting English gentleman" was Major Walter Hugh Rawnsley, a former High Sheriff of Lincolnshire and a fox-hunting man who was sixty-seven years old in 1921. Major Rawnsley had rented the Raasay shooting from Baird since the beginning of the First World War. After the Armistice he took on the Home Farm, and introduced his son, the twenty-nine-year-old Captain John Richard Chaplin Rawnsley, of the 15th King's Hussars, to the recreational delights and financial potential of Raasay. Captain J. R. C. Rawnsley took out a lease of the island's sheep runs at Glam and Fearns.

Once the raiders had set up camp at Fearns and Eyre they cautiously brought down their wives and families. In the subsequent words of their lawyer, Donald Shaw, they "took possession of the lands from which their forefathers had been cleared, they removed [the sheep farm's] stock very carefully and avoided any unnecessary loss. They offered fair rent for the lands." Even at that time of widespread Hebridean land skirmishes, the Raasay Raids attracted a great deal of national and local attention and sympathy, which both the shoemaker and the raiders were careful not to jeopardise.

With an eye on the media and an ear to the mood of the time, the Scottish Board of Agriculture, emboldened by a postwar Land Settlement Act which gave it some ability to purchase land for crofting compulsorily from reluctant owners, was in protracted negotiation with both Baird and the people of Rona about the creation of crofts in Raasay.

Matters soon escalated. As the number of squatters grew in March and April, William Baird & Company and their current tenant sheep-farmer, Captain J. R. C. Rawnsley, resorted to the law.

Interdicts were issued against five of the men, ordering them off Baird's land in Raasay. They were never likely to heed them. On 12 July the sheriff-substitute at Portree in Skye found the five guilty in absentia of breach of interdict and issued warrants for their arrest. When, six weeks later, those men had neither given themselves up nor evacuated the south end of Raasay, a detachment of police landed on the island.

The policemen would have been visible from Fearns for a long time before they disembarked. Upon arriving there they discovered that the raiders had "erected several rude houses for the occupation of themselves and their children, and the numbers of the invaders [had] been considerably augmented within the last week or two". The five indicted men, however, were nowhere to be found. They were, the officers and the press were told, "in hiding" in "the hills and caves of the island".

That would have been daunting news for the authorities. Raasay is not a large island, but its topography is as wild and inscrutable as any of the Hebrides. As the most superficial examination of history would have told the officers and their superiors, men who knew that landscape, and who had the support of virtually every other inhabitant, could have remained at large indefinitely in this place without a permanent police or military presence.

But they were not interested in becoming outlaws. They wished, merely, to be crofters. "The men repudiate any suggestion", reported a correspondent to *The Scotsman*, "as to their being regardless of law and order, but they contend that the course they have taken was the only one open to them in the circumstances ... They express regret that the Board of Agriculture has delayed so long to enforce its powers … If the Board were to assure them that they would get land peaceably and legally, the men say they are willing to do everything possible to conform with the order of the Court and to show their respect for law and order. They say, however, that they could not remain any longer in Rona …"

The prime minister, David Lloyd George, happened that September to be on vacation in Gairloch on the neighbouring Ross-shire mainland. That normally unremarkable fact became celebrated, not only in Raasay but internationally, owing to the troublesome and extremely public peace negotiations with President Eamon de Valera's provisional government in Ireland, which Lloyd George conducted partly from his Wester Ross holiday retreat, and which led to him convening in Inverness on 7 September 1921 the first British Government Cabinet meeting to be held outside London, and the only one until January 2020 when Boris Johnson mustered a celebratory Brexit cabinet in Sunderland.

Lloyd George, who in 1921 was immersed in lengthy translations of de Valera's Gaelic-language stipulations and assertions of Irish independence, suddenly received in Gairloch another long complaint from a smaller and hitherto less troublesome province of the residual British Gaidhealtachd.

John M. MacLeod, the shoemaker, took the opportunity of the prime minister's proximity to write – in English – and tell him that just twenty-five miles away men who in 1914 had "responded willingly to the call of duty" were even now being "hunted like vermin for asserting their right to live in the country which gave them birth, and in defence of which they fought so well".

John MacLeod received a quick acknowledgement and the assurance that David Lloyd George would give the matter his attention. An offer to send a delegation from Raasay to Gairloch, in a small but pointed echo of the conference which Lloyd George was attempting to set up with the Irish, was politely declined.

On Monday 19 September the five Raasay fugitives handed themselves in to a second visiting detachment of police officers.

They were taken to Portree amid "some pathetic scenes, their wives, children and friends following them as far as they could". Upon their arrival in Skye "a considerable crowd, obviously in sympathy with the arrested men, followed them all the way to the [Portree] prison gates". Two days later, at 9 p.m. on 22 September, the five men's case was adjourned until 6 October and they were released pending trial. "Although the hour was late,' reported *The Scotsman*, "a number of their friends, who had been awaiting anxiously the result of the Court, received them with cheers, and the men were carried shoulder high to the Caledonian Hotel, Portree, where they stayed overnight." Early next morning the five were piped down to Portree harbour, where they boarded the steamer back to Raasay. It discharged them at the iron-works' pier, and an hour later they were back in Fearns, where "the community now number[ed] about 40".

The cases of Malcolm MacKay, John MacKay, Donald MacLeod, John MacSwan and Donald MacLeod were duly heard by Sheriff George Donald Valentine, an Ayrshire man who had settled in Skye, two weeks later in Portree. Before passing sentence the sheriff conceded that "in some respects the position is difficult", but that he was obliged to uphold the letter of the law. Sheriff Valentine found in favour of the pursuers, William Baird & Company and Captain Rawnsley, and sentenced each of the men to be fined £15. If after twenty-one days the fine was unpaid, they would be sent to prison for forty-two days.

They did not have that kind of money. But even if the £75 had been raised from their supporters across the United Kingdom – as was certainly feasible – there was never any question of the Raasay Raiders compromising and handing over the fines. Their cause had become a moral crusade. And so, on the afternoon of Wednesday 9 November 1921, the five men were taken under police escort to Inverness Jail. They were met at the town's railway station "by ex-servicemen, who loudly cheered them as they entered the conveyance to take them to prison".

A week later, the government attempted to seek a compromised solution, suggesting to the imprisoned men's lawyer, Donald Shaw, that they relinquish their squatted holdings at Fearns in return for a promise of new land elsewhere. The five men refused. "It is impossible", they wrote from Inverness Jail on 17 November, "for us to give any undertaking because we have no place to go to and as you know our families are in Raasay, our cattle is there, our peats and potatoes is there and we cannot bear to see our children exposed to the four winds of Heaven."

They were released, all five of them, on the morning of Tuesday 20 December. They were cheered from the gates of the jail to Inverness Railway Station, where they boarded the train to Kyle of Lochalsh. They received another "rousing reception" at Kyle that afternoon. They caught the steamer to Raasay and disembarked at around 6 p.m. They were met at East Suisnish by "a large crowd of sympathisers, who had been patiently waiting at the pier for the arrival of the boat. They gave the men a warm welcome. In honour of the raiders, bonfires were lighted in Raasay and Skye, and threw their lurid glare all night across the stormy waters that separate the islands from the mainland."

The five men returned that December, not to Rona, but, naturally, to their families and friends in Fearns. That left them still in breach of interdict and therefore still liable to be rearrested and reimprisoned. But the landowners and the Board of Agriculture had had enough bad publicity. Two months later, early in February 1922, William Baird & Company offered, through the servicemen's representative Donald Shaw, to rehouse the five men and their families, pending their permanent resettlement on crofting land, rent-free in the deserted company mining cottages at Inverarish. The men accepted, and on 10 February horses and carts belonging to Baird transported their household goods from Fearns and Eyre down past the empty mineworks to the village – and former prisoner-of-war camp – of Inverarish.

A year later, in February 1923, Baird sold all of Raasay, Rona and Fladda but the mineral rights, the mine works, Raasay House, the Home Farm and other estate assets to the Scottish Rural

Workers Approved Society, whose trustees promptly sublet the land to the Board of Agriculture. The selling price was £16,150, which amounted to just over half the sum that George Rainy had spent seventy-seven years earlier, and almost exactly a quarter of the £65,000 that Edward Wood had paid for the islands less than fifty years before, in 1876. Security of crofting tenure and the prospect of compulsory land resettlement had made Highland crofting estates dubious investments.

The Board of Agriculture promptly created new holdings at Fearns, Eyre, Suisnish, Inverarish, Brochel, Glame and Oscaig. The island of Rona quickly emptied. The census of 1921, the year of the first raids, showed ninety-eight people living there. Ten years later there were only sixteen. And in 1951, the first census after the Second World War showed Rona once again to be empty of everybody but its lighthouse keepers.

The state, through the Board of Agriculture in its different iterations, up to and including the 21st-century devolved Scottish Parliament's Ministry for Agriculture and Connectivity, would continue as the landlord of the Raasay crofting estate. William Baird hung on to the mineral rights and the superfluous iron mine, including the pier and the village of Inverarish, until 1941, when the terraced former mining village and prisoner-of-war camp was sold piecemeal to local families. Ironically, at a time of domestic metal shortages in a world war, the iron mine's infrastructure was dismantled and recycled as scrap.

Inverarish settled into an invaluable role as a hub of the island, offering starter homes to young people and retirement homes to the elderly, as well as dwellings to some working crofters who walked unusual distances to their crofts. Its sturdy, sheltered little cottages often served all three functions at the same time. Inverarish became a rarity in the Highlands: a conurbation of owner-occupied housing which was at least as Gaelic, and often more so, than its satellite crofting townships.

In 1937 the Board of Agriculture ceased letting Raasay House to shooting tenants and opened it as a nationalised country hotel, with optional fishing and shooting for guests, on the model of publicly owned railway hotels which had been built beside stations throughout the country. That rare beneficial legacy of Victorian private landowners, their tree plantation schemes in the south, had transformed an ordinarily beautiful Hebridean island into an exceptionally lovely place – as well as making much of the south end of Raasay an outdoor aviary which was home to a multitude of woodland and estuary birds – and the Raasay Hotel built a steady reputation and employed local women for over twenty years.

In 1960 the hotel's longstanding manager and her son left for Skye. The Department of Agriculture and Fisheries in Edinburgh was flummoxed by her departure and decided that their quickest and easiest course was to close the hotel and then sell the building as a going concern. A forty-four-year-old man from Sussex named Dr John Green had recently sold the uninhabited island of Scalpay, south of Raasay, which he had owned since 1957, as "my wife found it too isolated". Hearing of Raasay's sudden availability, Green sold Scalpay, and the neighbouring islets of Longay and Guillamon in the Scalpay Estate, for £23,000, making in non-inflationary times a profit of £12,000. He then approached the Department of Agriculture and Fisheries and discovered that as far as they were concerned Raasay was in a buyer's market. He asked them to name their price and with little more to-do, the department sold to John Green for £4,000 the properties of Raasay House, Borodale House, the Battery and 10.5 acres of land which included points of access to William Baird's pier. Over the following years he would collect like football cards miscellaneous plots of Raasay land and even the mineral and salmon fishing rights. Dr Green never owned more than 113 acres of the 17,250 acres of Raasay, but they were strategically crucial acres, and all of them were put into cold storage.

Everything that John Green touched turned to dust. He was undoubtedly a fantasist. Green had invested several thousand pounds in connecting Scalpay to the National Grid, for no obvious purpose. He insisted that Raasay House would reopen as a bigger and better hotel than ever, with peacocks and other decorative creatures roaming the grounds. Some peacocks actually were imported – they died.

Without visiting the island more than twice and never spending a night there, and while owning many of Raasay's assets but hardly any of its surface area, he almost broke the spirit of the place and left even sensible Ratharsaich wondering if there was a hidden agenda in Edinburgh or London which involved the desertion and complete depopulation of Raasay. The first James Bond movie, *Dr No*, came out in 1962, and the name of its eponymous supervillain was quickly transposed, in Raasay, then in the media and then in the national imagination, onto the Sussex stockbroker who had apparently bought Raasay. He became the shining exemplar of the Highland curse of absentee landlords.

Raasay House did not reopen. Fully furnished and ready for occupation when John Green bought the property, within a very few years it became a torn and haunted echo of its former self. Its large windows broke, ushering the Hebridean weather onto soft furnishings, library books, and polished tables and chairs. Luxurious bedrooms were ravaged by water and wind. "Allegedly," wrote Calum MacLeod of Arnish in his account of *The Cruel Clearance of Raasay*, "it was broken into quite often, and anybody could purloin whatever he fancied … when I last visited Raasay House, truly it looked as if it had been overtaken by open judgement." Only its solid Raasay stone and masterwork kept Raasay House standing.

John Green also managed to delay by several years the introduction of a dedicated six-day ferry service between Skye and Raasay, by objecting to a slipway, an office and a waiting room being built, firstly at Clachan, and then by the Suisnish pier. The small roll-on roll-off vehicular ferry which was first mooted in 1972, would not run from Portree until 1975, and not from its intended departure point at Sconser until 1976, because Dr No had said No.

Unrepentant to the last, when he was visited at his Sussex home in the January of 1977 by the two most formidable Highland journalists of the twentieth century, Brian Wilson and Derek Cooper, John Green insisted that his actions and his intentions had always been positive and honourable. An unholy alliance of the Ratharsaich and the Highlands and Islands Development Board had, he said, frustrated all of his ambitions for the island and rejected hundreds of thousands of pounds of his own investments.

In the war of attrition between Dr John Green's fantasies and the patience and bank balance of the Development Board, the latter finally won. In 1979 they bought Green's portions of the old Raasay estate, including the sporting and mineral rights, for £135,000, bringing everything back into public ownership at a profit to Dr No of approximately £130,000. Raasay House, said the HIDB in 1977, "is now in such disrepair that it would be impossible for the Board to convert the building into an hotel at reasonable cost".

In 1961, the year of John Green's purchase, the population of Raasay was 223 people. In the first National Census after his departure, in 1981, it had fallen to 153, its lowest total in recorded history.

★

In September 1934, the twenty-three-year-old son of the Oscaig tailor, arrived back in the north-west with a first-class degree from Edinburgh University and a certificate from Moray House Teachers' Training College. Sorley MacLean began his first job as an English teacher at Portree High School, which he had earlier attended as a student.

For the 400 people of the Raasay islands, the 1930s could have offered a short summer of stability. MacLean's journey through those years followed its flight path from what his fellow poet W. H. Auden, who had also known the First World War, described in

1939 as "clever hopes" which were reduced in "a low dishonest decade" to an unthinkable Second World War. Sorley MacLean had been seven years old when the First World War ended. He was only twenty-eight when the Second World War began.

Six Raasay men died on active service in the Second World War. MacLean came close to being a seventh. Family responsibilities had prevented him from following his heart and enlisting in the Republican International Brigades in the dress rehearsal of the Spanish Civil War in 1936 and 1937. The British state itself prevented him from joining the Cameron Highlanders in 1939, as there was a shortage of teachers at home. In September 1940, he finally got his way and was drafted into the Royal Corps of Signals and sent with an artillery regiment to North Africa.

He was wounded twice before November 1942, when a landmine blew him thirty feet into the air. Shipped home to recover in Inverness's Raigmore Hospital, he was honourably discharged from the army ten months later, resumed teaching in the autumn of 1943, met and married Renee Cameron, and pursued education, family and poetry.

Sorley MacLean's own educational trajectory from Raasay to Portree to university at Edinburgh, Glasgow or Aberdeen, to teaching at increasingly elevated levels, was not unusual in the 1920s, and would become commonplace as the century progressed. But in MacLean's generation it was experienced only by a minority, of which the MacLean siblings, the seven "Oscaig scholars", were a large and notable portion.

Many Ratharsaich, particularly in the north of the island, experienced in the twentieth century lives which were materially little different from their medieval forebears. Julia MacKenzie, nee Cumming, was born in Eilean Taighe in 1923 and was raised there and across the tidal narrows in Kyle Rona. Throughout the later 1920s and the 1930s she walked along a worn path over the rough land, to and from Torran School, barefoot in summer and in boys' tackety boots in winter, to her homes on the northern edge of Raasay. "To many today," she would write at the end of the century, "life on our island may seem primitive, but believe me, it was a very happy, carefree life."

They had no electricity, of course, or tap water – the children carried from a spring each day's supply of fresh water, with two draws on Saturday so that the Sabbath would be unspoiled. Their father tilled "tiny cuts of land" on Eilean Taighe with a cas chrom, or foot plough, and they ate potatoes and cabbage but could not recognise a carrot. They dried and cured fish which they netted offshore, and cut peat for a year's fuel. In the middle of the 1930s Julia MacKenzie went away to Portree High School, and after the Second World War was declared she joined the Auxiliary Territorial Service, the women's branch of the British Army. Julia was posted first to Surrey, "which seemed like going to China".

After the 1872 Education Act prescribed schooling for all between the ages of five and thirteen years, most children of the Raasay croft learned only English, and then literacy in English, numeracy and whatever other subjects could be squeezed into the curriculum by their invariably hard-pressed teachers, at their nearest elementary school in Clachan or Torran. For a few years before the 1872 Act was enforced, churches or charitable societies, or concerned individuals, provided informal hedge schools in Fladda, Kyle Rona and even in Rona.

What would become the High School in Portree was built after 1872 to satisfy another precept of the Act, to offer education into their mid-teens to children who could sit the Higher School Leaving Certificate examinations which were mandatory for entrance to universities and several professions. The institute was first named Portree School, then Portree Secondary School, becoming Portree High School in 1957.

As large numbers of children in the county of Inverness then lived as far from Portree as Sleat, Strath and Trotternish in Skye, as well as the independent islands of Eigg, Muck, Soay, Canna, North Uist, Harris and Raasay, even as teenagers they could not be expected to commute daily to and from school. Some, but far from all, would find lodgings with family and friends. Many would simply not bother to continue with secondary education, and so, in 1924, a hostel for girls was opened in the school grounds. It was sponsored by a grant from the Carnegie Dunfermline Trust, which was a Scottish philanthropic arm of the Scottish-American steel magnate Andrew Carnegie. The facility was therefore named the Margaret Carnegie Hostel, after his only child and heiress.

Nine years later, in 1933, an equivalent accommodation block for youths was built and opened on the same school estate. It was also assisted by the Carnegie Trust, whose chair at the time was Edward James Bruce, 10th Earl of Elgin, and great-grandson of the 7th Earl of Elgin, the British ambassador to the Ottoman Empire who 130 years earlier had procured the Acropolis Marbles from occupied Athens. In deference to both of them, it became the Elgin Hostel for Boys.

When young Sorley MacLean and his brothers were Portree High School pupils there was no hostel provision. They were boarded with relatives and family friends. His return to Portree as a newly qualified teacher, and his consequent commission as a young, single man to resident supervisory adult among the teenagers in the Elgin Hostel was his first experience of the place. It was not the happiest of times for the young poet. "As you may see by the address," he wrote from the hostel to the older poet Hugh MacDiarmid in May 1935, "I am now staying in an institution, a hostel for boys from outlying districts at the school. It is rather an unsatisfactory place for work but I had more or less to enter it as there was no other teacher available."

At that time, before his identity developed and his literary legend spread, Sorley MacLean referred to himself as Sam MacLean. Names became a problem as the Scottish Gaidhealtachd found itself in an Anglophone world which often failed to recognise its appellations. Not unusually, Sorley MacLean had been christened Samuel MacLean, when in fact his name would have been more accurately rendered as Somhairle MacGill-Eain, and the forename Somhairle derived not from Samuel but from the Norse Sumarliðr, or Somerled. His parents shared a widespread concern that the Scottish authorities would recognise neither Somhairle nor its phonetic transliteration of Sorley, and so the Hebrew first name Samuel was conjured out of Old Testament history and imposed on Gaelic Highland boys.

In a region with a surfeit of Donald John MacDonalds and Calum MacLeods, let alone Sam MacLeans, nicknames had become commonplace. In the twentieth century, everyday cognomens largely replaced the ancient Gaelic patronymics, wherein fathers and grandfathers and great-grandfathers were proudly invoked until the subject's unique lineage and identity were beyond dispute. People might more pithily become Donald Bàn, Willie Eyre, Calum Mòr or Murdo Beag, after their hair colour, their place of birth, their size or their seniority.

At some point after 1933, the Elgin Boys' Hostel offered its own alternative. Each year a self-appointed panel of senior hostel boys assembled, assessed and re-christened the new intake. The future Portree chemist Donald Alec MacLeod arrived from Staffin in a fashionable duffle coat and so became Toggle. The initials of the future Gaelic development officer Allan Campbell from Colbost in north-west Skye made him Volt. For unknown reasons, as cricket was not a common sport in the twentieth-century Highlands, other boys got Yorker and Googly.

A boy from a family of hoteliers named Hilditch was graced with Ben Drain. "For a number of years," wrote the former deputy headmaster of Portree High School, himself a Portree kid called Ian George MacDonald, "boys from Broadford were given names of alcoholic drinks. I believe this arose from the innocuous naming of Sandy Sutherland as 'Shandy', thus consigning his relatives to be for ever 'Toddy', 'Brandy' and 'Cossack', after the brand of vodka."

Specialisation occurred. Boys from the Outer Hebrides of North Uist and Harris were named after such birds as the skart (shag), plover and peewit, possibly as an indication of how they got from their homes to Portree.

By some similar logic, new arrivals from Raasay became fish. They were suddenly, and for life, Crùbag (crab), Giomach (lobster) or Rionnach (mackerel). Norman Gillies of Inverarish was dubbed Skate. Andrew Gillies of Bailechuirn was suddenly Cuddy. Andrew's older brother, John William, had already become Bradan, which is the Gaelic word for a salmon.

Not only did Bradan's and Cuddy's schoolmates and neighbours know them forever after as Bradan and Cuddy – some of them either forgot, or had never known, them under any other name – so also did their siblings, their wives, their children, occasionally their reluctant mother, and always such a Nobel laureate as Seamus Heaney, whose sherpa in Raasay was introduced to him not as John William, but as Bradan Gillies.

Further educational legislation in 1883, 1918 and 1945 extended secondary schooling to all children, and the school leaving age was raised to fourteen, to fifteen and then to sixteen years. That caused increased patronage of Portree High School and both of its hostels, and some concern in far-flung parishes and islands.

While most urban Scottish children and parents welcomed the new provisions and potentials, crofters from islands such as Raasay, Eigg and North Uist found that their teenagers, who had for centuries been key components of the life and work of their communities, were only available at weekends, and often only during school holidays. Many of them effectively left home at the age of twelve years.

In the township of Arnish in northern Raasay, in 1962 Calum MacLeod's twelve-year-old daughter Julia received a letter from the education department of Inverness County Council. It ordered, she recalled, "'Thou shalt have two skirts, four blouses, one tie, one dressing gown …' And so when I was twelve all that was packed in a trunk and shipped off to Portree High School, along with me. I'll never get over the move to Portree, it was awful. I don't think anyone is ready at twelve to sever all ties. I became one of sixty-seven girls, having been the only girl in school all through my primary."

Julia's misery was compounded by the fact that the sporadic ferry service and the absence of a motor road for the last two miles of her journey from the pier meant that she was hardly ever able to get back to Arnish. Julia was boarded in the Margaret Carnegie Hostel for Girls for the whole of her secondary years, except for school holidays and occasional long weekends. Julia MacLeod would never return to live in northern Raasay.

"You were taken away at twelve," she said, "and you left school to do something else, somewhere else. I mean, what would you come back and do in Arnish? Milk half of the cow – let your father milk the other half? What would you do?"

Julia's father, Calum MacLeod, had manifold reasons for building the motor road between Castle and Arnish, and they changed with the seasons, but he was undoubtedly spurred by his daughter's removal from home. He was also aware that three decades earlier, when he had been twenty years old in 1931, a petition from 100 adults in north Raasay to Inverness County Council requesting just such a facility was rejected. After 1931 the population of the district haemorrhaged, until the late 1960s when the departure of the last dozen people from Fladda and Torran left only two people in the whole of northern Raasay, other than the three peripatetic Rona lighthouse keepers. Those two people were Calum MacLeod and his wife Lexie.

Inverness County Council's reason for not building the road – that it would entail too great a cost for too few people – was self-fulfilling. The longer they failed to extend the Raasay spinal route, the fewer people lived beyond its northern end. Calum MacLeod never accepted either that bald cost-effective equation, or the council's estimations of cost. To prove both points, he built it himself.

As he worked and as the last people left, new motivations fuelled his fire. The ancient civilisation of Fladda was disappearing before his eyes. Lexie MacLeod developed chronic incapacity, and he charged himself with ensuring that a doctor and an ambulance could at all times reach their home. Furthermore, Southern Raasay received mains electricity from the national grid via an undersea cable from Skye in 1956, but there was no suggestion of the trackless north ever being connected.

He never completed the road, for the simple reason that he never stopped maintaining and improving it. But it was negotiable by motor vehicle in the early 1980s, and in the New Year's Honours List of 1983 Calum was awarded the British Empire Medal.

This merit was officially given to him as a reward for his decades of "community service" both to the post office and to the Northern Lighthouse Board, decades which stretched from his time as a deckhand on the Rona lighthouse tender in the 1920s to his retirement in July 1975, when the Rona light was automated. Letters of congratulations – more than sixty of them – flooded into Arnish from the rest of Britain, from the USA, Canada and Australia.

Calum MacLeod, wearing his full lighthouse dress uniform, was officially invested with the British Empire Medal by the lord lieutenant of Ross and Cromarty, Admiral Sir John Hayes, at a ceremony in the new hotel in Borodale House in southern Raasay in April 1983. Apologies for their unavoidable absence were received and noted from Queen Elizabeth II, from Mr Russell Johnston MP, and from the convener of the Highland Regional Council, Mr Ian Campbell of Sligachan in Skye.

Mr Alastair Henry of the Department of Agriculture took the opportunity to comment on the "extremely good order" of Calum MacLeod's croft. A cousin of Calum's from Brisbane in Australia travelled to be in attendance. In his presentation speech, Admiral Hayes remarked that he had been a shipmate of Calum's late brother Ronald on board the aircraft carrier HMS *Indomitable* during the Second World War.

Calum himself would muse that he was not the first member of his family to receive a medal. "My cousin was the famous Captain Donald MacRae," he said afterwards, "the Sydney harbourmaster who was decorated twice before his death in 1962. He led an Australian contingent in the Dardanelles [during the First World War], and was said to be the last man out of Gallipoli, with a captured Turkish machine gun under his arm! His mother was born and brought up on what is now my very own holding in

Arnish, and until his death Donald MacRae had more Gaelic than English."

If Captain Donald MacRae's medal-winning feats had been clearly defined in the bloodbath of Gallipoli, his cousin Calum's was a concealed award.

Calum MacLeod's great achievement by 1983 was acknowledged to be the creation of his road, not his service to the Northern Lighthouse Board. But to have confirmed an emblem of twenty years' active agitprop against local and central government as sound reason to be offered the British Empire Medal might have set an embarrassing precedent.

The citation said that he became Malcolm MacLeod, BEM, for maintaining supplies to the Rona light, and latterly for working as local assistant keeper there for eight years. But the whole world knew that he had become Malcolm MacLeod, BEM, for building Calum's road.

Following the presentation ceremony in the Isle of Raasay Hotel on the afternoon of Saturday 23 April 1983, the entire official contingent drove north, and made its way in stately convoy along the finished road between Brochel and Arnish. "They were very charmed with it," said Calum MacLeod. "But I never thought I'd end up with a British Empire Medal." The establishment had, in a roundabout way, apologised.

Calum MacLeod himself personally illustrated the last parable of Calum's road. For centuries the people of northern Raasay had been buried in the island's cemetery in the low hills behind Oscaig in the south of the island. It was too great a distance even for those people to walk a coffin road, so the men took a boat with the remains of the departed down the coast to the landing places at Clachan or Oscaig, while the women watched from the shore.

Calum MacLeod died outside his house of a suspected heart attack in 1988. The hearse from Portree in Skye drove all the way to his door. He was the last of his kind to leave his community, down the road he had built himself.

10

In Its Beginning Was Its End

"Where the Crofters Union and the Highland Development Board saw community buyouts as a form of liberation, a door opening to a free and accountable tomorrow, Raasay crofters saw simply the state trying to wash its hands of its responsibilities to the island."

IN 1977 the young academic Richard Sharpe was pessimistic about the future of human life in the Raasay archipelago. At the end of *Raasay: A Study in Island History*, he wrote:

> The 20th century, has seen little but decline and decay. Depopulation has reduced the number of inhabitants to about 150, a half of them over 60 years old. The school and post office at Torran closed in 1966. Now, apart from two families at Arnish and holiday homes on Fladda and at Brochel, no-one lives further north than Balachuirn. In the last fifteen years development has been more often blocked than encouraged, but if the island is to retain an indigenous population, change must come soon.
>
> Raasay remains a microcosm of the Highlands and Islands in the 20th century. Crofting is declining. Transport difficulties threaten to cut the island off. The native population moves away and outsiders buy up houses for

> summer homes. It cannot yet be seen whether solutions will be found for these problems …

In 1973 Derek Cooper made a thirty-minute documentary about Raasay. The maternal half of Cooper's family was from Lewis and Skye, and in print and broadcast journalism he had an understanding of and urgent care for the Hebrides. The greater part of his Raasay documentary was devoted to Calum MacLeod's exertions on his road between Brochel and Arnish. He chose to title the programme *The Island That Nearly Made It.*

That was uncharacteristically enigmatic. If "made it" meant "survived", it implied that Raasay had fallen short. "Nearly" suggested that there had been a time in the recent past when Raasay could have breasted the tape, but failed to do so.

Neither one of the inferences stood up. The people of Raasay had come through hard times before. Just two centuries earlier units of soldiers had killed their livestock and set fire to much of their island. Not very far beyond living memory, a callous landowner had tried to deport them like criminals to the colonies.

In fact, the title of *The Island That Nearly Made It* reflected the despair of many Ratharsaich in the 1970s. They had endured the First and Second World Wars, a prisoner-of-war camp and an aborted attempt at massive industrialisation, only to be delivered into the hands of a faintly bonkers land speculator who specialised in the Hebrides and had only an occasional relationship with the truth. Raasay House had been left to rot, and the authorities appeared to find it impossible to build a slipway in the island for a small ferry. Meanwhile, the Inner Sound between Applecross and Raasay had become a torpedo testing range, which was served from a naval base at Kyle of Lochalsh and a military installation on Rona. They were not a paranoid people, but they were wary.

The return to public ownership under the Highlands and Islands Development Board in 1979 signalled a first return swing of the pendulum. The pressing matter of Raasay House was tackled by turning it into an outdoor-cum-adventure centre, as were appearing throughout the Highlands to give groups of city schoolchildren a view of the sea.

Schoolchildren did not require linen bedsheets, polished floors or even much furniture, and no attempt was made to restore the derelict mansion to its condition before the Green era. A sticking plaster was applied to the Raasay House wound.

In 1981 an extended and converted Borodale House was opened as a fifteen-bedroom hotel, with a public bar, under the management of the former ferryman Alastair Nicolson and his wife Isobel. Alastair Nicolson's formerly private enterprise ferry service between Sconser and Raasay was adopted by Caledonian MacBrayne and incorporated into the state-owned company's network of Hebridean routes. That progression guaranteed the continuation of a lifeline service, and the provision to Raasay of half-a-dozen salaried year-round jobs with the possibility of promotion up the employment ladder of a large shipping company. In 2010, with the 100-year-old iron mine pier at Suisnish crumbling into the sea, a new jetty, slipway and terminal complex was built by Highland Council and the Scottish Government at Churchton Bay, beneath the startled eyes of MacGilleChaluim's mermaids and beside the Pictish hieroglyphs which had for over a millennium directed visitors to the security of Moluag's chapel. To pursue bridges across the centuries, a new low-emission hybrid diesel and electric powered ferry was dedicated to the island in 2013. She was christened MV *Hallaig*.

In 1990 a Conservative government once again decided to try to shrug off its ownership of some crofting estates. The prospect was presented of places such as Raasay being delivered back onto the open market. Anxious to forestall that possibility, the Highlands and Islands Development Board and the Scottish Crofters Union between them commissioned a study into possible community buyouts in Raasay and Skye. A meeting was convened in Raasay to discuss the matter with officials.

The men in suits who took the CalMac ferry to Raasay met a uniformly negative response. Community buyouts would shortly gain momentum in the west Highlands and western islands, with estates from Assynt to Eigg to Lewis being purchased by their residents, assuming a democratic autonomy and taken off the free market merry-go-round, possibly forever.

In the early 1990s, however, selling the idea to Raasay betrayed an insensitivity to the island's recent past. Where the Crofters Union and the Highland Development Board saw a form of liberation, a door opening to a free and accountable tomorrow, Raasay crofters saw simply the state trying to wash its hands of its responsibilities to the island. As the Ratharsaich were, by and large, right in that assessment, and as the Department of Agriculture and Fisheries was regarded almost everywhere as a decent crofting landlord – it did not, at least, try to deport its tenants to New South Wales – the proposal was stillborn.

It would occasionally be revived, with no more success. In 1995 the sporting rights in Raasay were surrendered by an heir to the Highlands and Islands Development Board. Skye & Lochalsh Enterprise, which was comprised of a group of clerks in an office in Portree, was unsure why it had the Raasay shooting rights, and was equally uncertain what to do with them. A solution was reached when a Crofters Association was formed in the island which took over the rights on a peppercorn lease from the Scottish Office, and then from the Environment Ministry of the Scottish Parliament in Edinburgh.

For eighteen years Raasay crofters periodically sold trout fishing permits to visitors, uncontroversially escorted German riflemen around the island, culled the modest deer herd on their common grazings and supplemented both their diet and their income with fresh venison. It was a settlement low in hard-headed business appeal, but high in common sense. In 2013, inclining more to the first than the second, the Environment Ministry decided to put the sporting lease up for auction. A stalking partnership of former soldiers in Ayrshire bid £3,000, which was more than the

£1,150 offered by Raasay crofters, and they were duly handed the right to shoot deer and woodcock, and fish the lochs on the estate's hills and grazings.

It was both a practical and a symbolic insult to the indigenous people in an island of roe deer. "It seems incredible that we are facing the same situation that Raasay faced 50 years ago," said one member of the Raasay Crofters Association. "We thought these times were past in the age of community buyouts and local control."

As had been amply demonstrated on those same shores in the recent past, there are few more formidable foes than a crofter scorned. A media campaign was pursued against the unfortunate Environment Minister, an Edinburgh economist named Paul Wheelhouse, who represented the lush south of Scotland. In a self-confessed "unprecedented step", four Free Church of Scotland ministers from Skye wrote to Scottish parliamentarians, saying, "You will all be aware that it is difficult to make money at the margins and the Raasay Crofters' Association have made great progress in developing the sporting rights in Raasay to the benefit of the crofters and the community. The benefit certainly outstrips the mere £2,000 which is at stake. The Free Church has historically supported crofters' rights against oppressive landlords. We consider this recent development a gross injustice against the local crofters of Raasay."

Few Scottish governments would relish being compared by the crofters' Church to an oppressive Highland landlord. Paul Wheelhouse did his cause no favours by driving to Raasay, tweeting like a tourist about the pretty scenery in the Highlands and then suggesting to the crofters that if they were unhappy with the status quo they should explore the potential of a community estate buyout. The last proposal sounded more like a protection racketeer than a responsible politician – "buy it from us and you won't have us to worry about any more" – and Wheelhouse was ordered by First Minister Alec Salmond to go back to South Ayrshire Stalkers, buy them off with whatever was needed – they settled for £9,000 – and return the rights to the Raasay Crofters Association. He did it in twenty-four hours.

They might not have been ready to buy and manage all of their islands, but as if to show willing, Raasay's people gradually accepted the management and ownership of most of the island's assets other than the crofting estate itself. In 1999, in order to access public money for restoration, the outdoor centre at Raasay House became the property of the Raasay House Trust, a representative body which in 2007 became the Raasay House Community Company.

A complete multi-million-pound restoration of Raasay House, which would add high quality guest bedrooms to the adventure centre facilities, began in 2008. On a January night in 2009, with the work effectively completed, in an astonishing echo of the punitive arson of Captain Ferguson and Lieutenant Dalrymple in May 1746, the building caught fire and was gutted by an inferno which, once again, was watched with horror and pity from along the east coast of Skye. When the ashes settled, only the facade and the west wing remained.

Once again, it was rebuilt. Insurance premiums underwrote yet another comprehensive renovation. Raasay House began its third life, as a hotel and outdoor centre, in the spring of 2013. Borodale House, which had taken over the burden of the island hotel for thirty years, closed and was converted into an expansive distillery which also offered visitor accommodation and guided tours, as well as providing fifteen salaried and several seasonal jobs. The population of Raasay in 2021 crept back up to 187 people, which included the highest proportion of working age adults for many decades.

In common with most of the rest of the west Highlands and Islands, the Raasay archipelago reached their peak recorded population in the National Census of 1841. Then the islands of Raasay, Rona, Fladda and Eilean Taighe reported a combined citizenship of 1,126 people, with 987 of them in Raasay.

Also in common with most of its neighbouring parishes, Raasay then began a long decline which bottomed out 140 years later in

1981, when there were 152 people in Raasay, none at all in Fladda and Eilean Taighe, and just three lighthouse keepers in Rona. It revived slightly in the following decades without exceeding 200 inhabitants.

★

Ratharsaich were proud of their Gaelic. Kurt Duwe's studies of the strength of that language in different parts of Scotland show, perhaps unsurprisingly, that in 1881 every single one of 176 people in Umachan, Arnish, Kyle Rona and the rest of northern Raasay spoke Gaelic, with 44 per cent of them speaking nothing but Gaelic. The same applied to the 60 inhabitants of Fladda and Eilean Taighe. In Rona, 90 of 176 people were Gaelic speakers. Only in southern Raasay did the figures slightly decline to 84 per cent. Kurt Duwe reports:

> Most communities in this part of the island were overwhelmingly *Gàidhlig*-speaking – especially those with a crofting background. Notable exceptions were of course the residents of Raasay House and their associated servants at the time. "In original census report terms, the district had a population of 268 persons of all ages. 191 enumerated inhabitants spoke 'Gaelic and English' and 34 were counted as monolingual *Gàidhlig*-speakers. This led to an 'official' share of Gàidhlig-speakers of 84 per cent. This figure was an under-estimate of 5.5 per cent compared with the more realistic figures considering only the usually resident population. In total 26 inhabitants were enumerated with no 'G' or 'G&E' marked on their registration sheets. Among them was a crofter's family at Feàrn with 8 blank entries in the language column. This return, however, might have been a registration error as all family members were recorded in the 1901 census as either 'G' or 'G&E' speakers.

> "A second important entry of non-*Gàidhlig*-speakers was of course produced by the inhabitants of Raasay House where nine out of ten members of the household apparently ignored the local language around them. In this category also falls the family of the local gamekeeper and the head gardener with six additional 'English only' returns."

Compared to the rest of the Inner Hebrides and the western seaboard of the mainland, Raasay's Gaelic presence held up well in the second half of the twentieth century. The millennial census of 2001 recorded 70 Gaelic speakers in a population of 194 residents. The numbers fell away over the following two decades.

The altered demographics of a slowly reviving 21st-century island accelerated various kinds of change. In 2024 a short notice appeared in the April edition of the *Free Presbyterian Magazine*. "Sadly," it read, "services in Raasay no longer take place." The alphabetical list of places of Free Presbyterian worship in the same publication ran, without its usual interruption by a parish beginning with the letter R, from Portree straight through to Shieldaig. This most Highland of Protestant congregations was finally lost to the island and to the world.

Dr James Tallach would be the last Free Presbyterian minister in Raasay on the current record. In 2009 he translated to the Church's Stornoway congregation, ending his own ministry of thirty-four years, and more than a century of devotion to the island from the Tallach family which had given Raasay two long-serving ministers, two schoolteachers – the mother and daughter each named Margaret Tallach, the younger of whom tended to the students at Raasay Public School in Clachan for almost fifty years between 1908 and 1954 – and her sister, the relief nurse Katie Tallach.

There were only funerals left to conduct, some of which Reverend Tallach returned from Lewis to administer. When he left there was a sign by the gate to the island's play park and football field. It read: "Please do not use this playing field on Sundays." Shortly afterwards it disappeared in the night, silently and unannounced. The playing field was nonetheless still not used on Sundays. The Raasay Sabbath remained, for the moment, almost as unpolluted, restorative and serene as its surroundings. In some households its soundtrack was still the King James Bible.

Without a minister, the Free Presbyterian manse remained empty and the church was largely unused. But that consecrated plot of earth was not officially returned to lay Raasay while Calum Gillies was alive and living in Raasay.

Calum Gillies was born in Fladda in 1928, one year before the Free Presybterian church was raised above Clachan Bay by the missionary and stonemason William MacSween. He was raised in Fladda, across the bay from the cliff overhang cave which had sheltered the earliest inhabitants. Calum Gillies became a fisherman, attending Free Presbyterian services at the school building in Fladda, before he and his Lewis-born wife "retired" from Fladda to the south of Raasay in the middle of the 1960s. They raised two sons there. When he was eighty-seven years old, Calum was able to see and hear two passenger ferries in the Sound of Raasay, saluting each other with horn blasts as they crossed.

The MV *Loch Seaforth* and the MV *Hallaig* were each skippered by those two sons.

He died in 2024. The ninety-five-year-old Free Presbyterian church overlooking Clachan Bay was kept open for his funeral. That funeral was its very last service. In its beginning was its end.

Bibliography

Alston, David, *Slaves and Highlanders: Silenced Histories of Scotland and the Caribbean*, Edinburgh: Edinburgh University Press, 2021

Boswell, James, *The Journal of a Tour to the Hebrides with Samuel Johnson, L.L.D.*, London: White, Byrne and Cash, 1785

Clarkson, Tim, *The Picts: A History*, Cheltenham: Tempus Publishing, 2008

Cooke, Peter, Angus MacDonald, Morag MacLeod and Colm Ó Baoil, eds, *The Eliza Ross Collection: Original Highland Airs Collected on Raasay in 1812*, Skye: Taigh na Teud Music Publishers, 2022

Dinsley, Margaret Anne, "A Comparative Study of the Responses of Three Highland Communities to the Disruption in the Church of Scotland in 1843", PhD thesis, The Open University, 2005

Draper, Laurence and Pamela, *The Raasay Iron Mine 1912–1942: Where Enemies Became Friends*, Dingwall: Laurence and Pamela Draper, 1990

Duwe, Kurt C., *Gàidhlig* (Scottish Gaelic) Local Studies, Vol. 12: *An t-Eilean Sgitheanach: Port Rìgh, An Srath & Slèite*, 3rd edition, June 2024

Fairweather, Nick, *Exploring Raasay*, Edinburgh: Thirsty Books, 2015

Forbes, Alexander Robert, *Place-names of Skye and Adjacent Islands*, Paisley: Alexander Gardner Ltd, 1923

Forbes, Rev Robert, ed. by Henry Paton, *The Lyon in Mourning, or a Collection of Speeches, Letters, Journals, etc, Relative to the Affairs of Prince Charles Edward Stuart*, Edinburgh: T. and A. Constable, 1896

Garvey, John, *William Daniell's Isle of Skye and Raasay, An Artist's Journey in 1815*, Leicester: Matador, 2009

Gazin-Schwartz, Amy, *Raasay: the ACFA Archaeological Surveys 1995–2009*, Glasgow: Association of Certified Field Archaeologists, 2018

Hutchinson, Roger, *All the Sweets of Being: A Life of James Boswell*, Edinburgh: Mainstream, 1995

———, *Calum's Road*, Edinburgh: Birlinn, 2006

Johnson, Samuel, *A Journey to the Western Islands of Scotland*, London: W. Strahan and T. Cadell, 1775

Lawson, Bill, *Lewis in History and Legend: The East Coast*, Edinburgh: Birlinn, 2011

Lethbridge, T. C., *Gogmagog: The Buried Gods*, London: Routledge & Kegan Paul, 1957

MacAlister, Florence, *Memoir of the Right Hon. Sir John McNeill, G.C.B.*, London: John Murray, 1910

MacCowan, Roderick, *The Men of Skye*, Glasgow: John Macneilage, 1902

MacCulloch, John, *The Highlands and Western Isles of Scotland*, Vol. III, London: Longman, 1824

Macdonald, Norman and Cailean Maclean, *The Great Book of Skye*, Vols I–III, Portree: Great Book Publishing, 2014, 2016 and 2018

MacKay, Angus, *A Collection of Ancient Piobaireachd or Highland Pipe Music*, Aberdeen: Logan & Co., 1838

MacKay, Rebecca S., *Every Nook and Cranny: Placenames. Part I, Raasay, Rona, Fladda and Eilean Taighe*, Guildford: Grosvenor House Publishing, 2013

———, *Every Nook and Cranny: Placenames. Fact and Fiction, Raasay, Rona, Fladda and Eilean Taighe*, Guildford: Grosvenor House Publishing , 2014

MacKenzie, Julia, *Whirligig Beetles and Tackety Boots*, Yorkshire: Blaisdon Publishing, 2000

MacKenzie, William, *Old Skye Tales: Traditions, Reflections and Memories*, Edinburgh: Birlinn, 2002

McKirdy, Alan, *Landscapes in Stone*, Edinburgh: Birlinn, 2022

Macleod, Alistair, 'From Rona to Cambridge', a memoir, unpublished

MacLeod, Calum, *Fàsachadh An-Iochdmhor Ratharsair: The Cruel Clearance of Raasay*, Glasgow: Clò Àrnais, 2007

MacLeod, James Lachlan, *The Second Disruption: The Free Church in Victorian Scotland and the Origins of the Free Presbyterian Church*, East Lothian: Tuckwell Press, 2000

MacLeod, Norma, *Raasay: The Island and Its People*, Edinburgh: Birlinn, 2002

McNeill, John, *Report to the Board of Supervision on the Western Highlands and Islands*, Edinburgh: Murray and Gibb (for HMSO), 1851

MacSwan, Duncan, 'Rona Revisited after Forty-two Years', a memoir, unpublished

MacSween, Ann, *The Brochs, Duns and Enclosures of Skye*, Newcastle upon Tyne: Northumberland Archaeology Group, 1985

Malloy, Robert B., *The Isle of Raasay*, Massachusetts: Grace Malloy, 1975

Martin, Martin, *A Description of the Western Islands of Scotland*,1703

Middleton, Roy, "Raasay and Rona in nineteenth-century Scottish Presbyterianism", *Scottish Reformation Society Historical Journal*, 13, 2023

Miers, Mary, *The Western Seaboard: an Illustrated Architectural Guide*, Edinburgh: Rutland Press, 2008

Miket, Roger, and David L. Roberts, *The Mediaeval Castles of Skye and Lochalsh*, Portree: MacLean Press, 1990

Morton, H. V., *In Search of Scotland*, London: Methuen, 1929

Morton, J. D. and A. S. Baird, 'Geology of the Isle of Raasay', School of Earth and Environment, University of Leeds, 2015

Napier Commission of Inquiry into the Conditions of the Crofters and Cottars in the Highlands and Islands of Scotland, Vols I–V, London: HMSO, 1894

Nicolson, Alexander, *Handbook to the Isle of Skye and Adjacent Islands*, Glasgow: Archibald Sinclair, 1936

Nicolson, John, *I Remember: Memories of Raasay* Edinburgh: Birlinn, 1989

———, *The People Must Go*, Bedale: Blaisdon, 2008

Noble, Gordon and Nicholas Evans (eds), *Picts: Scourge of Rome, Rulers of the North*, Edinburgh: Birlinn, 2022

Quine, David A., ed, *Expeditions to the Hebrides by George Clayton Atkinson in 1831 and 1833*, Waternish: MacLean Press, 2001

Reckitt, B. N., *Holoman House, Isle of Raasay, Some Notes on its History*, Raasay, 1997

Sharpe, Richard, *Raasay: A Study in Island History*, London: Grant & Cutler, 1977

Sharpe, Richard, *Raasay: A Study in Island History. Documents and Sources, People and Places*, London: Grant & Cutler, 1978

Skene, William Forbes, *Celtic Scotland: a History of Ancient Alban*, 3 vols, Edinburgh: Thomas and Archibald Constable, 1880

Stack, Prunella, *Island Quest, the Inner Hebrides*, London: Collins, 1979

Tallach, Revd James, 'Raasay Congregation – a Brief History', *The Free Presbyterian Magazine*, September 2001

Thorneycroft, Wallace, 'Note on the Upper Lias of the Western Islands in reference to the iron ore deposit therein', *Transactions of the Edinburgh Geological Society*, vol. 10, 1914, pp.196–204

Transactions of the Gaelic Society of Inverness, Vol. XXXVI, Inverness: Inverness Gaelic Society, 1941

Turner, Barry C., *Dr Green of Sussex and the Island of Raasay*, Dornoch: Inkandstuff, 2009

Whyte, Christopher and Emma Dymock, *Sorley MacLean, Collected Poems*, Edinburgh: Polygon, 2011

Wilson, Susan R., ed., *The Correspondence Between Hugh MacDiarmid and Sorley MacLean*, Edinburgh: Edinburgh University Press, 2010

Index

INDEX

INDEX